# 1st Bedfordshires

# 1ST BEDFORDSHIRES

## PART TWO: ARRAS TO THE ARMISTICE

STEVEN FULLER

Published in 2013 by Fighting High Ltd,
www.fightinghigh.com

British Library Cataloguing-in-Publication data.
A CIP record for this title is available from the
British Library.

ISBN – 13: 978-0957116320

Designed and typeset in Monotype Baskerville
11/14pt and Monotype by Michael Lindley
www.truthstudio.co.uk

Printed and bound in China by Toppan Leefung.
Front cover design by Michael Lindley.

# Contents

# Foreword

The second volume of Steven Fuller's history of the 1st Battalion the Bedfordshire Regiment takes us through some of the fiercest battles of the First World War, from Vimy Ridge, Passchendaele and Ypres to Arras and the Second Battle of the Somme.

In view of the horrendous number of casualties, each chapter contains biographical details of some of the dead and wounded, together with accounts of many acts of bravery for which medals were rightly awarded. Life behind the front line is also included, while the battalion alternated between the trenches, supporting roles and periods in reserve.

The book also summarises the battalion's history post-war with service in Northern Ireland, Aldershot, Malta and war service in Greece, Egypt, Syria, Tobruk and Burma. The year 1958 saw the battalion merge with the 1st Battalion Essex Regiment to form the 3rd East Anglian Regiment, while in 1964 the three regiments forming the East Anglian Brigade were merged with the Royal Leicestershire Regiment to become the first Large Regiment of Infantry in the British army; the 3rd East Anglian Regiment became the 3rd Battalion (16th/44th Foot) of the Royal Anglian Regiment. Finally, in 1992 the 3rd Battalion disbanded, being folded into the 1st and 2nd Battalions. D Company (Bedfordshire and Hertfordshire) of the 2nd Battalion are today the direct descendants of the pikemen and musketeers who were raised in 1688.

The battalion's padre wrote to a friend in 1917, illustrating the courage shown by men in the battalion, remarking that 'The British soldier is the absolute limit in true nobility. I have just helped in a poor fellow with his leg off at the thigh and the other foot off, and, probably, may lose a hand, and yet ... he says he's "fine"!'

Asked by Marshal Foch, in the presence of Marshal Haig, whether the colonel of a Bedfordshire battalion could be sure that his men would hold the line during a desperate situation when no reserves were available, the colonel's reply summed up the entire regiment's determination and reliability: 'I am a Bedfordshire man; I know the men of the County, and I know that they will not betray the trust you have placed in them. I am going back to tell them what is expected of them, and though many of them have not been under fire before, I vouch for them. ... They will hold the line.'

**Sir Samuel Whitbread, KCVO**

*President – The Bedfordshire and Hertfordshire Regiment Association*

# Introduction

The Bedfordshire Regiment's long history stretches back to 1688, when a foot regiment was comprised of musketeers and pikemen. Their record of faithfully serving a succession of twelve monarchs took them across the British Empire when it was at its zenith, from the Far East to the New World. Having been engaged in numerous battles and campaigns, as well as long, costly garrison spells on the Fever Isles and other such debilitating posts, their history certainly proved full of casualty-riddled events, but none was remotely comparable to their involvement in the First World War.

Being mobilised from their garrison posting in Ireland when war broke out in August 1914, the 1st Bedfordshires had served in the 15th Infantry Brigade of the 5th Division from the opening engagement at Mons. Days later, they had stood firm among the thin defensive line at Le Cateau, conducted rearguard actions during the retreat to Paris, before finding themselves heavily engaged on the Marne, the Aisne, at La Bassée and during the First Battle of Ypres.

After five relatively quiet, if uncomfortable, months on the front lines, which included them fraternising with their enemies during the remarkable Christmas Truce of 1914, April and May 1915 saw them heavily engaged in the capture and subsequent defence of Hill 60, on which Private Edward Warner won a posthumous Victoria Cross. A year of trench life on the Somme and at Arras had given the battalion time to rest, rebuild and reorganise before being called on to take part in several phases of the Battles of the Somme (1916).

Initially holding the line at High Wood, they soon assaulted, captured and held the heavily fortified village of Longueval before following up with the storming of another heavily fortified position called Falfemont Farm.[1] A more limited role was played in the assault against Morval before their tour of the Somme came to a close and the division were withdrawn from the battlefield entirely.

Two years into the war and with a casualty list already comprised of many thousands, the 1st Bedfordshires had become a tried and tested, reliable battalion within the highly regarded, veteran, 5th Division. But their war was far from over.

# Chapter 1

# Winter in the Béthune Sector: October 1916 to March 1917

*'Picture, if you will, a real cold winter's night. ...'*

During their tour of the Somme, the 5th Division had lost 559 officers and over 11,100 men between mid-July and the end of September, having been charged with breaking several particularly tough defensive positions. Despite many reinforcement drafts received during the campaign, most of the 5th Division's battalions were at around half strength, including the 1st Bedfordshires who were only able to muster around 500 officers and men.

After a pause on the fringes of the Somme battlefields while the division concentrated, the battalion moved 60km west by train, to billets in Longpré-les-Corps-Saints on 29 September, but after a day's rest were moving once again, this time 80km north-east to Béthune. This sector would be their home until mid-March 1917. After alighting at Fouquereuil, the travel-weary battalion moved in to billets at Les Loges, 4km north-east of Béthune. At the same time, the division were transferred into XI Corps of the First Army.

While resting, Captain and Adjutant Harry Willans rejoined, having recovered from his wound over the summer. Lieutenant Colonel Walter Allason took the opportunity for a spell of leave to the UK, being temporarily replaced as the commanding officer by Major Montague Walter Halford. Old hands from the 1914 campaign took the chance to visit the graves of their chums who had fallen at Givenchy, as they had not returned to the area since being rushed north to stem the German advance around Ypres that October.

On the 5th another move took them to billets 500 metres east of La Couture, where they remained until the 10th. Half of the battalion were posted to Seneschal Farm, the balance being held 1km to the south in the King's Road, off the Rue du Bois. While taking their final rest before returning to the front, Captain John Jenkins Moyse rejoined, having recovered from the shrapnel wounds to his legs sustained six months earlier.

As the officers reconnoitred the front lines opposite Festubert in readiness for their move back into the trenches, specialist training began to replace the Lewis gunners and bombers lost in their recent fighting on the Somme, as there were not enough left to support the battalion while holding the line.

The division started their move into the front lines, which ran from south of the La Bassée canal to north-east of Festubert. The 95th Brigade held the southern sector with the 13th in the centre and the 15th to the north, each brigade holding two battalions in the front trenches, one in support and one in reserve.

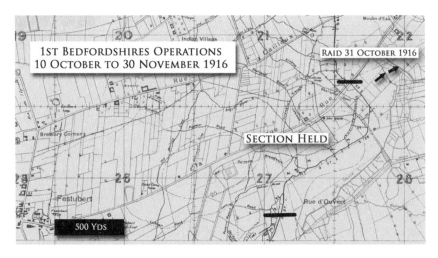

In broad daylight on 10 October, the Bedfordshires took over a wet 1km section of the front-line trench system, running from the Quinque Rue (Rue de Lille) to the Lothian Road communications trench, 1,200 metres east of Festubert. Their section was in an exposed salient jutting into the German lines, with most of the southern half inaccessible by daylight and much of the northern half comprised of breastworks as the ground was so sodden. The duckboards were noted by Lieutenant Colonel Allason[2] as being so loose that after heavy rains, many would work themselves free; with the water being so dirty and obscuring the trench floor, several Bedfordshires found themselves taking unwelcome cold baths.

Other than considerable work improving their defensive lines, nightly wiring parties from the Warwickshires, working fatigues provided by the Argyll and Sutherland Highlanders and the occasional sniper's shot ringing out in the damp air, their tour was uneventful. The men were even bemused by the appearance of a visitor to their trenches in the form of a young local girl who brought the papers round to them every morning, and farming carried on behind the lines as though the war was a far-off event.

Once relieved on the 16th, the Bedfordshires returned to their old billets and worked on the local roads, drainage and their billets during the day, also providing wiring parties for the front lines each night. A concert troupe was formed by Second Lieutenant Sullivan and Sergeant Green and the soft ground saw rugby football become the sport of choice for the time being. Their second tour in the front lines between the 20th and 23rd was equally as inactive, the fatigue duties and recreations repeating once in support from the 24th to 28th.

New gas masks were issued on the 26th, with each man in the battalion having to pass through the training 'Gas House' in Essars to ensure they understood how to use them. Orders were also issued at army level for each division to conduct at least two raids per week, which provided an outlet for the men's creativity as there were no hard and fast rules on the structure or purpose of individual raids. The Bedfordshires' turn soon came round and planning and training for a raid against the German lines went ahead despite the weather; this included two trial runs by day and another under cover of darkness. Given the losses suffered on the Somme, the Bedfords not only had trouble selecting experienced men for the raid but were hard pressed to find enough experienced bombers, so training using live bombs was also provided as most of those taking part had little or no experience.

Back in the front lines on 28 October, A Company held the southern section with the 13th Brigade to their right and C Company in support in Richmond Terrace. A composite company under Captain Charles Morris were held in the Old British Line trench, comprised of around eighty men from B and D Companies who were to be involved in the raid. The rest of B and D Companies not committed to the raid were holding the northern half of the battalion lines, with the 1st Norfolks to their north. Other than an occasional sniper's shot, the quiet period continued, although on the 30th A and C Companies swapped positions during the day.

### Trench raid: 31 October 1916

By the evening of the 31st conditions were perfect for the planned raid to proceed. The raiding party under Captain Morris was let loose with the implicit instructions of killing as many of their counterparts as possible, bombing as many dugouts as they could identify and damaging as much of the German trench system as was feasible given the time. Split into four composite platoons of around twenty men, each platoon had one officer and was further divided into four sections of one NCO and four men each. Every platoon also had a Bangalore torpedo detachment, although in the event no opportunities arose for their deployment. Faces were blacked out with burned cork, equipment was dulled with soot and oil, with each man being issued with two bombs, and the novel idea of electric torches being secured to the rifle stock was tried. A report on the operation remarked how 'it caused much hilarity and certainly raised morale'.[3]

Second Lieutenants Robert Wright[4] and John Kingdon led their two platoons on the right half of the raid, with Sydney Draper and Arthur Woodford's platoons advancing on the left flank. Machine Gun Officer John Kingdon also coordinated covering fire and ensured the trench system on either side of the raid was swept with fire, the raiding party itself being given express orders not to fire and give their positions away while in No Man's Land.

Under a moonless Halloween night sky, the raiding party set out at 7 p.m. and advanced unseen across the 200 metres of No Man's Land that separated them from the German lines. At 7.50 p.m. the two left-hand platoons had cut through the German wire and moved into the trench system via old drainage ditches, surprising a patrol from the 6th Bavarian Regiment once in the trenches. The three survivors were captured and bomb stops were set up on each flank of their positions, while the remaining sections explored dugouts or moved east along the communications trench. The four-man teams moved carefully through 100 metres of trench that took them to the support lines, but met no more German troops, while a further team linked up with the right-hand platoons.

To the right, Second Lieutenants Wright and Kingdon's platoons had encountered a thick belt of wire before being held up by a German machine-gun post out in front of the trench system. The German infantry rushed from their dugouts and added their own fusillade of rifle fire and bombs, wounding many and forcing the forty men to ground. After bombing the machine-gun post, they moved in support of the left platoons, entering the trench system further north. Attempts to progress south along the trench were thwarted by a strong defensive contingent and Captain Morris called for the retirement. After the wounded were evacuated, rearguard sections moved back through one another and an attempt to follow up by German troops was stopped by a Lewis-gun team.

Some 450 metres to their south Second Lieutenant John Sullivan led a small group of six men in a demonstration against the German lines to take the focus from their colleagues. Leaving the lines at 6.30 p.m., his small section bombed and drove a three-man listening post back before waiting until the sounds of fighting could be heard from further north. After silencing the listening post, they made as much noise as possible, attracting the attention of the German defenders, who opened fire. After several volleys, Sullivan's men retired noisily, drawing German fire as they did so.

Once the raiding party were back in their own lines, it was learned that Second Lieutenant Wright and seventeen men were wounded, one was dead and a further two were wounded and missing, having been seen helping one another back towards their own lines. At 2 a.m. a full search was carried out along the path of the raid and although the body of 18-year-old Private Ernest Baalham[5] from Lawford in Essex was recovered, neither of the missing could be found. Witnesses later confirmed they were seen entering Shetland Trench, where a German Minenwerfer exploded, so it was assumed they had both been killed in the explosion. The next day another body could be seen in front of the German wire, although attempts to recover it the next night were futile.

The Bedfordshires lost in the raid included another of their pre-war veterans, Private Herbert Durant[6] of Bloxworth in Dorset, who had been fighting in the battalion since Mons in 1914. The 28-year-old Private Frank Kefford[7] from Biggleswade had been with the battalion since November 1915 and was initially classed as wounded and missing; despite rumours in his home town that he had been captured, Frank was later confirmed as having been one of the two killed by the Minenwerfer shell. Private Harold Oclee[8] from Bedford was also killed, all three comrades being remembered on the Loos memorial to the missing.

Several letters of praise filtered down from brigade, divisional and corps commanders, with Second Lieutenant Wright being awarded a

Military Cross, his citation reading: 'Although wounded he led a raid and forced his way through the enemy wire under heavy fire, entering the enemy trench. He showed marked courage and determination throughout the operations.' He would not return to the battalion, serving in the 6th Bedfordshires once he had recovered until wounded a third time, finally being killed in the 2nd Worcestershires just weeks before the armistice, in September 1918.

Herbert Dicks of Kettering won the Military Medal during the raid. One of the Derby Scheme enlisters, Herbert had only joined the battalion in September 1916, winning his medal six weeks after his arrival. On 4 November, Lieutenant General Haking, commanding officer of XI Corps, presented Herbert with a medal ribbon in France but he had to wait almost a year to receive the medal itself in a ceremony in Kettering while on leave. His local paper recorded how 'in the course of some exciting and perilous work, he picked up a wounded comrade who happened to be lying just outside a German trench, and carried him back to the British lines, while a little later on he bounded "over the top" and fetched another "Tommy" into comparative safety. Not until he returned home, however, for the leave he has just concluded, did his relatives learn that he himself had been wounded in the knee.'[9]

## A fourth winter in the trenches

Around this time a curious rumour started spreading through the division,[10] which claimed that 'some of the old hard-fighting divisions, of which the 5th was one, were to be sent for the winter somewhere to the back of beyond, or even home, for an honourable rest, called "the King's Rest"'. In the event no such luxury came their way but it was a welcomed topic of conversation for several days.

Routines took over once again, the Bedfords alternating between four days in the line and four in support, their positions not changing throughout November. The issues of finding gumboots and oiling the men's feet became paramount as the month progressed, the trenches being badly waterlogged regardless of how much drainage work was carried out.

Lieutenant Colonel Walter Allason took command of the brigade between the 6th and 10th, attending the First Army commanding officers' conference on the 12th, when Major Moyse assumed command until his return. After another spell in support between 27 and 30 November, the battalion were warned for a new section of the line, their officers visiting the area the day before taking over.

Arriving in the front trenches between Richebourg l'Avoué and Neuve Chapelle early afternoon on 1 December, sporadic trench mortar fire broke their otherwise relatively quiet tour. A different defensive scheme operated in this section, determined by factors such as the closeness of the opposing lines, which made the laying of wire in No Man's Land impossible. Within the new scheme, strict orders were also issued not to fire at anyone approaching in the darkness without warning, to avoid accidents. An enemy raid against the battalion next to the Bedfordshires on the 2nd heightened the awareness along their lines, leading to just the type of accident they were trying to avoid.

At around 2 a.m. on the 3rd, Lieutenant Colonel Allason and his orderly were touring the trenches when they approached a section commanded by a recently arrived second lieutenant. Convinced that the approaching figures were a fresh raid after they did not respond to his challenge, the new officer shot his colonel in the stomach. Fortunately it was not fatal, although it would signal the end of Allason's time in the battalion until he returned as its commanding officer after the war, serving as brigadier and in command of a battalion in the Bedfordshire Brigade on the Rhine in 1919 in the interim.

Major John Moyse assumed command of the battalion until the arrival of Lieutenant Colonel Francis Noel Butler on the 18th, who had recovered from a serious bout of influenza early in 1915, which had forced his resignation as Lieutenant Colonel of the 5th Bedfordshires.

A well-earned rest period started on 5 December that saw the men billeted in the École de Jeunes Filles in Béthune until the 20th. The routine of training, inspections and local leave began, broken only by a parade in the Municipal Theatre to issue medal ribbons on the 17th. Second Lieutenant Samuel Norrish was presented with his Military Cross ribbon, earned on the Somme a few months earlier; Private Herbert Fish[11], a maltster in a Baldock brewery before the war, had a Distinguished Conduct Medal ribbon pinned to his tunic that he had won in the 7th Bedfordshires' July attacks; Corporal Harold McHugh[12] and Private Christopher Cross[13] were both presented with their Military Medal ribbons.

News of more Military Medals arrived during the month as Corporals Frank Bradley[14] from Australia and Arthur Faulder,[15] in addition to Old Contemptible Lance Corporal Frederick Payne,[16] were all rewarded with medals.

On 18 December Second Lieutenant William Martin Stantan joined, having been briefly attached to the 16th Warwickshires since recovering from a wound in September. The following day saw Lieutenant Albert Grover transfer from the 2nd Bedfordshires, who had recovered from wounds received at Festubert in 1915 and a badly broken leg early in 1916. Orders also arrived for a move back to the trenches and company officers reconnoitred the new section of the line they were to take over as the men prepared for the relocation.

By early afternoon on the 20th, the Bedfords were in position, spread around several close-support keeps in the Cuinchy area, south of the La Bassée canal. Demanding fatigue duties filled the next two days and other than a heavy Minenwerfer bombardment about 9 a.m. on the 21st, which only managed to destroy the officers' breakfasts, no harm was done. Several more days of fetching and carrying followed, with rest spells being spent in 'rat infested hovels', until the battalion moved to take over an 800-metre stretch of the front trenches on Christmas Eve. With their northern flank resting on the canal and within sight of the ground they held at such a high cost in October 1914, the line stretched to 100 metres south of the road running east from Cambrin and faced the notorious Brickstacks position. Although an improvement on their billets, the front-line trenches were noted as being in a dreadful condition with some sections impassable, the entire forward sector being nothing

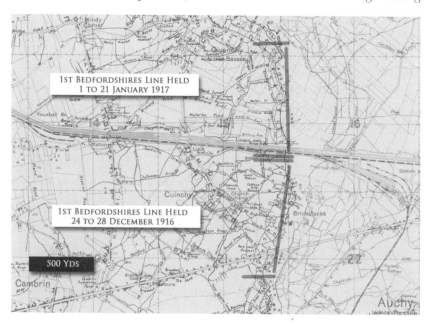

more than a mass of saps and joined up lines of craters, only approachable via tunnels. Under their feet were a myriad of mineshafts and counter-mining efforts, adding to the already unpleasant position. Just after their relief was complete, British artillery started their three-day 'Christmas barrage', the din and destruction being added to by retaliatory trench mortar fire from both sides. Between the weather, condition of their lines, the artillery duel, nests of German snipers watching for every unguarded movement and the German posts being just 20 metres from their own in some places, Christmas 1916 promised to be uncomfortable.

There was no let-up in the barrage throughout Christmas Day and Boxing Day, and although the German response was limited, it still managed to blow some sections of trench in. Relief for those men in the forward saps, close to the German positions, proved difficult and a constant stream of working parties to repair trenches and wire kept the battalion busy. On the 25th, Major Moyse was lucky enough to be given leave and Second Lieutenant Fred Girling was sent to England with a skin infection on Boxing Day, as officers from the Cheshires and Norfolks arrived to prepare for the Bedfordshires' relief.

The appearance of the first relieving parties mid-morning on the 28th signalled the end of their festive tour and the battalion were moved 5km west, into billets in Le Quesnoy and at the Girls' School in Beuvry. Their restful Christmas break proved to be an unusual few days, which saw several problems surface regarding their allocated billets. The town major in Beuvry initially insisted that B Company were in fact from the Kents of the 95th Brigade and tried to turn them out, losing the opening round to a loud and incredulous company of tired soldiers pointing out what they considered to be 'the bleedin' obvious'. Not to be outdone, the town majors from both villages moved the C and D Company officers from their billets in Le Quesnoy in favour of officers from other units and, despite a move to the Girls' School, division overturned this and put them into some very poor billets. Further, D Company were ousted in favour of some Gloucester officers and by the time the moves and grumbles had fizzled out, the allocated baths at Le Quesnoy were closed and would not be reopened.

Problems with baths continued throughout the 30th, but at 2 p.m. the battalion forgot about the past few days and settled down to their Christmas dinner. A draft of ninety-one men joined at Beuvry that afternoon, followed by seventy-one more the next evening, who were left in the area under Major Halford for further training when the battalion moved forward the next day.

On their return to the front lines, the battalion took steps to hold the left sub sector, running from the Red Dragon Crater east of Givenchy to the La Bassée canal. The few surviving veterans of the 1914 battle hardly recognised the area, as the village was nothing more than a low mound of rubble; the once open fields of crops they had fought in had since been replaced with mud, trenches, mine craters and the debris of three years of static siege warfare. A routine of three or four days in the line followed by the same in their Christmas support billets developed, with regular bombardments, mine detonations and fighting patrols keeping the entire divisional line busy.

A British mine exploded just north of the Bedfords on the 4th, causing an instant retaliatory bombardment from German guns. The northern sector was hit hard with three Bedfords being killed and a further seven wounded in the shelling.

Other than what had become the usual sporadic trench mortar bombardments and daily bombing duels between parties holding opposing saps, their last two tours in the front from the 9th to 12th and 17th to 21st were relatively quiet. Gas caused some discomfort but no casualties on the 18th, with repairing their trenches and keeping warm being the main focus of their efforts.

A break in Feuillade Barracks, Béthune, between 22 and 31 January followed, with the cold hampering most of the planned training other than the expected route marches and some musketry practice.

The men naturally needed distractions when on duty so close to the front lines over such an extended period and in the depths of winter so, not to be inconvenienced by the closeness of their foes, impromptu entertainments sprung up, often at very short notice. Titled 'A concert in France',[17] one of the members of such a troupe shared an event in a letter home, complete with cryptic phrasing intended to bypass the ever keen censor's eyes:

*Picture, if you will, a real cold winter's night, a half-moon struggling to shine through a snow laden sky, the air full of downy flakes, and ever and anon the fitful flashing and deep booming of not-far-distant guns, the high toned hum of a plane, the rattle of a Lewis, the banging of transports on a cobbled highway ... and then imagine a cosy room, bare it may be of finicky upholstery, but cosy in its warmth and light; a piano, a willing company to give their talent, and a crowd of red, healthy looking British faces wreathed in smiles. Then, mayhap, you will get a notion of what our concert was like.*

*We hadn't rehearsed much. True it was that Mr. Sullivan, of a famous Battalion not unconnected with Beds and Hunts, a talented and well known impresario, had coached us for an hour or so in the afternoon, but some of us had 'our doubts' about what sort of show it would be to place before the Colonel and the other officers present. We need not have had those doubts. It was a real tophole success, and the lads enjoyed it to the full, despite the boom of cannon, the roar of shells, the 'Kr-r-r-rupp' of Fritz's souvenirs, the rattle of machine guns, the banging of transports and the attendant devilish noises of a great war continuing outside among the silent snowflakes.*

*Among the artists, 2nd Lieut. Sullivan from this battalion, was splendid with his monologue, stories and songs. Sergt. Green, well known as the manager and promoter of numerous concerts at Landguard, was greatly enjoyed, especially in 'Follow the Sergeant'. In harmony, Ptes. Crawte, Spencer, Bolger, Cotton and Barnwell of the Bedfords, were exceedingly good, and made a fine super beauty chorus. The brothers Franks were worth a good deal more than two Francs in their American duet and dance, and Ptes. Evans and Parrott sang together tunefully. Solos were also given by Ptes. Crawte, Barnwell, Wooding, Evans, Cartledge and Parrott, Corpl. MacHugh (sic) and Sergt. Hancock, while Lance-Corp. Wilden gave some clever impersonations.*

On 1 February the battalion moved 7km north-east to brigade support positions at Le Touret, where the men waited in freezing cold billets for orders to take over the lines once more. While waiting, Second Lieutenant William Arthur Spencer Ogden joined fresh from training in England and once again a routine developed of three or four days in the same section of trenches they had held in October 1916 and several days in billets at Le Touret.

Before moving to the front, two more gallantry awards were issued in the theatre in Béthune, with Captains Harry Willans and Allan Beale both receiving Military Cross ribbons for gallantry during the Somme campaign. Within a week both officers were also promoted, Captain Willans being appointed as the brigade Staff Captain and Captain Beale becoming the battalion Adjutant. Both officers would go on to win more awards before the war was over. Allan Beale's promotion to Staff Captain in early 1918 ensured he did not return to the battalion, serving instead on the 15th Brigade staff until gassed in May 1918. He still managed to see service in Constantinople and Russia before resigning his commission in 1922, being awarded the MBE and Croix de Guerre in the process. Harry Willans also saw service on the brigade staff, adding the Distinguished Service Order to his medal collection in 1918; he also survived

the war and served into the Second World War, finally being killed in an aeroplane crash at Tobruk in 1943.

On their final day before moving back into the front lines, a game of football was organised. During the game Second Lieutenant Frederick Booth, who had been with the battalion since September 1916, caught his foot in a rut in the ground, fell and fractured his leg, also rupturing the muscle. This innocuous event ensured Frederick spent fifteen months in England before being pronounced fit again, although the remainder of his service was spent away from the front.

The front-line tour from 5 to 8 February was quiet, but a German sniper caught Captain John Moyse as he was moving between his exposed posts in No Man's Land and, although he was conveyed back to the Casualty Clearing Station in Béthune, he died from his wounds, aged 32.

The 19-year-old Harry Bashford from Kent[18] was among the new arrivals with the battalion, having joined on the 4th. He described the line as one made up of sandbag breastworks rather than trenches, as the position was so close to the canal, in spite of the winter being remarkably cold and freezing everything solid. Rotating through three-man teams, duties were split into one hour manning the firestep with two hours spent huddled in dugouts trying to keep warm. Harry and his new comrades 'amused' themselves by putting morsels of food on to their bayonets and spearing any of the hordes of rats sharing their hovel, adding how the rats 'grew to massive sizes ... 18 inches long'.

Their penultimate spell in the trenches between Valentine's Day and 18 February was typically quiet, broken only by an attempted German raid on their lines on the 17th. On a very dark night, a German party of around 40 men slipped between two Lewis-gun-team posts 130 metres apart. Explosions in the darkness alerted the left-hand post who sent a

Very light into the sky, illuminating the party as they crept through the broken section of wire. After opening fire on the group, all but one officer and six men retired into No Man's Land. Their determined bombing assault continued despite their officer falling and they moved along the Bedfords' front trench until stopped by Lieutenant Geoffrey de Carteret Millais's bombing party. During the exchange, Sergeant Frederick Groom[19] from St Albans, who wrote of his experiences on Hill 60 in May 1915, was killed. While the duel flared up, Second Lieutenant Arthur Creasey mounted a Lewis gun at the junction of Shetland Road and Cover Trench, firing into the party. He pinned them, killing two and wounding the remaining four, who scrambled over the parapet and into the darkness of No Man's Land.

As this was unfolding a second party of around forty Germans approached a post further north. Waiting until they were 40 metres away, the Bedfordshires' Lewis gunners opened fire and brought their raid to a premature end, killing at least three and wounding others.

William Brown was awarded with a Military Medal after the raid, his war coming to a close following a wound sustained during the Third Battle of Ypres later that year.[20]

After another spell in support, the battalion's final tour on the front in this sector from 21 to 25 February was uneventful, although the casualties continued, with Private Arthur Thetford[21] from Norwich being killed on the 22nd. On the last day in the front trenches reports arrived that the Germans had withdrawn from the area in front of the Third and Fifth Armies, back to positions behind what was called the Hindenburg Line. In case the same was happening in the 5th Division area, patrols were sent forward but quickly established that their counterparts were still in permanent residence.

Another 48 hours in the now familiar billets in Le Touret saw their tour east of Festubert come to an end and on 27 February the battalion moved into crowded but comfortable billets in Beuvry, just east of Béthune. The weather improved and a mixture of training and local passes kept the men occupied until the officers disappeared to reconnoitre a new sector on 3 March.

During the reconnaissance of the new front lines, 35-year-old Second Lieutenant Walter Thomas Smith was killed. Walter was a native of Staffordshire and had been a grocer before enlisting into the Worcestershire Regiment in November 1899, aged 18 years. With service in the South African wars and many years in India, he had recovered from a wound in April 1915. Promotion to Regimental Sergeant Major in April 1916 was followed closely by being commissioned into the regular army the same month. Initially serving in the 8th Bedfordshires, Walter was wounded in the face in September 1916 and posted to the 1st Bedfordshires once recovered, arriving on 16 February 1917. Just two weeks later he was killed by probing German artillery as he was evaluating the section of trench they were preparing to take over.

The battalion were back in the front lines around Cambrin between 5 and 8 March, returning for their second and last tour there from the 13th to the 17th. The 66th Division had recently arrived from England and were sending platoons and companies into the 5th Division lines for training throughout March, in readiness for them taking over the entire sector. Training the new arrivals as they shadowed the Bedfords in their daily duties, in addition to the usual snipers, trench mortars and working fatigues kept the men busy and, on what would be their penultimate day in the front lines for a month, the opposing German unit launched a raid on the Bedfordshires' lines.

At around 8 p.m. on 16 March German artillery opened up a bombardment on the Bedfordshires' trenches. Within moments, British artillery was replying, turning the hitherto quiet section into a deafening cacophony of high-explosive shell bursts and flying debris. Two minutes into the rain of shells, lookouts spotted between thirty and forty German soldiers trying to force entry through the barbed wire around a post called Boyau 5. A fierce rifle and Lewis-gun fire was directed at them and the party retired back into No Man's Land without having made it through the wire barricade. No further attempts were made to approach the English lines and an officer patrol ventured into No Man's Land once the shelling had died down, finding two dead German soldiers.

On 17 March the Bedfordshires were relieved and initially moved back to support positions in Annequin, where they organised and quickly re-equipped in case needed by the new arrivals at short notice. However, no alarms were raised so two days later a 5km march west took them to billets in the orphanage at Béthune, where they remained on a six-hour notice to move for a week while the division concentrated. Platoon-level training, fitness, cleaning up and general fatigues kept the men busy, with opportunities to explore the local delights in Béthune presenting themselves once the day's work was complete.

Private Harry Bashford was among the men enjoying a rest in the shell-damaged town, who baked their uniforms in an attempt to rid them of some of the lice that had taken up lodgings in the folds and seams of their clothes. When baths were allocated, four men shared each tub, leaving newcomers like Harry to think 'What a wonderful shot that would have made for the family album.'

A self-confessed 'naive country boy' who had led a 'sheltered life' to that point, Harry was typical of many young men serving at the time. Having never really ventured out of his local area before joining the colours and eager to explore this strange land, he wandered into the town centre with a group of like-minded pals, where he came across a curious red lamp that warranted further examination. Quickly learning the purpose of the lamp, he later remarked that 'These young ladies are not renowned for giving their services …' and wanted nothing to do with such activities, whether others around him chose to or not, adding 'these young men had either wives or sweethearts but with no more than a 50/50 chance of seeing them again, who could blame them for this indulgence'. A further move was made on 25 March, with the entire division retiring from its support position, the Bedfordshires finding themselves in Allouagne, 10km west of Béthune. Despite bad training facilities and billets, platoon training continued in earnest, the men having seen such activities before and understanding that an offensive was imminent. At the end of March training advanced to company level and by 3 April it was being carried out as a full battalion. Although no confirmation was needed, a practice assault across a flagged course on the 4th made it crystal clear that their 1917 campaigning season was about to start.

During bomb-throwing training led by Acting Captain Robert Guthrie Forbes on 30 March, one of numerous accidents occurred, typical of the dangerous climate even while removed from combat conditions. In subsequent witness statements, his assistant, Corporal Weston,[22] explained how the men were given instructions to stand behind the protective barricade and wait for orders to throw. Once the grenades had been released, the class ducked behind their wooden boards and Corporal Weston heard his officer quietly remark, almost to himself, that he had been hit in the right shoulder.[23] After six months with the battalion, 36-year-old Captain Forbes was returned to the UK to have the two shrapnel fragments removed and would not be fit for general service again until the autumn.

April Fool's Day saw Lieutenant Colonel Butler leave to command an Essex battalion. A career officer and South African wars veteran with a Military Cross to his credit, Lieutenant Colonel Percy Reginald Worrall stepped into Lieutenant Colonel Butler's shoes, in which position he would remain until early the following year.

News also arrived of an old friend of the battalion when it was learned that Brigadier General Francis De Gex had died on 2 April while serving as the camp commandant at Rouen. The 55-year-old's service in the British army went back to 1882 and, with medals for campaigns including South Africa, had commanded the 1st Bedfordshires between 1909 and 1913.

Leaving XI Corps, a 6km march south-east on 7 April saw the Bedfordshires billet in Bruay-la-Buissière and under the orders of the Canadian Corps, with a further 12km move south to Cambligneul the next day leaving them in reserve to the Canadians, who were lining up opposite the hitherto impregnable Vimy Ridge. On 8 April, Easter Sunday, Major Reginald Le Huquet joined as second in command, just as the battalion were placed on a one-hour notice to be ready to move, and when orders came to dump blankets and haversacks at Brigade HQ, every man expected to be going into action at any moment. However, the brigade were held in position in response to a scare that the Germans were about to launch a massed attack in the area, so training continued, with the officers heading 13km east to scout positions around Givenchy-en-Gohelle and the route there from Mont-Saint-Éloi.

Although the sound of massed artillery and the ever reliable army grapevine told the Bedfordshires of the British offensive unfolding 15km further east, the 5th Division were held as the Canadian reserve, waiting for orders that would take them into their next battle.

Chapter 2

# The Battle of Arras:
# 9 April to 16 May 1917

*'When I went over this piece of ground I was surprised, for it was worse than the Somme for shell holes. They all joined one another.'*

The initial enthusiasm for the war had long since waned on the home fronts of the belligerent countries as the scale of losses continued climbing with each new battle. On the Western Front in 1916, the British Somme offensives had achieved limited success, but at a dreadful cost, while the French focus had been drawn to the slaughter at Verdun, which had seen the loss of around one million soldiers from both sides and halted any offensive ideas the French may have had. Nevertheless, Allied politicians and generals had been planning how to break the German lines since the weather had stopped all serious offensive actions the previous November.

Russian involvement in the war was wavering on the Eastern Front with their staggering losses becoming an increasingly dangerous factor in the country's willingness to continue fighting, but another participant was about to join the spreading conflict.

Before the Battle of the Somme, Germany had considered Britain as a predominantly naval power, viewing France and Russia as their main enemies. The Somme changed this perception and led to Germany's introduction of unrestricted submarine warfare in January 1917, in an attempt to starve Britain out of the war. Across the Atlantic, public opinion towards Germany had grown increasingly negative following the introduction of this new, extremely risky strategy. High-profile American civilian shipping losses had caused outrage and the sinking of seven merchantmen early in 1917 had been the final straw. On 6 April America entered the war. Although both sides knew it would take some time until a significant degree of their military might could be brought to bear on the European battlefields, the news certainly served to increase the Allies' morale.

Back in France, Robert Nivelle had taken over as the Commander-in-Chief from Joseph Joffre in December 1916 after the costly fighting at Verdun. Flamboyant and confident, Nivelle announced that he would break the German lines in a massive onslaught and promised to end war within forty-eight hours at the cost of a relatively meagre 10,000 French casualties. In support of this major blow, British and Commonwealth forces would be committed 80km to the north where they would break through the formidable Hindenburg Line around the French city of Arras.

The Battle of Arras was planned as a preliminary attack, designed to draw off German reserves and direct their focus from other areas of the front. Unknown to the Allies, Nivelle's all-important element of surprise had been lost when, on 4 April, a German raid into the French trenches had returned with secret documents detailing the coming offensive. Unbeknown to the assembling French troops, they would be advancing towards well-prepared and fully reinforced German lines.

However, for the time being this was an undetected factor and the opening British attacks of what would be called the Battle of Arras took place on Easter Monday, 9 April 1917, between Vimy in the north and Bullecourt to the south.

In the northern sector, the Canadians captured the 'impregnable' Vimy Ridge on the heels of a heavy bombardment that destroyed German defensive positions, the 13th Brigade of the British 5th Division going in with the 2nd Canadian Division. British divisions in the centre carried significant gains but the British and Australian assaults in the southern sector enjoyed less success as they came up against the German 'elastic defence' concept, which limited their momentum.

In the 5th Division area, although the 13th Brigade were involved in the opening day of the battle, the 15th and 95th Brigades were held in reserve, ready to move in support of the Canadians at a moment's notice. Under these conditions, training continued in the Bedfordshires' billeting area for several days until move orders saw the division relieve the 4th Canadian Division. The Bedfordshires were posted to brigade support at Villers au Bois on 13 April as the senior officers and NCOs scouted Vimy Ridge and Givenchy-en-Gohelle to the east. That day also saw Lieutenant Percival Hart and Second Lieutenant Basil Williams rejoin, along

THE BATTLE OF ARRAS

with Second Lieutenant Frederick Hague who had recovered from wounds received in the 2nd Bedfordshires.

As the division continued the advance against the German lines, at 2 a.m. the following day the Bedfordshires marched east to the Zouave Valley, west of Vimy Ridge. As they constructed a road running from Tottenham Tunnel to Givenchy that would take four days to complete in dreadful conditions, 19-year-old Second Lieutenant Douglas Hood of Golders Green was killed by a shell, the track being named Hood Track in his memory. Douglas had been with the battalion for over a year, helping to organise their recreation at every opportunity, and despite getting his aviator's licence with the Royal Flying Corps, chose to serve in the infantry. Second Lieutenant Leonard Dolman, a teacher from Suffolk, was also wounded by a shell splinter in his right shoulder, having been with the battalion just a matter of weeks; he would be back on the Western Front in October, only to receive his third and final wound while in the 8th Bedfordshires during Christmas week, dying on New Year's Eve. Private Sidney Short[24] from Norfolk was also killed and a further four were hit by shrapnel as they worked, including another of the 1914 Old Contemptibles, Frederick Eames[25] of Watford, who died from his wounds the next day.

Between the intense, never-ending fatigue duties, the men took the opportunity to write home, many proving to be fateful last letters, including one penned by Second Lieutenant Thomas Fletcher. A popular officer who was well liked among his peers and the men alike, Thomas had returned from working in Shanghai, China, when war had broken out, joining the 1st Bedfordshires in September 1916 while they fought on the Somme battlefields. A notable cheerful, upbeat and almost carefree man, Thomas's tone must have been a surprise to his parents as they read his letter a few days later.[26]

*Since I last wrote I have had the most strenuous period since coming to the front. It has been a matter of working at high pressure during every minute of darkness and often during daytime as well, and no chance for sleep. Have not had my clothes off for a fortnight. The country where we are is part of the Hindenburg Line. More I cannot tell you. I thought I had seen the limit of destruction in the matter of shell fire on the Somme, but this has been the most terrific bombardment since the commencement of the war, as so sudden had been our push that a wounded man told me that the Germans were absolutely panic stricken when our men went over the top. The next few days will be a dangerous time for me, and I shall not be able to write you again. These few lines will only be sent to you in case it is my last opportunity. Well, dear mother and father, my heart is too full to write more. You will always have the consolation that I am quite ready to give my all for the cause I came home to fight for. If it is God's will to call me, I shall meet you all by and by in the land where all is peace and happiness.*

A Company's Chris Runham from Biggleswade was another who wrote home between the fatigues, discussing the local band and how he had met fellow band member George Boness days earlier, remarking how 'we are in a warm part of the line, and have been busy clearing up the mess they made of the Germans a little while back'. His letter was published in a local paper almost a fortnight later, the family and publishing staff unaware that Chris was among those posted as missing after the battalion's attack on 23 April, his parents having to wait until August 1918 for confirmation of his death.[27]

By the time orders arrived to move forward at 6 p.m. on 17 April, a dozen more men had been lost to shelling and the general advance on the divisional front had been brought to a standstill by a heavily engineered defensive line. The Bedfordshires had relieved the Norfolks and a group of Canadians on the open ground between Givenchy and La Coulotte by 2.30 a.m., in staggered positions between 200 and 500 metres from the German trenches. Their first and most pressing task was to deepen their shell holes and connect them, thus forming a basic defensive line from which to repel any counter-attacks. This task kept them busy until relieved on the evening of 19 April, with the battalion having lost remarkably few men considering their exposed position and the heavy bombardments they were subjected to. A day's rest at the Bois de la Folie was followed by two in the Zouave Valley preparing for action, their operational orders finally reaching them late on 21 April. Twenty-four hours later the battalion were marching across Vimy Ridge under cover of darkness, with another difficult task ahead of them.

## La Coulotte: 23 April 1917

The Battle of Arras had been raging for two weeks, with British and Commonwealth casualties mounting at an alarming rate once they started coming across unmolested, reinforced and well-sited German positions. The latest phase of the battle, later named the Second Battle of the Scarpe, saw nine divisions attack on a 16km frontage running from Bailleul to north of Bullecourt. As a supporting action, the British 5th Division were assigned the task of taking the Thelus Line at the northern edge of the battle zone, to the east of the Vimy Ridge.

Facing the division was a well-crafted defensive line. Three thick belts
of wire ran from the electricity works 500 metres north-west of La
Coulotte, through the village itself and on to Acheville some 6km to the
south-east. Behind the wire were two trench lines with numerous bomb-
proof dugouts and machine-gun emplacements, both in turn supported
by reinforced concrete and steel structures to their rear including defensive positions constructed around a railway embankment at the far-
thest northern point of the divisional sector, at the electricity works, the
houses in La Coulotte, a water tower, and a factory, in addition to several
independent structures that would have been completely innocuous in
peacetime. With well-plotted, mutually supportive fields of fire and a
flat, open expanse over which the attackers had to advance, the defending Germans held the advantage as the 95th Brigade lined up on the
northern half of the 5th Division front with the 15th Brigade taking
positions opposite the village. In the brigade's ominous pre-battle report,
La Coulotte was described as a 'veritable fortress'.

Overnight the assaulting battalions took up places around 270 metres
from the German lines, with the Duke of Cornwall's Light Infantry  on
the northern flank, then the Devons of the 95th Brigade, with the Bedfordshires next and on the southern flank the 1st Norfolks. The 16th
Warwickshires held supporting positions, with the rest of the division being
held back in reserve. The Bedfords faced north-east towards La Coulotte

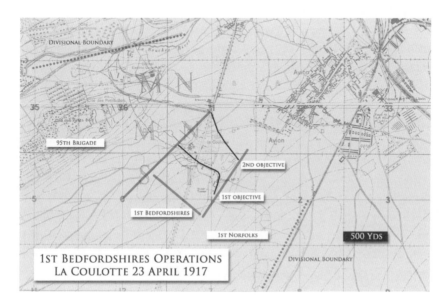

1ST BEDFORDSHIRES OPERATIONS
LA COULOTTE 23 APRIL 1917

itself, with the water tower and Fosse No. 7 on their right flank and the road running from Givenchy to La Coulotte on their left.

At 4.45 a.m. on St George's Day, the two brigades advanced behind a creeping barrage, each battalion progressing with two companies in front and two in support. On the Bedfordshires' front, B Company held the northern half, with D Company as back-up, while A Company advanced to their south, aided by C Company. It was not long before the entire line reached the thick belts of wire but to their dismay, they had not been cut by the British barrage. Small groups hacked their way through with cutters or bayonets but the barrage had left them behind long before they were in a position even to consider attacking the German trenches. The Bedfordshires could see lines of German defenders holding their hands up ready to surrender, but once their machine gunners got to work on the beleaguered British trapped at the wire, they soon took up their weapons and added to the deadly hail of fire being directed at the attackers.

Among the early casualties, Second Lieutenant Vernon Edward Curry of Old Trafford in Manchester was killed, aged 24. In a letter to his widow,[28] Lieutenant Colonel Worrall wrote that Sergeant Reginald Humphries[29] saw him fall during the initial advance, his death being instantaneous.

Unable to get through the unbroken belts of wire and losing heavily in each new attempt, much of the British line took cover in shell holes, where they remained under heavy shell fire all day until darkness gave them the opportunity to retire.

According to a later statement,[30] Private Edgar Gurney[31] saw Second Lieutenant Ackroyd hit by a bullet around 5 a.m. close to the German wire, where he remained motionless. Private Gurney was soon wounded himself and made it back to the dressing station, but his platoon officer did not and was initially posted as missing, believed killed. Second Lieutenant Thomas Noel Ackroyd, a former Inns of Court soldier from before the war, was 24 years old and is remembered on the Arras memorial to the missing.

Just after 5 a.m. on the 15th Brigade front, a few platoons of Bedfordshires from A and C Companies on the right, along with a handful of Norfolks, found and exploited a gap in the wire south of the water tower and to the north a group from the DCLI held their gains along the railway embankment, but any attempts to support the stricken troops led to heavy casualties, so was abandoned.

One of those killed during the advance from the wire into the water tower trench was Corporal Frederick Hazelton[32] from St Neots. Described in a letter to his father, a Baptist pastor, as having a *'quiet, retiring nature, kind and generally beloved',*[33] the 23-year-old librarian and Sunday school teacher had been with the battalion since the previous August.

Undaunted by the hail of fire being directed at them, the groups of Bedfordshires, bolstered by the handful of Norfolks now in the German lines around the water tower, organised themselves into bombing parties and started clearing the trenches yard by yard, using their reliable tactic of bombers and bayonet men working together. However, their advances came to an abrupt halt once they reached concrete emplacements that had no approaches, being encircled with thick, untouched belts of wire. Platoon commander Lieutenant Harold Bird had made it into the trench with most of his men and survived to write to the parents of the 21-year-old Lance Corporal James O'Brien[34] of Letchworth, explaining how he had fallen while in charge of a section of bombers assaulting one such machine-gun post.[35] In spite of these unassailable positions, elements of C Company had broken into the second trench lines before 8 a.m., with some even making it into the houses south-east of the village.

Later in the morning orders arrived for A and C Companies to cover their northern flank as no contact could be made with the two companies to their north, and a patrol was sent out to try to identify where the left-hand companies were. Lance Corporal Frederick Rowley[36] of Edgware volunteered to take the patrol out into the fire-swept open ground but was unable to make contact, winning the Military Medal for his bravery during the patrol and throughout the day.

At 10 a.m. the German barrage increased in intensity, not easing up until around 7 p.m. Under this barrage, B and D Companies on the left of the battalion line broke through the first belt of wire, only to find a deeper belt awaiting them. Under shell and machine-gun fire, they started the process of overcoming this new obstacle, regardless of their mounting casualties. Enfilade fire caught the right section of their lines unexpectedly from their open right flank, a German platoon having crept along an unseen communications trench to outflank them. Lieutenant Robert Hunter, who was pinned to the right of their position, reported how he watched helplessly while the men became surrounded 'like rats in a trap'. Being bombed from three sides, the small party of survivors had little option but to surrender as most had already become casualties in the close-quarters fighting.

While this was developing, the left-hand platoons continued their advance and by late morning had made it as far as the second trench before being halted by a significantly stronger force. Second Lieutenant Arthur Woodford was wounded during the exchange and made it back to report that they were managing to hold on to a short communications trench running parallel to the Givenchy to La Coulotte road. Captain Charles Morris, in command of B Company, was killed while he rallied his men and led another attack from the front against the machine guns dominating the second trench line. Captain Morris had already been wounded in the 2nd Bedfordshires at Neuve Chapelle and again in Serbia while attached to the Royal Irish Fusiliers, but although he was listed as killed in action it was later learned that he died as a prisoner of war at Malmaison on 7 May, a week before his 22nd birthday.

Once news of Captain Morris's death was known, Captain William Chirnside assumed the initiative, having already been extremely busy during the assault. Heavy casualties had not stopped him leading his men from the front to their objectives and despite suffering from shock after being buried by a heavy-calibre shell, he held his men in position against successive counter-attacks.

With mounting casualties, no support and a dwindling supply of ammunition, C Company's attacks on the right ground to a halt and the defenders, realising the situation, grew in confidence. By 11 a.m. just one hundred Bedfordshires remained in the German lines and no support could make it through to them.

Corporal Herbert Ball[37] of St Neots was among those who had forced their way into the German lines, but was wounded during an exchange of fire. No further news was heard of him, leaving Second Lieutenant Ernest Hanssen to write home to Herbert's mother after the battle. Explaining the events[38] he wrote, *'Unfortunately another portion of the attack was held up and many of these splendid fellows (among whom, your son has always been most prominent) were surrounded and compelled to surrender. It is very probable that your son is one of these, and it is most likely that he is now a prisoner of war in German hands, but otherwise in the best of health.'* Sadly, enquiries into his whereabouts revealed that three days later Corporal Ball died from wounds in German hands.

Messages from C Company eventually made it back to Battalion HQ, in the hands of the Mons veteran Sergeant Samuel Baxter,[39] who had already been wounded in the stomach but carried on fighting until he was ordered back against his will. On arrival, Sergeant Baxter urgently requested bombs and reinforcements and was recommended for the

Distinguished Conduct Medal although he was later awarded with a Military Medal. Lieutenant Colonel Worrall, realising that no support was being moved forward from divisional reserves and fearing for his entire battalion, requested permission to retire. At 1.30 p.m. the request was refused so Lieutenant Horace Everett was sent forward with a thrown-together squad of those left in Battalion HQ, carrying 700 bombs between them. In his group was Private James Sinclair[40] of Wisbech who was largely responsible for the party making it to the front lines despite being under heavy fire. During the battle he also voluntarily carried two urgent messages with a complete disregard to his own personal safety and was noted for laughing and joking with his comrades as the intense German barrage fell around them, thus raising the spirits and determination of all those in the bomb-carrying party. James was recommended for the Distinguished Conduct Medal but settled for a Military Medal and promotion to Corporal.

Back in the water tower trench, constant counter-attacks were thrown at the isolated survivors and gradually forced the Bedfordshires back along the trenches they had battled so hard to win. Having already fought courageously all day, the battalion's entertainment maestro Second Lieutenant John Sullivan saw the arrival of Horace Everett and 700 bombs as a perfect opportunity, instantly organising and leading a counter-attack, thus keeping the numerically superior German troops at bay. Urgent efforts to get their wounded back were made and a desperate bayonet charge was planned and led by a Norfolk sergeant in an attempt to relieve the pressure. By 3 p.m. it was clear that the few survivors had little choice but to retire, as they were in danger of being completely overwhelmed. Under the cover of yet another ferocious counter-attack from Second Lieutenant Sullivan and a small group of bombers, a band of around sixty surviving Bedfordshires and Norfolks could be seen re-tiring back through the smoke and barbed wire under heavy fire, seeking the dubious cover of shell holes until darkness would allow them to slip away. Soon after their arrival, the determined figure of Lieutenant Everett again appeared, hauling more bombs with him in readiness for their defence. John Sullivan won the Military Cross and Horace Everett was awarded a bar to add to the Military Cross he had won just months earlier.

On the left side of their attack, the remnants of B and D Companies who had not made it into the German trenches were pinned in front of the wire under relentless artillery and machine-gun fire, with the isolated group of survivors still holding on in the German trenches. Lieutenant Geoffrey Millais was among those constrained in the ragged line of shell holes close to the German trenches and kept the German gunners' attentions fixed on his position throughout the day to enable the parties on either side to develop their assaults. Although later recommended for the Military Cross, he was mentioned in despatches for bravery instead. Old Contemptible Sergeant Walter Hilliard[41] was also among the trapped band of men and set a stoic example to his platoon, rallying and steadying them while under heavy fire. He was recommended for a Military Medal, but no award was made.

Second Lieutenant Thomas Murray Kilpin Fletcher was wounded during D Company's attack and his servant, Private Robert Brown[42] of Baldock, was killed trying to bring his wounded officer in. Private Brown had already been wounded three times in the war and Lieutenant John Kingdon of their company wrote to Brown's widow,[43] remarking how Private Brown and his officer were like two good friends and that his self-sacrifice had not gone unnoticed. Despite his servant's best efforts, Second Lieutenant Fletcher was also killed soon afterwards. Days later, not long after receiving a letter penned by Thomas just before the battle, his parents received two letters in the same delivery by a cruel twist of fate, one of which was an official letter from the War Office, so demanded their immediate attention. It contained notification of their son's death in action, which must have been made even worse by the fact that the second letter was an untidily written note from their son. In communications with the War Office, who requested a copy of the letter to establish his will,[44] his father wrote *'It was simply a short note. A farewell message, as he felt sure it was his last. He knew our men were in a position that meant this and we knew he would never surrender. I don't like the idea of sending away his last letter.'* The note had been removed from Thomas's tunic and sent on to the addressee, having been written while he was wounded and hopelessly pinned down.

The dwindling platoon hemmed into the German communications trench at the northern end of the battalion lines under Captain Chirnside stubbornly held out, the captain only arranging their retirement after specific orders arrived pulling them back. Taking care of the wounded first and moving them out as opportunities allowed, he held the men in place by personal example, sharing the firing line with them while continually organising their defence and with a complete disregard for his own safety. Later that afternoon a protective barrage landed on the

German second lines and, taking advantage of the smoke it created, Chirnside's band retired back to rejoin the main line in No Man's Land. After the battle Captain Chirnside was understandably recommended for the Distinguished Service Order, but a bar to his existing Military Cross from Gallipoli was issued instead.

To the south, the 1st Norfolks had a similarly bad time of it, with only a few groups making it through the wire, some also getting as far as their second objective. Enfilade fire from the south stopped all attempts to support the advanced parties, with a withdrawal from the German lines being the only option open to them.

As the rearguard conducted their stubborn withdrawal, Captain James McKay, RAMC, attached to the 1st Bedfordshires, along with stretcher-bearers Richard Hoar[45] of Hemel Hempstead and Frederick Sapsford[46] of the Bedfordshires, worked tirelessly in the open while under heavy fire, evacuating thirty casualties between them. Captain McKay won the Military Cross, with Privates Hoar and Sapsford both getting the Military Medal.

Once the battalion started to gather and take stock of their situation, Second Lieutenants Illingworth and Hart were identified as being wounded and missing. Lance Sergeant Edward Flitton[47] and seven men volunteered to venture back to the German lines and search for them.

Second Lieutenant Percival Hart, a 23-year-old former chartered accountant, was discovered suffering from wounds to his legs, chest and arms, probably the result of a close-range grenade explosion. He was moved back to No. 32 Stationary Hospital and on 28 April was reported as being dangerously ill. After a long struggle against his wounds, Percival died in Wimereux on 3 May, having only rejoined the battalion a few weeks before after recovering from wounds sustained on Hill 60 two years earlier.

Second Lieutenant Frederick Illingworth, a 21-year-old former shipping clerk from Liverpool who had served in the King's Liverpool Regiment as a private from 1913, had already recovered from two separate wounds, but the third was to prove too much. He could not be found during the search and remained listed as wounded and missing until his body was discovered in June and buried 1,000 metres south-west of Avion. Although the location was reported, it was later lost and he is remembered on the Arras memorial to the missing.

Lance Sergeant Flitton's bravery during the battle itself and in the subsequent search for the missing officers was noted, his commanding officer recommending him for the Military Medal, but no award was made to him or any of his squad.

Four more second lieutenants were also wounded. William Martin Stantan from London was hit by a machine-gun bullet which passed through his right thigh a day after his 20th birthday, his second wound of the war; Arthur James Fyson of Luton was wounded when high-explosive shell splinters entered his left thigh, groin and buttock; Frederick Hague was also hit, having rejoined just ten days earlier and would return again three months later; Harold Augustus Deacon, who had been with the battalion since the previous summer but was hit by an explosive bullet in the left buttock, would endure several operations, survive pneumonia in 1918 and resign on account of ill health in 1919.

Among the long list of casualties from the other ranks were Military Medallist's Corporals Frank Bradley from Australia and Harold McHugh from Royston. Frank was killed in the assault but Harold was hit by shrapnel in the left arm and hand while dressing the wounds of another comrade. His second wound of the war, Harold was sent back to Mile End Road hospital in London to recover, giving him a welcomed break from the fighting.

Several recommendations were made for gallantry medals after the action, which went unsatisfied, the men receiving nothing whatsoever. Company Sergeant Major Walter Freer,[48] a regimental veteran of eighteen years whose service included the South African wars, was put forward for the Distinguished Conduct Medal for his stirring leadership under intense fire; Private Charles Vowles[49] from Taunton was also recommended for the Distinguished Conduct Medal for carrying messages under extremely heavy, close-range fire and would be commissioned as an officer in the 2nd Bedfordshires a year later; Lance Corporal William Smith[50] from Stevenage laid a communications cable in the open under heavy fire to keep messages flowing back to Battalion HQ and, having completed his task, he advanced again, only to be wounded. He remained in the battle throughout the day and, only when relieved, was treated and moved back through the casualty system, dying on 7 May at Boulogne; Lance Corporal George Bland from Arlesey continued organising and fighting in his Lewis-gun team despite being injured in the left side, left shoulder and right thigh, and was recommended for a bar to his Military Medal, which was not granted. In a letter to his mother, he remarked how 'the bounders' gave him his second wound of the war while he 'was trying to get away'.[51]

Arthur Izzard from St Albans was more fortunate in that he was awarded with a Military Medal for bravery. A pre-war reservist and veteran of the 1914 fighting, Arthur was wounded during the final actions of the war, dying from his injuries on 30 January 1919.[52]

One of the survivors and veteran of the 1914 fighting, Algernon Breed from Shefford, known as Algy, wrote after the battle that he had *'been in it again on the Ridge, but lucky to get off once more. We put up a good show, and are keeping up the name of the regiment. I am in my seventh year of service now, but can see no hopes of finishing yet. When I went over this piece of ground I was surprised, for it was worse than the Somme for shell holes. They all joined one another. They were our shells that did it, and there were not many holes that were not as wide as a road in Bedfordshire. Harry Brice and George Endersby are all right, but they tell me that Corporal Dilley is killed.'* [53]

The battalion's jungle drums were accurate and, although initially posted as missing, George Dilley from Luton was later presumed to have been killed, as was David Dilley from Biggleswade. Both are recorded on the Arras memorial to the missing, along with most of their comrades who fell that day.[54]

George Howlett from Luton, winner of the Distinguished Conduct Medal on the Somme, was also wounded. George had returned to the battalion on 2 October 1916 after recovering from his wound from 6 September, only to be injured a second time at La Coulotte. George's time with the battalion had come to an end as, once he had recovered, he was commissioned and attached to the Royal West Kents, where he served out the remainder of the war. In 1920, George would resign his commission and enlist into the ranks of the Royal Air Force, retiring in 1937 with the rank of Sergeant Mechanic and going on to serve in an administrative capacity during the Second World War.[55]

Fourteen-year veteran George Gazeley from Westoning picked up his fourth wound stripe of the war, which was to be his last as he was retained for service in England once he had healed. His leg was hit by shrapnel in four places and in April 1919, George was discharged on completion of his second period of service, with several long service stripes and an array of campaign medals to go with the Military Medal he had won at Longueval on the Somme.[56]

Arthur Jackson from Eaton Bray was also killed. Arthur was the second son his parents had lost, the first having died almost five years earlier to the day when he went down with the *Titanic*, on which he served as an assistant boot steward.[57]

During the long day, the 15th Brigade lost 36 officers and over 700 men, the 95th Brigade some 30 officers and 850 men, with neither brigade being able to hold their objectives. Of the 1,600 divisional casualties, the 1st Bedfordshires lost 11 officers and 320 men, which equated to almost half of the entire brigade's losses over the two weeks at Vimy, with the Norfolks losing a further 15 officers and 220 men. In the main assault to their south the picture was just as grim, with British casualties running to around 10,000 of their best assault troops, for the reward of precious few gains.

In his post-battle report, Lieutenant Colonel Worrall made it clear that, although extremely pleased with the conduct of his men, he was not especially happy with the day's events from a tactical perspective, remarking that *'The whole undertaking seemed to be most hazardous. I considered the Water Tower Trench to be key to the situation and so attacked it frontally and in enfilade. Had I not got this footing, my Battalion must have been wiped out by Water Tower Trench if we were held up by wire.'*

The brigade report was also understandably critical of the overall plan being allowed to proceed, spelling out several 'lessons to be learned'. Remarking how the assault illustrated *'the impossibility of carrying out an enterprise of the above nature without sufficient preliminary bombardment'*, further criticisms on the *'difficulty and danger of hastening on a "show" at the eleventh hour'*, in addition to *'the unreliability of aeroplane reconnaissance as far as wire is concerned'* were recorded. Finally, encouraging subalterns who had carried out patrols to *'express their true opinion'*, the report added the telling remark *'The Subaltern officer is only too ready to accept personal danger in carrying or patrolling but is often afraid of rendering a discouraging report and thus run the risk of being considered "faint hearted".'*

Two more weeks of the bloodiest and most pointless fighting of the war followed but although the Battle of Arras officially carried on until 16 May, the 1st Bedfordshires would not be called on to take further part in offensive actions. By mid-May the British had suffered over 150,000 losses, equating to their highest daily casualty rate of the war. Although sources vary, those on the German side were estimated at around 120,000.

With promises of a stunning victory, the Nivelle offensives further south had started on 16 April, finally grinding to an inglorious halt on 9 May, with the French penetrating 4km into German lines and having accounted for around 160,000 German defenders. The French admitted to 93,000 casualties, although it is possible that the figure was twice as high given that they lost 120,000 during the first five days alone. Their massive losses overloaded the French medical system and widespread unrest rippled through the French army, turning into mutinous behaviour in almost half of the French infantry divisions. Around 30,000 French troops simply refused to move into the front and support lines on 27 May, instead retiring to the reserve areas in protest.[58] The act signalled that the French army disagreed with the way the war was being waged but they did not refuse to fight. General Haig wrote in his personal diary[59] how an entire brigade marched on Paris after looting a supply column, another convoy was looted, and one French village was even occupied, forcing French cavalry to retake it with force.

In the aftermath, over 23,000 French troops were convicted of mutiny and although over 500 were sentenced to death, less than one in ten sentences were actually carried out.[60]

Nivelle was sacked and disgraced, the unenviable task of keeping the French army in the field and restoring morale falling to General Philippe Pétain. Along with more regular leave for his troops, Pétain also agreed that all offensive operations, for the immediate future, would be suspended.

Added to this, Russia had experienced the first series of revolutions in March and a Provisional Government had been established to calm the strikes and rioting, with their part in the alliance looking unsteady at best. So, with their two major allies both reeling from internal unrest, British and Commonwealth forces would have to bear the brunt of any offensive actions for the foreseeable future.

Chapter 3

# The Vimy Sector:
# 24 April to 3 September 1917

*'What a horrid war! . . . You people at home, I think, paint it with a deal*
*of glamour, just as of old we used to think what a jolly life the pirate must*
*have had, but that's all bunkum. The fact is that it is absolutely beastly*
*and all boredom.'*

Until early September the Bedfordshires would remain in the Arras sector,
with much of their time in the front-line trenches being spent around
Oppy, 10km north-east of Arras itself.

Late on 23 April the two battle-worn brigades were relieved, the Bedfordshires retiring to a camp at Berthonval, many instantly falling asleep
after their arduous ordeal. On 24 April a move to Cambligneul, 15km
due west from Vimy, was followed by two days of resting, reorganising
and cleaning up.

After a further move 4km north-east to Gouy-Servins on 27 April the
battalion were kept busy with brigade games and specialist training, two
companies even being allocated baths in Camblain-l'Abbé. During the
sporting distractions, the Bedfordshires beat the 1st Devonshires 2–1 in
football but were not placed in the brigade horse jumping competition.

The battalion's reverend captain wrote to a friend of his in the UK
after the Battle of Arras, illustrating that even those with the staunchest
of faiths and beliefs were unable to consistently maintain the 'business as
usual' attitude shown throughout the country, especially having seen and
done so much. Having been at the front supporting both of the regular
battalions since the outbreak of war, the reverend was serving in a general hospital at the time, having a 'rest' from the front, although not from
the constant trials of being a reverend in such a costly war.[61]

*What a horrid war! I am for the line quite soon again, now. You people at home, I think, paint it with a deal of glamour, just as of old we used to think what a jolly life the pirate must have had, but that's all bunkum. The fact is that it is absolutely beastly and all boredom. The poor old Padre gets worst off going through the pockets of and burying the dead, then writing home to say what fine fellows they all were. I had my turn at Loos etc. However, if I must go up, Kismet! Just carry on and trust. But it's a weird feeling to the man with any sensibility when you follow the lads over the top. Don't believe the people who say they don't have the 'wind up'. Why I didn't float upon the atmosphere, I don't know … R [censored, but should read Rouen], where I am now, is not a bad spot … we have just had another batch of mangled humanity in, and I have had a rough time. … The British soldier is the absolute limit of true nobility. I have just helped in a poor fellow with a leg off at the thigh and the other foot off, and, probably, may lose a hand, and yet he says he's 'fine'! The Padre's convoy from this lot will be a fat one. One poor fellow has hung wounded on the wire in front of the Hindenburg Line for three days and he tells me he was conscious all the time. You would not credit the tales of wanton destruction that one hears that the Bosche has committed on the retreat – absolutely fiendish. There is not a bush – currant or rose – even left.*

Major General Reginald Stephens, in command of the 5th Division, inspected the battalion on 26 April and was joined by the Canadian Corps commander Lieutenant General Sir Julian Byng during their church parade on 29 April.

The process of rebuilding the battalion got under way with Second Lieutenants Charles Whitfield and Harold Henry Reynolds joining on 28 April, Captain Eric Fanning arriving the following day, and trickles of other ranks returning after treatment for slight wounds. Nevertheless, by the time they were back in the front lines ten days later, they could still only muster a 'trench strength'[62] of around 400.

A four-day spell back in Cambligneul from 30 April included night training in readiness for attacking over open ground, and orders arrived on 3 May for the division to relieve the 1st Canadian and 2nd British Divisions in the line from Fresnoy to Oppy, where they would be moved into Lieutenant General Congreve's XIII Corps. Their new corps included the veteran, regular 2nd Division, the predominantly northern 31st Division and the renowned 63rd (Royal Naval) Division, which included the 4th Bedfordshires. That day also saw Lieutenant Colonel Francis Butler leave to assume command of the 11th Essex, the rest of the battalion moving 14km south-east to an open field north of Roclincourt.

Training continued as the officers scouted what would be their new lines, with the battalion running into the 4th Bedfordshires on 5 May; they had been heavily engaged at Gavrelle with the 63rd (Royal Naval) Division. Repairing tracks and roads took much of the spare time up, although an impromptu football match against the 4th Bedfordshires was squeezed in on the 6th.

## The Arleux–Fresnoy sector: 8 to 24 May 1917

At 9.30 a.m. on 8 May move orders arrived, taking the battalion into close support to the 13th and 95th Brigades who had been attacked overnight and forced from Fresnoy-en-Gohelle. With fierce fighting continuing in and around the village, the bulk of the Bedfordshires remained in an old German trench 2km west of Bailleul while the officers scouted the positions they were to take over the following morning.

The 15th Brigade were to adopt their standard defensive scheme while in the Arleux sector, with two battalions in the front, one in support, one in the reserve line 600 metres east of Willerval. At 8.15 p.m. on 9 May the Bedfordshires moved forward, into brigade reserve trenches east of Willerval, thus signalling a spell in the line that would last until 24 May. With only 400 men left to hold the line, each company was organised into two platoons instead of the usual four, with an additional Lewis-gun section being attached to each platoon to strengthen their defensive capabilities. Gas and heavy shelling greeted them that night, continuing throughout the following day, while fatigue parties carried stores forward for those in the front trenches. By the time the battalion moved to take over the front lines on 13 May, ten more men had been lost to shelling.

At 10 p.m. on 13 May the Bedfordshires started to relieve the 1st Cheshires in the left subsector, astride the Arleux-en-Gohelle to Fresnoy-en-Gohelle road, 100 metres east of the edge of Arleux village. Four hours later the uneventful relief was complete and A and D Companies under Captain Montague Halford spread out to hold the 600-metre section of the front lines, with B and C in support. Little more than a series of completely unconnected rifle pits with no link to each other or to the units on either side, the front line threatened to be dangerous and liable to a continued German attack at any moment. Fortunately their spell east of Arleux was uneventful, allowing them to start the process of connecting the holes and forming a defensive trench line. Over the next two days the entire front line was put to the task of digging the front and communications trenches, wiring and establishing strongpoints. In wet, uncomfortable weather on 16 May, B and C Companies under Second

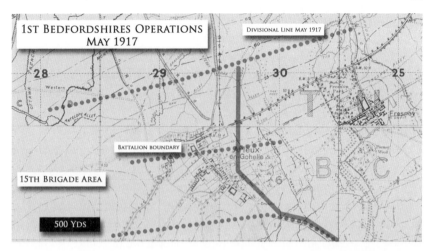

Lieutenant James Hope took over the front line, named Britannia and Brandy trenches, with A and D Companies retiring into Arleux in support.

Although relatively quiet overall, nightly fighting patrols were sent out all along the brigade frontage, their intention being to engage any Germans they came across. Other than a thick mist that stopped any observation, 17 May was equally uneventful and the next evening saw the Bedfordshires moved into brigade reserve south-west of Farbus Wood.

While in reserve the work continued, with digging communications trenches filling many hours of each day. Heavy shelling accounted for twenty casualties during the work including Second Lieutenant William Ogden who was knocked over by a close explosion on the 19th, which peppered the right side of his legs, arms and face with tiny shell fragments. Although William would recover, a more serious wound in January 1918 while serving in the 6th Bedfordshires caused his retirement through ill health.

The Bedfordshires were back in the left subsector from 21 to 24 May, with A and B Companies initially holding the front lines under Lieutenant Millais of B Company. Regular fighting patrols met with no resistance and a patrol under Second Lieutenant Whitfield on 22 May was unable to penetrate German wire so instead lay in front of it for ninety minutes before withdrawing at 2 a.m. On 23 May Lieutenant Colonel Worrall returned from a short leave and elements of the 17th Royal Fusiliers from the 2nd Division scouted the positions in readiness for the entire division's relief. Second Lieutenant Edgar Nailer and his scouts advised the incoming relief of their routes and the lie of the land, while Second Lieutenant John Dalton, a recent arrival from the Artists Rifles, took a fighting patrol out overnight to prevent prying eyes seeing the replacement process but, once again, met no German patrols.

Overnight on 24 May the Bedfordshires were relieved, and by 5.30 a.m. had marched 8km south-west, back to the familiar camp at Roclincourt, where they would be held in corps reserve for almost three weeks.

## Corps reserve: 25 May to 15 June 1917

Cleaning up, resting and refitting started almost immediately, followed by inspections and familiarisation with the reserve area. Lively inter-platoon football matches sprung up on the 26th, and the 27th was busy with a church service, scouting the area, working parties and the arrival of a draft of eight men. After working parties and parades, the final of the inter-platoon football tournament was played the next day, 13 Platoon of D Company winning the enthusiastic game.

As Lieutenant George Blanchard was sent to the field ambulance suffering from a lingering hernia, Second Lieutenant George Sharpin assumed his duties as the Transport Officer, with Lieutenant Millais also taking over as Acting Adjutant, while Second Lieutenant John Kingdon took the small group of new arrivals to the corps draft training school. George Blanchard's hernia would ensure he could not return to the front line again, keeping him in service at the Ampthill Command Depot between hospital visits until demobilised in January 1919, when he returned to his life as a Devon farmer.

Other senior officers went to Écoivres, 35km west, to a lecture on patrolling and self-defence, with Lieutenant Colonel Worrall in turn addressing the officers and NCOs the next day on their duties.

Late that afternoon, once the day's work was done, D Company took the rest of the battalion on in another football match and at 7.30 p.m. Captain Sullivan's entertainment troupe gave an open-air concert to the raucous amusement of all within earshot.

Parades and working parties filled 30 May, with bayonet fighting training for the officers and sergeants at 2 p.m. Lieutenant Ernest Hanssen and a selection of company sergeants scouted the line east of Willerval in preparation for the expected move into that area, returning in time to see the Bedfordshires beating the DCLI 2–1 that afternoon. Second Lieutenant Horace Everett and two men were sent to Wailly, where they watched a display by tanks, but did not return until late that evening.

The work and parades continued the next day and many of the battalion paused to watch a German aeroplane shoot down British observation balloons to the east that afternoon, the observers parachuting to safety to the hearty cheers of those watching. At 6 p.m. another match was played, the Bedfordshires losing 2–0 to the 11th East Lancashires.

On their final day in reserve, 1 June, German aeroplanes homed in on the camp in the early hours, bringing them all to a hasty 'stand to', those veterans from September 1916 vividly recalling the damage they were capable of inflicting on unsuspecting troops. After the usual working parties a mounted gymkhana was held in the afternoon and news came that a draft of fifty-eight men had arrived at the XIII Corps training department, with fifty of them joining the battalion the next day.

From 2 to 9 June the battalion were stationed in the reserve camp east of Willerval, from where they mounted daily working parties to construct a strongpoint west of Arleux-en-Gohelle. On 3 June the Bedfordshires and Norfolks paraded at 12.30 p.m. for the King's birthday and later that night German aeroplanes bombed the transport at Écurie, repeating their raid again the following night. Shell fire wounded two men on the overnight working party late on the 3rd, and a draft of thirty-four arrived on the 5th.

CQMS Frederick Halsey went on ten days' leave to England on the 5th but would not return, having been commissioned into the 7th Bedfordshires. A veteran of the South African wars with seventeen years of service in the regiment, Frederick Halsey was killed by a shell wound to the back in Glencourse Wood, two months later. Initially left with the dressing station, his body was lost but rediscovered after the war and interred in the Hooge Crater cemetery, Belgium.[63]

With the Battle of Messines in full flow 50km to the north, the 15th Brigade were relieved by the 95th on 9 June, the Bedfordshires moving 30km north-west by bus to Camblain-Châtelain, east of Béthune. Being out of range of German guns and all but the most determined aeroplanes, the brigade trained and relaxed. A swimming parade was called before breakfast on 10 June with a church parade at 11.15 a.m. That afternoon three officers arrived at the battalion: Captain Hugh Pearse rejoined having been wounded in the 1st Bedfordshires in 1915, spending almost a year in the 2nd Bedfordshires before becoming ill in March 1917 and returning to the 1st Battalion again once he had regained his health; Lieutenant Arthur Nugent Waldemar Powell, who had been wounded in the battalion on Hill 60 in 1915, and served in the Essex Regiment in the interim before returning to the 1st Bedfordshires; and Second Lieutenant Percival Denis Sisley, who was joining the battalion as a newly commissioned officer.

Bad weather stopped training on 11 June, the battalion taking their pursuits indoors and straight into a lecture given by Major le Huquet on trench orders, followed by Lieutenant Colonel Worrall's address on wood fighting. Subalterns added their own smaller lectures before impromptu competitions in bugle calling, turn-out saluting, marching songs and the like developed. By the end of the morning's activities, B Company had fared the best until the afternoon competitions ventured outside, into more physically demanding sporting challenges. A Company had carried the day by the time 'fall out' was called, the men having enjoyed the day's distractions.

The following morning saw the battalion march to the Bois des Mottes for wood fighting training but they had returned for dinner and brigade sports by the afternoon, when they were greeted by seven reinforcements. The date of 13 June started with widespread training, including on the rifle range, bayonet fighting, rifle grenade practice and bombing practice. Another competition beckoned in the afternoon, the brigade horse show being the main event. The Bedfordshires came second in the wrestling on horseback event, with Lieutenant Colonel Worrall's horse 'Angel Face' coming third in the jumping but winning the VC race. Lance Corporal Hiley came a respectable second in the cross-country race, with the battalion transport proudly winning the general service wagon turnout and coming third in the battalion transport turnout.

On their last full day in corps reserve, musketry and rifle meetings took precedence as orders had arrived for a move in the morning, the battalion understanding that the focus and intensity of their recent training meant they were going 'over the top' once again.

### Oppy Wood: 28 June 1917

Despite it being a collection of shattered tree stumps, littered with the debris of battle and with the village itself behind the wood nothing more than low piles of rubble, Oppy was nevertheless a formidable defensive position. Comprising carefully sited trenches, machine-gun posts, reinforced dugouts and thick belts of wire, the wood had already withstood assaults from the veteran 2nd Division on 28 April and the 31st Division on 3 May. Added to this, in the two unmolested months since the last assault, the position had been strengthened and interlocking fields of fire perfected.

Orders for the 5th Division to relieve the 2nd Division in the left sector of XIII Corps' line from 13 June arrived, with the 15th Brigade starting

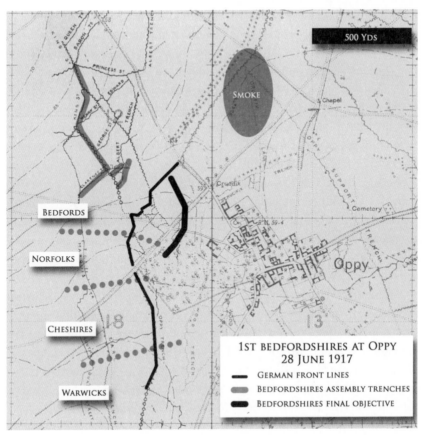

their relief on the 15th. Returning to Roclincourt again by bus on 15 June, the Bedfordshires were moved into the divisional reserve area ready for their return to the front lines, their brief holiday over. At 7 p.m. on 16 June the Bedfordshires took over the left sector of their brigade line, facing the north-west corner of Oppy Wood. Learning the ground was their chief objective during the four days in the line so patrols, scouting parties and constant observation became major elements of their daily routine. Casualties continued from German shell fire with Second Lieutenant Robert Moore Hunter being severely wounded on their last day in the line in addition to four men; Lieutenant Hunter was hit by shrapnel in the chest, abdomen, left arm and left knee and, although his active service was over, retained administrative positions until being discharged in 1918.

That evening, Second Lieutenant Harold Winning Fleming joined but found himself moving back into reserve again the following evening once the Bedfordshires returned to Roclincourt.

On the 19th, Second Lieutenant Harold Bird was sent back to the field ambulance suffering from trench fever, nervousness and headaches, and would not return to the battalion again, going on to serve in the Royal Air Force until resigning his commission in 1920.

A day resting and cleaning up was followed by five days of intense training over a prepared course mimicking the imminent operation, with a contingent of 20 officer candidates being attached for three weeks of training from 23 June. A much needed draft of 105 men joined the next day, with a further 10 following a day later.

Among them was Private Harry Bashford, who had been recovering from an attack of scabies in a base hospital, caused by the insanitary conditions of trench life. He had been *'put in chamber and steam filled the room ... allowed out looking like boiled lobsters'*. Most of those who accompanied Harry were new to the front and he would later remark that *'these newcomers, they couldn't have arrived at a worst time'*.

Trained, prepared, and having absorbed fresh drafts, the arrival of move orders on the 26th saw the Bedfordshires make their final preparations before proceeding to assembly positions in readiness for the operation. Second in command Major Montague Halford, Captains William Chirnside and John Sullivan were left with the battalion transport, along with Acting RSM Cecil Walker, CSM Spicer and sixty-six NCOs and men, who collectively formed the details left out of the attack.

While preparing to move into positions ready for the attack overnight on 27 June, ammunition was issued, including bombs. Unfortunately, an accident left sixteen men wounded before they had even made it into the battle zone.

In the days leading up to the assault, several variations of orders had been issued, one even marking their objectives out as being the village of Neuvireuil, 1km further east from Oppy. However, their final instructions left the 5th Division the task of attacking the wood, with the 31st Division taking trenches to the south. The division deployed just the 15th Brigade, with all four battalions in line, and with the specific objective to take the trench system lining the western edge of the wood only. The Bedfordshires held the northern section of the brigade sector and were tasked with taking the trenches on the north-western face of the wood, with the Norfolks, Cheshires and Warwicks respectively positioned to their south and securing the entire length of Oppy trench to a point some 500 metres south of the wood. Each battalion lined up with two companies in front and two in support.

Throughout 28 June routines continued, giving the impression of business as usual to German observers, other than a spectacle witnessed by groups of Bedfords as they quietly prepared for battle: 2km to their north the sky was filled with a dense black cloud as British engineers 'treated' German positions in Fresnoy with burning oil, a dreadful weapon developed in response to the German Flammenwerfer.

At 5.10 p.m. a heavy German bombardment fell on the brigade's assembly trenches and by the end of the fifteen-minute inferno, the brigade had taken 'heavy casualties', most being in the Bedfordshires' section. Then ninety minutes later, after a hot, dry day, the weather broke.

In the cooling rain, the Bedfordshires took up their final positions. C Company were to advance on the left, supported by D Company who also had orders to swing to their left and form a defensive flank, while B Company were to take the right, with a single platoon from A Company in direct support. In all, 348 Bedfordshires were all that could be mustered for the assault.

After the disaster at La Coulotte, British artillery were issued very specific orders and given enough time to prepare and carry them out. To that end, at 7.10 p.m. British artillery opened up with an intense bombardment, the wire being all but obliterated. In accordance with their orders, the defensive trenches were left largely intact, thereby giving the attacking troops time to consolidate and prepare for counter-attacks. At the same time a smoke barrage was unleashed to the north-east of the Bedfordshires, providing a protective screen against lethal, aimed machine-gun fire bowling them over as they advanced across the open ground.

Knowing that an attack was forming in the British trenches, German artillery opened their own counter-bombardment on to the assembling troops. Huddled in the trenches was Harry Bashford, who was near to the group of fresh drafts that were being held back from the initial assault.

*These newcomers, they couldn't have arrived at a worst time and they just went berserk. A case of mass shell shock. It was. It was one of the most distressing scenes I've ever witnessed. They just ... Haywire. The whole lot. Thrashing about, bashing. You know, this imaginary thing that if you go this way you'll miss a shell, you know, and we all did it at one time or another but you're better standing still as you're just as likely to be hit wherever you are. ... And our platoon Sergeant, my goodness he'd got a string of ribbons, an old timer. I said he'd obviously sought courage from the rum bottle, 'cos as far as I remember, he was left behind when we went over. I don't remember seeing him ... whether he went over or not, I don't know.*

Regardless of the smokescreen, the Bedfordshires were met with a hail of machine-gun and rifle fire as soon as they went 'over the top'. In the moment of uncertainty that followed, 31-year-old Second Lieutenant Trotter rallied his men and led them from the front as they streamed through the gaps in the wire with a loud, throaty cheer, leaving their fallen where they were. He was hit by a shell fragment in the thigh before reaching the trench but his leadership inspired the men to continue without him, winning him the Military Cross, but losing his left leg in a subsequent operation six weeks later. Trotter's men fell on the defenders with the ferocity of determined, highly motivated soldiers and within five minutes the entire brigade had advanced into the German positions closely behind their creeping barrage, the three battalions to the south of the Bedfordshires meeting little resistance and gaining complete dominance immediately.

In the Bedfordshires' section, the objectives were a little deeper into the German lines so took longer to overcome, C Company running into a strongly defended 'maze-like' trench and requesting reinforcements at 7.25 p.m. Captain Hugh Pearse quickly evaluated the situation and personally led his reserves into the fray, causing sixty-three defenders to surrender and the position to fall within five minutes. He continued to show *'splendid dash and determination in the attack and skilfully organised the work of consolidation afterwards'*, thus winning the Military Cross.

Private Harry Bashford was among the parties working their way through the German trench system.

*When we reached the German front line where they were all in these deep dugouts, we noticed quite a few Germans retreating down the communications trench. This was really the first time I remember shooting at Germans ... then we turned our attentions to the deep dugouts. Over the entrance were these waterproof sheets so, without exposing ourselves, we pulled them aside and threw two Mills bombs in and down the steps. Well, the effect of two grenades exploding in such a confined space was pretty ghastly and I felt almost guilty about what I'd done. ... These Germans came out very badly wounded and surrounded, with the usual cry of "Kamerade".*

Parties immediately advanced 200 metres into the wood, with the intention of setting up forward defensive posts in shell holes that would blunt the expected counter-attacks. Second Lieutenant Ernest Hanssen, the battalion's Lewis-gun officer, hurriedly moved his teams from positions providing supporting fire to the new line of posts in the tangled wood.

Harry Bashford's platoon had advanced into the rear section of the German position, leaving the mopping-up parties to complete the task of clearing any remaining dugouts.

*When we reached their further trenches, they were almost obliterated and we just wondered what casualties the Germans must have suffered. But eventually, we made a front line of sorts, from which a communications trench was dug and from which three listening posts were established.*

*My Sergeant told me to leave the equipment at the first post which we were establishing and move on to the second. The sound of this minenwerfer was heard. It was an ominous sound – whomp, whomp, whomp as they turn over and you can see the spark on the front of them as they do it, you know. It exploded just a few feet from where I had left my equipment, folding the trench in and burying it, but luckily not me. I think the only thing I lost was a safety razor which I had brought from home.*

As the battalion advanced further into the defensive system, a bombing attack was also launched along Fresnoy trench to secure the approaches against any surprises, several dugouts being overcome during the expedition. By the time this trench had been overrun, the position was all but secure and Captain Pearse sent a message back reporting that fifty-one German prisoners had already been taken.

Just as the Bedfordshires started organising the newly won position for defence, the hot, sultry day was broken by a thunderstorm and heavy rain, drenching the troops within moments.

At 8 p.m. the three platoons of A Company that had been initially held in support were moved to the open left flank and ordered to dig in and keep a careful watch for counter-attacks from the north-east, while back at HQ, a curious message arrived from the commanding officer of B Company, who reported *'Great fun. Objectives taken.'*

Just before 8.30 p.m. a fresh German retaliatory barrage started pounding their positions but as the trenches had been left untouched by the British bombardment, enough cover was found to keep casualties to a minimum. By then the dugouts had also been completely cleared of the last hidden knots of defenders and the Norfolks sent a report back to Brigade HQ stating that the Bedfordshires *'had reached their objectives and taken 63 prisoners, besides killing numerous Germans'*.

News reached Battalion HQ at 8.30 p.m. that Second Lieutenant Charles Owen Whitfield had been wounded and by 8.40 p.m. D Company had sent back 20 prisoners. But by now, just 160 Bedfordshires were left in the front lines and messages started filtering back to HQ requesting reinforcements to enable them to hold the extended section of line they were left in command of.

By 9 p.m. the brigade were completing their consolidation and, to their south, the 31st Division had enjoyed similar success, ensuring the operation came to a smooth close. In a welcomed change to the norm, no counter-attacks came their way overnight, the defenders having abandoned the position they had fought so hard for since April.

At 10 p.m. 18-pounder shells from a British battery started falling short, landing on A Company's trenches. Although remedied by short, sharp words with the forward observation officer, who in turn corrected the error, the same happened to C Company around 11.30 p.m.

Mons veteran Sergeant Herbert Hill[64] from Maulden, known as Bert, had been badly wounded in both legs during the initial advance. Realising they would not carry his weight, Bert had dragged himself into a shell hole, only to find it inhabited by four Germans who were telephoning information back to their own lines. As luck would have it, all four happened to be facing the opposite way as Bert slithered into the shell hole but the officer, glancing over towards the noise, saw him and reached for his rifle. Bert quickly grabbed it himself just as the officer fired, taking a piece of his finger off in the process. Wrestling the rifle from his enemy, the four Germans surrendered to the badly wounded but obviously determined British soldier who was threatening them with their own weapon. He covered them with the rifle as they marched back to the British lines, only 60 metres away, before sliding back into the shell hole in pain. The area remained under heavy shell fire overnight and, although he had managed to apply a tourniquet, Bert lost a lot of blood as he waited for stretcher-bearers to find him. After a long night, someone finally heard Bert's calls at 7.30 a.m., over twelve hours after he had been wounded, and recovered the immobile, semi-conscious sergeant. He was seriously ill in hospital for some time before recovering enough to be shipped home. Bert was medically discharged the following January, aged 24. Sergeant Hill was awarded the Military Medal for his gallantry, which was presented to him at Ampthill Park in March 1918 by the Duke of Bedford.

Over and above the 150 or more defenders killed, as well as those who were wounded but retired back to their own support positions, 2 German officers and 141 men were passed back to division as prisoners, along with a raft of captured equipment. However, the cost of this success was high, as 10 officers and 342 men from the 15th Brigade were lost in the attack, of which 3 officers and 117 men were from the Bedfordshires. Other than Second Lieutenants Trotter and Whitfield, it was later learned that Second Lieutenant James Kenneth Hope from Bedford dislocated his knee in the attack. James had slipped into a shell hole during the initial advance and, although continuing with operations for another hour afterwards, found that once the adrenalin had stopped, he could hardly move his left leg. A fortnight later he was returned to the UK for treatment, the rest of his war being served out in the Infantry Records Office, Warwick.

Two of the battalion's Old Contemptible Distinguished Conduct Medal winners were also killed in the fighting: 28-year-old Mons veteran, Acting Company Sergeant Major Walter James Summerfield,[65] who had won his DCM on Hill 60; and Sergeant William Falla[66] from Ipswich, who had been with the battalion since just after the Battle of Le Cateau in 1914 and had won his DCM at Ypres in November 1914.

In contrast, 19-year-old Private Herbert William Lovitt[67] from St Neots was also among those Bedfords killed in the assault. Jimmy, as he was known, had enlisted underage the previous September, his two older brothers already serving. After qualifying as a bomber, Jimmy had joined the battalion in May, only to be killed in his first battle.[68]

Lieutenant Colonel Worrall's post-battle report was full of praise for his men, when recounting their actions, the casualties they inflicted on their enemy and the men and equipment they captured, writing, '*I consider the pertinacity of my officers and NCOs and the valour of my men more than upheld the highest traditions of the Battalion I have the honour to command.*'

In his own report, Brigadier General Turner remarked that '*the morale of the troops in this brigade was always good, but after this operation it attained a standard of perfection, and all the troops are satisfied to know that they accomplished, in magnificent style, all that was asked of them, although expressing regret that the pursuit of the Bosche was not permitted*'.

As a result, another hoard of gallantry medals were issued, with Second Lieutenant Percival Sisley winning the battalion's third Military Cross of the operation, his citation reading: '*When his platoon was held up by superior numbers he showed both fine leadership and control, which resulted in heavy losses being inflicted on the enemy and his objectives being quickly gained and consolidated. His battle discipline was of an exceptionally high order.*'

Two more Distinguished Conduct Medals were issued to Old Contemptibles who had been fighting since Mons.

Acting Colour Sergeant Major Reginald Lansbury[69] from Bromley added the DCM to his Military Medal from 1916, *'For conspicuous gallantry and devotion to duty in commanding his platoon throughout an action, the success of which was largely due to his dash and able leadership. He has invariably shown unbounded energy and fearlessness, and can be relied upon in any emergency.'*

The 22-year-old Sergeant Reginald Puddefoot[70] from Chesham won the second DCM: *'For conspicuous gallantry and devotion to duty in leading his platoon to its objective through a very stiff fight in spite of the fact that he was shot through the thigh whilst topping the parapet. He continued to do excellent work until he was wounded for the second time, and his conduct has on all occasions been conspicuous by its excellence.'* Reg would be transferred into the 1st Lincolnshires once recovered, only to be killed in April 1918.

Two bars to Military Medals were also won: Sergeant James Sinclair[71] from Wisbech, who had cheerfully led a party at La Coulotte, won his bar, and was to go on to secure a further decoration before the year was out; Old Contemptible Sergeant Arthur Faulder,[72] who had been on the front since August 1914, was issued with a bar to complement the Military Medal won the previous year.

Seven more Military Medals were also awarded to men from the 1st Bedfordshires: Sergeant David Stone,[73] another veteran of Mons who would survive the war and go on to serve in the Bedfordshire Brigade in the British Army of Occupation in 1919; Acting Sergeant Harry Norman[74] of Potton and later Berkhampstead, who had been with the regiment since 1905 and had joined the battalion on the front in August 1914 – he had already recovered from wounds received on Hill 60 two years earlier and returned to the 1st Bedfordshires in September 1916; Mons veteran Corporal George Ilott[75] from Hertford, who would be adding to his medal collection before the war was over, rising to the rank of Acting RSM; 37-year-old Private Frederick Dighton[76] of Godmanchester, whose war would come to an unexpected end when a severely sprained ankle in October put an end to his time in the army; Private James Houston,[77] who had initially served in the 6th Bedfordshires, moving into the 1st Battalion having recovered from wounds; Stretcher-bearer Leonard King[78] of Diddington, who was one of five brothers serving with the colours; and Private William Clarke,[79] who had been with the battalion since the end of 1915.

Four gallantry cards were also issued: Sergeant George Neale[80] from Bushey, who had been in the firing line since Mons in 1914; Lance Corporal Arthur Cox,[81] who had been wounded in the 7th Bedfordshires' assault on the Somme on 1 July 1916 before joining the 1st Bedfordshires; Lance Corporal James Price,[82] who had initially served alongside Private James Houston in the 6th Bedfordshires before being transferred into the 1st after recovering from a wound; and Sergeant Reginald Humphries[83] from Tempsford, who was later commissioned as an officer and won the Military Cross in 1918.

On 29 June the Bedfordshires moved north along the trench, enabling the 1st Norfolks to take over their sector as the division aligned itself to make room for their anticipated relief. Other than occasional shelling, the next 24 hours was uneventful, giving the companies time to settle and reorganise in readiness for the incoming division. Although the battalion had expected to be away from the front overnight, their relief was delayed until columns of Scottish Borderers were seen filing along the communications trenches. Unfortunately half of the Bedfordshires could not be reached before dawn on 1 July, the stragglers rejoining the following night.

By the time the 15th Brigade left the line, their casualty report for June showed they lost 15 officers and 395 men during the month, with the Bedfordshires' losses amounting to 11 officers and 136 men.

### Trench life: 1 July to 2 October 1917

The Bedfordshires remained in the area until late September, spending relatively long spells of their battle-free summer in corps support and reserve areas. This was certainly appreciated, given that July and August were hot months and no one enjoyed marching along the winding, stuffy communications trenches towards the front lines, which became so uncomfortable that a brigadier general even reportedly stripped off to his trousers.[84]

Supplies for those on the front were often inconsistent in both regularity and quality, with water being a constant problem for the thirsty men that summer. Private Bashford recalled: *'We did really suffer quite badly from thirst, so it was very unfortunate that when the water did arrive, it was sometimes conveyed in petrol cans, which are very difficult to purge, and so the resulting drink was terrible. It was bad enough having to swallow it, but worst of all it had the unpleasant habit of repeating and one wondered what would have resulted from a belch near a naked flame.'*

Moving into camp near Roclincourt between 1 and 4 July, the battalion spent the time there resting, cleaning up and providing working parties for the Royal Engineers. While in camp on the morning of 2 July, one of their own was attached to the trench mortar battery still being held in the line. Corporal Sidney Wilson of Bourn, who had won the Military Medal the previous year, *'was sitting with one of his comrades under a shelter, when a shell landed on the roof, killing both of them instantly … only last Sunday he was invested with his Military Medal by the Corps Commander and well he earned it'.*[85] Sidney's brother, Gunner James Wilson, had also been killed previously, having been recommended for the DCM but being awarded the Russian Medal of St George instead.

From 4 to 9 July, the Bedfordshires were in reserve east of Willerval, where they provided daily working parties for the front lines. A draft of 152 experienced men joined them on 6 July, all having previously seen action in one of the six Bedfordshire battalions on the Western Front. That day, Second Lieutenant Harold Watson Wright was wounded and Private John Catlyn[86] of Old Buckenham was killed by shelling, but otherwise the tour was quiet.

William Wrenn was awarded the Military Medal on 9 July, having been with the battalion since August 1913. A veteran of Mons, William would survive the war unscathed and continue serving well into the 1930s.[87]

The battalion were moved back to the Écurie Camp on the 9th, remaining there until the 16th, with parades, training, working parties and drill taking up their time. They lined the Arras to Souchez road on 11 July to salute the King as he passed, and cricket was enjoyed the following day, their game against the Warwickshires ending in a draw. The 13th was broken up by Major General Stephens, their divisional commander, presenting a host of medals won at Oppy, but working parties continued until their move back to the support area around Willerval on the 16th.

With time to spare and the long, hot summer days helping to relax the men, letters inevitably started flowing. One of the more mischievous was from Private Charles Dukes, who shared his observations on the remarkable effectiveness of tanks with his fiancée:[88]

*They can do up prisoners in bundles like straw binders, and, in addition, have an adaptation of a printing machine, which enables them to catch the Huns, fold, count and deliver them in quires, every thirteenth man being thrown out a little farther than the others. The tanks can truss refractory prisoners like fowls prepared for cooking while their equipment renders it possible for them to charge into a crowd of Huns and by shooting out spokes like porcupine quills, carry off an opponent on each. Though 'stuck up', the prisoners are, needless to say, by no means proud of their position. They can chew barbed wire and turn it into munitions. As they run, they slash their tails and clear away trees, houses, howitzers, and everything else in the vicinity. They turn over on their backs and catch live shells in their caterpillar feet, and can easily be adapted as submarines; in fact most of them crossed the Channel in this guise. They loop the loop, travel forwards, sideways and backwards, not only with equal speed, but at the same time. They spin round like a top, only far more quickly, dig themselves in, bury themselves, scoop out a tunnel and come out again 10 miles away in half an hour.*

Between the 16th and 20th the Bedfordshires worked on support trenches around Willerval, although on their first day Lance Corporal Charles Cross[89] was mortally wounded by pre-targeted shelling, forcing them to move their camp 700 metres further west overnight.

During the month, a raft of replacement officers joined, bringing the officer corps up to somewhere near its full establishment despite the battalion overall being not much more than 50 per cent strength. Many were young men fresh from Sandhurst, including Second Lieutenant Paul Norman Jones Christie. In a letter home on 11 July, he updated his parents, doubtless belying any concerns they may have had with his dry humour: *'Dear Mummy. Tomorrow I am off up the line taking with me what the Adjutant is pleased to call a "small draft" to join the first battalion. I hear the Boches on their sector are absolutely demoralised at the prospect and "Kamerade" drill is being practised daily.'*[90]

Second Lieutenant Joseph Thornton Laughton joined C Company on the 12th; Second Lieutenant Robert Craigh Hare, a veteran CSM with seventeen years of service in the regiment behind him, and who had been commissioned in the field in July 1917, arrived at B Company on the 15th; Second Lieutenant Paul Norman Jones Christie joined C Company on the 16th; Lieutenant Geoffrey Arthur Anstee transferred from the 2nd Bedfordshires on the 24th, but would return to his original unit within weeks, later rejoining the 1st Battalion in 1919 after a spell as a POW in Germany; and Second Lieutenant William Arthur Jackson made his appearance and would remain with the battalion until a staff appointment with XIV Corps beckoned in Italy early the following year. On 26 July seven more second lieutenants also presented themselves: Frederick Hague and John Thomas Dickinson were posted to A Company; Sidney Allport went into B Company; Arthur William Matson and Alexander Edward Crookewit moved into C Company, although Arthur would soon transfer into the Royal Air Force and spend the final eight months of the war as a POW after his aircraft crashed behind enemy lines; and Frank Flavell and Joseph Cotchin joined D Company. Subalterns Allport, Cotchin and Crookewit had all been through No. 20 Officer Cadet Battalion together before being transferred into the 3rd Bedfordshires on 29 May 1917 and had arrived with the 1st Bedfordshires together.

On 22 July, the battalion returned to Écurie Wood Camp for six days where a 'programme of work, musketry and amusements' was established. In a further letter home on 20 July, Second Lieutenant Christie, although new to the battalion, shared an observation with his mother not often considered by those trying to keep the fighting men busy: '*Next week we are to have organized "intensive" games. Contrary to general belief they are not beloved by "the boys" who like to be left alone at times.*' His letter went on to share some of the ever-present gossip, often created by overactive imaginations with little else to amuse them. '*There is a very strong rumour in the battalion that peace is a matter of weeks now. How it arose I know not.*'

Leave was also granted to men from the battalion while away from the front with '*one Officer and umpteen other ranks*' going away every five days according to Paul Christie. He also remarked in a letter dated 27 July that '*Tonight we are for a Brigade Gas bag march – a form of amusement which I don't appreciate at its true value. The other evening the battalion marched into Arras to see a concert party yclept "The Duds". However there was a hitch and therefore no seats, so the C.O. decided to let them loose in the town for three hours, much to their joy, from 6 to 9pm. What is more they all turned up on time, a bit lively certainly and some had to be assisted home, but very creditable on the whole. The march home was full of melody including "We are the Bedford Boys", a variation of which Daddy knows I think!*'[91]

Between 28 July and 3 August the Bedfordshires were back in the line once more, holding the left subsector of the brigade front, between Arleux and Oppy Wood. A and D Companies held the front, with C and B in support. Although spattered with storms, making the focus of their tour repairing and draining, the only fatality during the tour was on 30 July, when Private Albert Andrews[92] of Ware was killed.

After his first tour on the front, Second Lieutenant Christie shared his initial impressions with his family, noting that '*War in the front line trenches is a damned silly business. You spend your time wandering up and down unprintably muddy trenches, getting them nicely drained, floored and revetted, when there comes some more rain and it is "as you were"*', his letter closing with the remark '*I really must stop now as I must go on duty in the nice trench. ...*'

With what local papers called the 'Chocolate famine'[93] taking hold at home and the Third Battle of Ypres opening 60km further north, the

battalion's quiet spell continued with the companies swapping their positions without any event, other than on 1 August, when Second Lieutenants Wilfred Haynes, Harold Charles Loe, a six-foot-tall former sergeant from the Black Watch, and Percy Daniels joined.

They were relieved on 3 August and posted to the Red Line, where
they remained for six days, providing working parties. A further relief on
9 August sent them to Kitchener Camp, returning to Écurie Wood Camp
between the 15th and 20th. Training and competitions resumed until sent
to the front lines south of Arleux again on 21 August.

On the afternoon of 24 August a heavy bombardment fell on the
battalion's lines, one shell killing three of the Bedfordshires instantly
early in the evening: John Catlin[94] of Bedford, John Bartlett[95] from
St Neots and William Uffindell[96] of Surrey. The 35-year-old John Bartlett
had initially enlisted in the Bedfordshire Yeomanry but was transferred
to the Bedfordshire Regiment on Christmas Day 1916. That day he set
sail for France and was posted to the 1st Battalion on arrival. John had
come through Arras and Oppy without a scratch, only to be killed by an
arbitrary shell during an otherwise quiet period.

Among the day's wounded was another Old Contemptible, Lance
Sergeant George Corbett[97] of Eaton Ford. The 18-year-old labourer had
enlisted in October 1901, initially into the Royal Artillery, although five
days later found himself in the Bedfordshires. After seven years with the
colours, including several years in India, George had transferred into the
reserves until he was mobilised once more when war broke out in 1914.
He had been sent home between January and April 1915 suffering from
frozen feet and, having overcome gas poisoning from Hill 60 in April
1915, had returned home again in August 1916 with the curious injury of
a needle in his buttock, caused during their spell in reserve. Lance Sergeant Corbett was back among his comrades again in January 1917 and
survived the assaults against La Coulotte and Oppy, but was seriously
wounded in the left hand and thigh during the shelling. George under-
went lengthy treatment at home, finally being medically discharged six
days before Christmas 1918, unlike his brother John who was lost on
Gallipoli.

From 27 August to 4 September the Bedfordshires moved into support
of the Vimy–Lievin line and provided working and wiring parties for the
front-line battalions. On the 30th, four more second lieutenants joined
the battalion, all having been commissioned together from the ranks on
26 June 1917: Edgar Francis Kirkman Graham, formerly a sapper in

No. 2 Canadian Tunnelling Company, who had also served as a lieutenant in the 2nd Bedfordshires between 1900 and 1904 and had won the Military Medal in 1916; Vivian Eric Farr of Bedford from the Royal Fusiliers; Leonard Jack Hobson, who had been on the Western Front since early 1915 as a private in the Cambridgeshires; and Howard George Baker, who had served in the ranks of several battalions of the Bedfordshire Regiment.

At the end of August all heads turned south one night as a huge explosion physically shook Roclincourt when a derelict ammunition dump exploded, creating a 25m crater and wounding some of the 63rd Division troops sleeping nearby. However, all remained quiet around the Bedfordshires and their only combat death of the month was from 2 September when 38-year-old Private John Fairey[98] from St Albans was wounded, dying three days later in the casualty clearing station at Étrun.

The Bedfordshires' last day in support was rounded off with a game of football, which saw them soundly beaten 4–0 by an artillery team, and the following day they marched back to Écurie Wood Camp. A 10km trek west to Frévin-Capelle on the 5th was followed by a further move 16km south-west to Grand-Rullecourt, where they remained for several days.

RSM Cecil Walker was taken ill and shipped back to England to recover, with CSM Walter Freer assuming the role of Acting RSM. Initially enlisting into the 1st Bedfordshires in 1903, the veteran of every engagement since August 1914 had been wounded on the Somme and in January 1918 would be awarded the DCM, the citation reading: *'For conspicuous gallantry and devotion to duty. He has rendered valuable service since the commencement of the campaign, invariably displaying great courage and resource in action, and setting a fine example of devotion to duty.'* Although his combat service was over, Cecil went on to serve as the RSM of a Young Soldiers Battalion, the Huntingdonshire Cyclists and the 5th Bedfordshires after the war until discharged in June 1929 and retiring to Billington. After spending 26 of his 45-year lifespan serving in the regiment, RSM Walker died from influenza on 10 July 1930. He lies in the Bedford cemetery, next to his former adjutant, Major Reginald Le Huquet.[99]

On 7 September the division handed their sector over and retired from the front lines completely. This signalled the start of a three-week period in corps reserve, which saw the men train, carry out fatigues and rest in the comfortable late summer weather.

Sporting competitions started up again, with the first inter-platoon football matches surfacing on the 9th, and another 5km move west came on the 10th, into billets at Beaudricourt, 28km north-west of Arras. Still under-strength, the battalion was reorganised into three platoons per company and a trickle of reinforcements turned up over the next two days: Second Lieutenant John Phillips Kingdon rejoined, bringing ten men from the corps' reinforcement camp with him on the 10th; and Lieutenant John Broadhurst Sproston arrived the following day with eleven more men from the base depot.

Training, lectures, drills, practice attacks and more inter-platoon football filled the next two weeks, the battalion realising they were being primed for offensive operations once more. Another officer made his appearance on 22 September, Second Lieutenant Frederick Arthur Garwood being posted to D Company, having served in the ranks of the battalion since October 1905.

Speculation about their future deployment proved to be justified after a series of moves in late September took them from their relatively quiet sector north of Arras, into the churned-up sector of the Western Front around Ypres. After a 12km march north to the railway station at Tincques, the Bedfordshires boarded troop trains that carried them 50km north-west to St Omer, and a final 6km march north-west of St Omer took them to billets in Zudrove, 1km south of Serques. Waiting in the billets were Second Lieutenants William White and Herbert Charles Hutchinson, with a further three second lieutenants arriving two days later: Albert Henry Wakefield, Arthur William Rope and Herbert Walter Cornelius.

On 28 September the division transferred into X Corps of the Second Army and marched 20km east to Staple. Another 14km trek east the next day took them to Le Thieushouck, 2km north-east of Cäestre, where the senior NCOs spent two days training over taped ground in readiness for their involvements in coming operations. The date of 2 October brought another move, this time 9km to Westouter, some 12km south-west of Ypres and back into the battle zone, where Second Lieutenant Alfred Edgar Oxley was waiting to join them.

Chapter 4

# The Third Battle of Ypres (1917): 31 July to 10 November 1917

*'It was a desolate sight. Just a vast expanse of mud and water filled shell holes … "Great God. This is an awful place."'*

By the summer of 1917, the Allied position in Europe was shaky. Russia was on the brink of a revolution, the French army were being held in an entirely defensive stance following the mutinies of the spring, and although the Italian army were conducting operations, the terrain they fought across was difficult and unforgiving. Similarly, the Axis powers were reeling from sustained losses, the effects of the long-term naval blockade to their economy and the uncertainty exhibited by Austria and the Ottoman Empire. However, the imminent withdrawal of Russia from the war gave the German planners the opportunity to consider moving dozens of veteran divisions to support their unsettled Austrian allies in addition to focusing their efforts towards the Western Front.

With neither side appearing to have a clear advantage, the pressure was continually being applied by the Allies, with the British and Commonwealth forces taking the fight to their opponents while the French army recuperated and reorganised.

It was under these conditions that the Third Battle of Ypres, also known as the Battle of Passchendaele (Passendale), was launched on 31 July 1917, the objective being to wear down German forces, break the German lines east of Ypres and sweep on to the North Sea ports. By the time the 5th Division arrived, a series of 'bite and hold' battles with specific, limited objectives had already been fought and the Germans had adapted their defensive tactics, making the final month of the battle a costly business.

## The Battle of Broodseinde: 4 October 1917

The 15th Brigade was to provide divisional support for the assaulting brigades and the Bedfordshires moved into their battle positions accordingly. After pausing for dinner in Ridge Wood on 3 October, details were left in situ while less than half the officer corps advanced with their under-strength battalion. The headquarters section comprised Lieutenant Colonel Percy Worrall, Captain and Adjutant Allan Beale, Second Lieutenants Sydney Draper and Harold Fleming, and supported by Regimental Sergeant Major Walter Freer. A Company advanced with Captain Hugh Pearse at their head, Second Lieutenants Harold Reynolds, John Dickinson and Edgar Nailer, and Acting CSM Wesley running the platoons. B Company was led by Acting Captain Gerald d'Avigdor, with Lieutenant John Sproston, Second Lieutenants John Dalton and Robert Hare, and CSM Henry Trasler heading the platoons. C Company was organised under Acting Captain Harold Loe, Second Lieutenants Joseph Laughton, Paul Christie, Leonard Hobson and Acting CSM Percy Folkard[100] as platoon commanders, while D Company was commanded by Acting Captain Geoffrey Millais, with the platoons spread between Second Lieutenants Joseph Cotchin, Edgar Graham and Vivian Farr, alongside Acting CSM Stone.

The battalion advanced east to positions in Sanctuary Wood that afternoon and, after scouting the line they were to take over, moved forward at dusk. They dug in on the eastern slopes of the ridge, littered with the shattered remains of Sanctuary Wood, and endured heavy shelling overnight while being held in support of the 13th Brigade, who went forward the following morning.

Private Harry Bashford, now 'number two' in a Lewis-gun team, remembered the overnight march to the front, being the first time he and dozens of his comrades had ventured on to the embattled Ypres salient: *'Of all the harrowing sights that met with me on the battlefield, mercifully most are forgotten but those of an unusual nature tend to stay with you. One such incident occurred going up the line. Two British soldiers were lying side by side. They'd evidently been close together when a large shell splinter had severed a left leg from one and a right leg from another, almost as cleanly as a surgeon. Not a sight to improve your morale when going up the line.'*

Once in position, Harry's team were *'quartered in a vacated German pill box. There was intermittent shelling during the night and one poor chap who'd evidently lost his nerve, shrieked as the shells burst. The nearer the shell, the louder he shrieked. Not a very restful night. In the morning, the shelling subsided and we were able to take stock of our surroundings. It was a desolate sight. Just a vast expanse of mud and water filled shell holes. Viewing the scene, one could only echo Captain Scott's words on his expedition to the South Pole when most of his men had died when he said "Great God. This is an awful place".'*

In spite of three days of heavy rain that threatened to turn much of the battlefield into an impassable morass, at 6 a.m. on 4 October, twelve British and Commonwealth divisions attacked along a 14km frontage, running between Houthulst Forest on the northern flank and the Menin Road to the south, their objectives being the Geluveld (Gheluvelt) plateau and Broodseinde ridge. The main thrust of the assault was from two Anzac corps and one British corps in the centre, with supporting assaults on either flank, including from the 5th Division at the southern-most edge of the battlefront.

The 13th Brigade's assault north of the Menin Road met with mixed success, but by 7 a.m. the first objectives had all fallen. Advancing behind their creeping barrage and pausing only to deal with the many pillboxes that peppered the countryside, the attack made it almost 1km before the West Kents on the right of the line were stopped in front of the heavily reinforced Polderhoek Chateau, supported as it was by heavy fire from the German garrison in Geluveld, who had repulsed their own assaults. By late morning it became clear that further attempts would prove futile so the Kents dug in and waited for relief.

By the end of the day's fighting, the centre of the battle front had advanced over 1,600 metres and the divisions had achieved most of their objectives, while both flanks' advances were held to around 1km. Losses amounted to around 20,000 on each side, with around a quarter of the German casualties being captured and the battle was hailed as the most successful of the entire autumn campaign.

Being on the flank of a large attack always drew heavy fire and this assault was certainly no different. After spending the entire day waiting for orders under heavy shell fire, that evening the Bedfordshires were ordered to move into positions north of the Menin Road. On their way to the front line, the few surviving 1914 veterans vaguely recognised the area they had paid so dearly to hold almost three years earlier, namely the shattered remains of the wood around the Herentage Chateau.

Arriving in the darkness, in an unfamiliar and desolate area that had been levelled by the heavy fighting and rain, the battalion set to organising themselves for a defence, despite being uncertain who was to their front or on either side. Second Lieutenant John Dalton took matters, and his own life, into his hands and reconnoitred the wasteland on the left flank of the battalion as no contact had been made with the unit expected to be to their north. Being in command of the northernmost platoon in the battalion line, '*he crossed very boggy ground to the right company headquarters of the battalion on our left, laid a tape from there a distance of about 300 yards to our left post, and got one of their companies to dig in and join up with our left. It was due to his action that our left flank was made secure.*' John was awarded the Military Cross for his initiative and bravery, which would continue for the rest of the month.

Even though they were not engaged in the direct assault, the battalion lost men to shelling on 4 October. A Company's Second Lieutenant Harold Henry Reynolds was killed, aged 20, having joined the battalion after La Coulotte. He was interred 1,700 metres south-east of Hooge but later exhumed and buried in the Hooge Crater cemetery. Second Lieutenant Edgar Nailer was gassed and suffered superficial facial burns, although he would return the following summer.

Two of the battalion's Military Medallists were also killed during the day's shelling. A Company's Sergeant Oswald Gentle of Baldock, who had won his medal at Longueval on the Somme, was the third brother to fall in the war. At just 23, Oswald was an Old Contemptible who had been fighting since Mons, and died soon after being '*very seriously wounded*'.[101] His comrade, Sergeant Bird, wrote to Oswald's widow that he '*left him with some stretcher bearers to be buried, as I had no time to do it myself*' but his final resting place was lost in the fighting and Oswald is remembered on the Tyne Cot memorial to the missing.

Also killed was George Bland, who had been on the Western Front since early 1915 and had won his Military Medal in 1916, even being recommended for a second MM at La Coulotte. He was among two Arlesey men fatally injured that day, the second being George Pike[102] who had already been wounded three times and was among four men killed instantly when a shell burst in their trench.

By dawn they had taken up positions in support of the Kents on the right of the brigade line, between the Menin Road and Veldhoek, within sight of the machine gunners holding Polderhoek Chateau. C and B Companies moved forward and took over a 600-metre stretch of the front line from Geluveld (Gheluvelt) Wood on the Menin Road, headed north-east towards Polderhoek Chateau, their left flank resting on Thick Copse, astride the Scherriabeek stream. A and D Companies were held in support and reserve, just 200 metres behind them.

The Bedfordshires spent the next few days consolidating their positions and digging a continuous series of front, support and communications trenches, all the while under heavy artillery and machine-gun fire as the rain continued falling steadily and the ground became even more waterlogged.

The casualty count carried on rising, with another eighteen Bedfords being killed by shelling and sniping between 5 and 8 October.

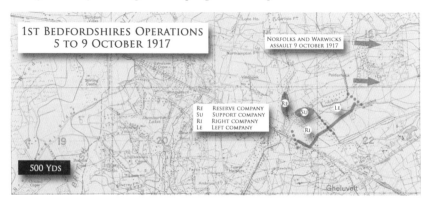

The 20-year-old Private Frederick Dollimore[103] from Letchworth was caught out in an unguarded moment when he was shot by a sniper on the 5th, having been with the battalion for five months. The sister in charge of the hospital in which Fred died wrote to his mother how *'he was admitted here on the 5th very ill indeed, with a severe wound of the head. Everything possible was done for him but he passed away at 5.45 a.m.'*

At around 6 a.m. on 6 October the bombardment became intense, with heavier-calibre German shells falling into their lines. Captain Hugh Pearse was wounded and 19-year-old Second Lieutenant Harold Winning Fleming of Hampstead, known as 'Margy' in the officers' mess, was killed.

Snipers were a serious problem in the area, as Harry Bashford recorded: *'It was difficult to locate either our or the enemy's positions and this is where the danger of snipers arose. Sometime later this was proved rather tragically. I was standing behind one of our officers at the top of steps leading down to Company HQ. He was using binoculars. Without hearing a shot fired, his steel helmet flew over my head and on picking it up I noticed a bullet hole just above the rim ... he collapsed in front of me. It was a mystery where this shot came from and this was reflected on this young officer's face as he died. That puzzled look will stay with me till the end of my days. It was terrible.'[104]*

Second Lieutenant Joseph Laughton of St Albans was injured on 7 October and admitted to 14 General Hospital in Wimereux on 9 October suffering from slight wounds and a contusion to his face and one eye. Second Lieutenant Edgar Francis Kirkman Graham was also hit by a rifle bullet that day, which entered his inner left thigh, passing straight through without catching any vital arteries and exiting his outer thigh.

Two more of the battalion's Mons veterans were also lost, with Private Alfred Barker[105] from Bedford, and Sergeant James Bush[106] of Bishop's Stortford both being killed, as were old comrades Privates Alfred Burridge[107] of Bedford and Frederick Chessum[108] of Dunton, both former Bedfordshire Yeomanry troopers who had transferred into the 1st Bedfordshires together.

By the end of a very busy spell in command of C Company, Acting Captain Harold Loe had won a well-earned Military Cross, his citation reading: *'For conspicuous gallantry and devotion to duty when in command of one of the front line companies during five days of operations. The line which he took over was in a very precarious condition but he threw out a defensive flank and made a long system of trenches. He was three times completely buried by shell fire. He also crawled out and dressed a wounded man who could not be got in owing to enemy snipers.'* [109]

### The Battle of Poelcapelle: 9 October 1917
The next phase of the offensive, the Battle of Poelcapelle, was launched on the same front as Broodseinde, with many of the same troops being used despite them already having been through the mill during the past week. Enemy artillery fire had been relentless against the brigade's lines, the ground had long become the notorious, glutinous mud now so familiar with the Ypres campaign of 1917 and the weather added to the men's discomfort, who were unable to keep anything dry.

It was no great surprise that the respite in the fighting had seen the defending German troops busily reorganising their defence. Other than the concrete-reinforced chateau that bristled with machine guns, the grounds that had once formed the picturesque park in which the chateau was set were strewn with carefully sited, mutually supporting pillboxes, each protected by wire, streams and marsh-like ground.

The Norfolks and Warwickshires were assigned to lead the attack while the Bedfordshires initially held steady on the southern edge of the line and provided supporting fire against the chateau, Geluveld and defensive pillboxes until orders arrived to take their own lines forward once the attack to their north had secured its objectives. Remarkably – despite the conditions they had endured, and with the brigade in a bad physical condition – they remained highly motivated.

After a 'wet and stormy night' the 15th Brigade went in to take the heavily fortified Polderhoek Chateau at 5.20 a.m., which had been re-inforced to the point of becoming a fortress. Things started badly when the opening barrage fell short, causing casualties among the brigade before they even started their advance, then the explosive curtain moved ahead at a rate considerably faster than their timetable had specified. Nevertheless, the two assaulting battalions moved in behind the creeping barrage, even managing to overrun several pillboxes in spite of being under heavy fire from the supporting positions and the chateau itself.

Through the smoke and confusion of the battle, the right company of the Warwickshires were seen crossing the Scherriabeek in front of the Bedfordshires' trenches. An officer sprinted through the barrage and re-directed the wayward Warwickshires, who were by now under heavy fire from Geluveld and restricting the amount of supporting fire the Bed-fordshires could provide by their presence.

It was not long before a mixture of casualties, heavy defensive fire, an intense bombardment and the impassable ground brought the brigade's attack to a halt and the survivors retired to their original positions, re-organising themselves into a defensive line overnight. Preparations for another attempt were made but, thankfully, it was called off before dawn came and the thinning ranks of the brigade settled into another uncom-fortable day of trench warfare, under sniper and heavy shell fire.

Between 4 p.m. and 6 p.m. on 9 October, 19-year-old Second Lieu-tenant Paul Norman Jones Christie was directing his platoon's fire to-wards Geluveld when a shell scored a direct hit on his section of trench, killing him instantly. Private Walter Berry[110] from Hatfield was in the trench and wrote to his officer's parents from hospital: *'I was wounded with the same shell and he had just sent for me to bring my gun as he saw a lot of Germans being relieved and I was busy firing at them and when I got my wound I turned round and see that my officer had gone and it was a great shock to every one.'* Although Walter recovered and returned to the front, he was killed in March 1918 in the 6th Bedfordshires.

Letters to Second Lieutenant Christie's parents in Much Hadham tell of him being laid next to his other fatally wounded officer comrades, *'buried in our cemetery hard by a famous road'* according to Lieutenant Colonel Worrall. As is the case with many of the fallen from that battle, his grave was lost in the fighting that churned the area up for another year and he is remembered on the Tyne Cot memorial to the missing. Lieutenant

Colonel Worrall's letter also remarked that *'Both his pals, Reynolds and Fleming, were also killed, so there is a big blank left in the battalion at the loss of these cheery boys.'*

Second Lieutenant Joseph Laughton had become good friends with Paul Christie and only learned of his pal's death a fortnight later. He wrote to Paul's parents: *'Dear Mrs Christie. I have heard with very great regret on my way to rejoin the Battn. about Paul. It came as a great shock to me as I was wounded two days before and have been in hospital since. Paul was a great friend of mine, we were at Felixstowe and came out to France together, and were in the same Company and both Hertfordshire fellows and so had a deal in common. Out here Paul always did his job extraordinarily well and in the most quiet way and never grumbled or made a fuss. He was a general favourite among the officers and men and will be greatly missed, especially by the few of us who knew him better and worked with him in C Company.'*

Another close friendship formed at Sandhurst was with Second Lieutenant Neville Goodman of the Worcesters, who added his own observations in another letter to Paul Christie's parents: *'I shall always remember him as the wittiest man I ever knew. For clean intellectual humour he was unrivalled and I often think of the many new "schools" if one may use the term, of jokes to which he introduced us. His influence on me, I know, was all for the good.'*

Second Lieutenant Joseph Cotchin of Ridgmont was also killed on 9 October, aged 31. Adding two years to his age, Joseph had joined the King's Royal Rifle Corps in 1903, aged just 17. Serving in several battalions during his career, he had already been wounded twice before being urged to apply for an officer's post and returning to England at the end of 1916. The newly qualified Second Lieutenant Cotchin had joined the 1st Bedfordshires in the field at the end of July but was killed during his first battle as an officer. He was laid to rest alongside Paul Christie and his grave was also lost in the subsequent fighting.

Nineteen more Bedfords were fatally injured during the day's heavy shelling, including several of their 1914 veterans and Private Tom Neale of Aspenden,[111] who had joined the battalion with his brother at Hill 60 in 1915 and had recovered from being wounded on the Somme, only to be killed while he sheltered in a dugout during the bombardment.

The following day, which was to be the battalion's last in the line until the end of the month, saw Boer War veteran Acting RSM Walter Freer wounded by shrapnel in his left eye, left ankle and left side of his abdomen, which ensured the end of his combat service, although he assumed duties in the depot for a further two years. CSM Henry Trasler, who had won the

DCM earlier in 1915, took on the Acting RSM role until mid-December, being commissioned in the field the following summer.[112]

Also wounded during their six days opposite Geluveld were Second Lieutenants Frank Flavell, who had been among the large officer draft to arrive at the end of July, and Samuel Norrish, who had won the Military Cross on the Somme a year earlier and would recover to rejoin the 4th Bedfordshires on 8 April 1918.

At 4.45 p.m. on 10 October the relief of what remained of the brigade started and just before midnight the Bedfordshires were replaced by the 7th KRRC, which had been Second Lieutenant Cotchin's old unit before being commissioned as an officer. They retired back to Ridge Wood and paused while the rest of the 5th Division's relief was completed, the promise of a well-earned spell in reserve beckoning.

Their brigadier described the attempted capture of the chateau and grounds as a 'gallant failure', heaping praise on his men's endurance and behaviour but criticising the planning that allowed his troops to be held in such poor conditions for so long before an attack; the lack of artillery preparation on the chateau or Geluveld; and their own artillery falling on the assembled troops before the assault had started.

Although the offensive itself was a failure overall, some gains were made in the north. British and French casualties totalled around 13,000 and much of the failure was attributed to the weather, poor artillery preparation and the same exhausted troops being used in the attacks who had been fighting for a whole week.

By the time the Bedfordshires were relieved, despite having been spared frontal assaults, they still lost 10 officers and almost 140 men in the rifle grenade, and sniping duels between 4 and 10 October. Although their count of confirmed German casualties attributed to them was equal to their own losses, it was another expensive action for the brigade.

### Rest and reorganisation: 11 to 25 October 1917

The exhausted and heavily depleted brigade were relieved by the 41st Brigade and sent back to rest for ten days, the 1st Bedfordshires spending the night of 11 October in Brooke Camp, Westouter, before moving to a billeting area 1,500 metres due east of Fletre, 16km south-west of Ypres. Several days were spent recuperating, cleaning up and refitting in farms and tents in the open countryside. After reorganising, Harold Loe was in command of A Company, John Sproston was the officer commanding B Company, William Chirnside took charge of C Company and

Frederick Garwood ran D Company. Mid-October also saw Captain Chirnside take over the battalion temporarily while Lieutenant Colonel Worrall spent time in hospital ill.[113]

However, Captain Sproston had been 'knocked about' by the shelling that continued throughout their relief and, after being buried by an exploding parados, he was blown over three successive times by high-explosive shells landing close to him. Shell fragments hit his backpack and penetrated far enough to cause contusions, with additional fragments piercing the outer flank of his left thigh. Although badly shaken, almost completely deaf in his left ear and suffering from the effects of concussion, he tried to carry on with his duties but was sent back into the medical system soon afterwards. Captain Sproston was finally returned to the UK a week later, once it was realised that he was unlikely to recover quickly, and was demobilised in May 1919, still having not completely recovered.

On 14 October a sports programme was implemented, with a draft of forty-five men joining the next day, just in time for a lecture explaining what part the battalion had played in their recent battle. A war game titled 'The Taking of Polderhoek Chateau' for the officers and sergeants was organised for the 16th, and the under-strength battalion enjoyed a lively concert that evening.

A full range of training and practice attacks against pillbox positions was introduced into their routines the following day, with a lecture rounding off the busy hours, the experienced men understanding that they were not finished in the Ypres salient just yet.

The 18th found the Bedfordshires demonstrating a 'modern attack' to the commanders and adjutants of their brigade in the morning, with a loudly supported 'rugger match' amusing the men that afternoon, their officers beating the other ranks 9–0. Lord Ampthill visited the battalion on 19 October, watching them engaged in specialist training and remaining with them to inspect them the next day, before they assembled and prepared for operations once more.

On 21 October, the Bedfordshires started their return to the front lines with a 12km march north-east to Micmac Camp, which lay 2km west of Dikkebus (Dickebusch), and the next night were back in range of the German guns at Ridge Wood Camp. Almost every time a battalion moved along what remained of the local roads or tracks in the salient, shelling followed them. Other than the more obvious result of men being caught by an enemy shell, indirect casualties also followed in the unhealthy, waterlogged landscape, as Private Harry Bashford was to find out as he and his team sought cover from an approaching shell as they tramped along a muddy trail in the darkness:

*As number two on the Lewis gun team, I had to carry the spare parts bag. This was quite heavy and as I dived off the road, the bag swung round, taking me into a large shell hole, with only my feet showing above the water. I was rescued by my pals and we continued as speedily as possible and eventually reached shelter for the night. I had no hope of a change of clothes for at least another 24 hours, and by this time was feeling pretty groggy. When we eventually reached permanent quarters, I reported sick. The M.O. didn't spend much time on me. Trench Fever was the diagnosis, which I suspect was a second cousin to pneumonia, I don't know. A label was fastened to my tunic, which I learnt later meant the magical word Blighty and hospital.*

Harry's time with the battalion was over, although he would return to the ranks of the 2nd Bedfordshires in the final months of the war, surviving without a scratch and living to a ripe old age.

Lieutenant James Charles Abbott Birch caught up with the battalion on the 23rd, having completed his time in a staff position in the 112th Brigade, just in time for their part in the battle to follow. The same day saw Lieutenant Percival Sisley leave, suffering from trench fever, which would see him back in England a week later, never to return to the battalion.

Leaving what cadre they could afford to in Ridge Wood Camp, the Bedfordshires moved to Stirling Castle and remained in position under shell fire, waiting for orders that would carry them forward once again.

**The Second Battle of Passchendaele: 26 October to 10 November**
The final phase of the autumn campaign around Ypres was planned as three distinctive assaults, each with their own specific, limited objectives. Rain had fallen incessantly throughout the month and, coupled with the ferocious fighting that had churned up the waterlogged ground, the entire area was almost impassable.

Nevertheless, on 26 October, British, Canadian, Anzac and French troops combined in an assault that heralded the next phase of the Third Battle of Ypres, with the Bedfordshires' corps on the extreme southern flank of the battle once more. The badly worn 5th Division was assigned the limited objective of capturing the elusive Polderhoek Chateau and the small spur south of the Scherriabeek stream, with three battalions from the 13th Brigade conducting the attack.

The Cheshires of the 15th Brigade held the static left flank of the narrow divisional sector, with the Bedfordshires in brigade support at the familiar Stirling Castle and the other battalions spread out around them.

During the build-up to zero hour, the Bedfordshires provided carrying parties for the Cheshires as German shelling continued, killing and wounding men daily. Among the casualties were Second Lieutenants Leonard Hobson, who was slightly wounded, and Alexander Edward Crookewit, who was badly wounded on 25 October. Known as Alec, the former Bedford grammar school boy died the following day, aged 31. The *'Intelligent, sober and thoroughly reliable'* chicken farmer from Kent stood almost six feet tall and had enlisted as a driver in the Army Service Corps in February 1915, before being commissioned and joining the 1st Bedfordshires on 26 July 1917. Alongside Joseph Cotchin and Sidney Allport, Alec Crookewit had been through training at No. 20 Officer Cadet Battalion before joining the 1st Bedfordshires with them in July 1917. Now just Allport remained.

Company Sergeant Major Sidney 'Spot' Chamberlain from Meldreth was also killed as he tried to recover some of his wounded men from the open. A soldier since 1903, Spot had been in the reserves when war broke out, arriving to reinforce the 1st Bedfordshires in August 1914 as a private. CSM Chamberlain was typical of many of the 1914 veterans, having been gassed at Hill 60, buried by falling masonry at Longueval, affected by shell shock and wounded at La Coulotte, even though he only counted the final wound as a real one, remarking how he had 'gone through the whole campaign without a scratch' before Arras.[114]

Private Samuel Spicer from Hertford[115] was also among the day's casualties, having been killed by a chance shell as he and his comrades moved through the trenches. A drayman before the war, Samuel was typical of the drafts sent to the 1st Bedfordshires during 1917 and had already been through the intense fighting at Arras, Oppy Wood and Ypres, in spite of his relatively short service. His final resting place was never found, and Samuel is remembered along with Spot Chamberlain and most of their other comrades who fell that day on the Tyne Cot memorial to the missing.

Also wounded during the shelling on 25 October was Albert Durham[116] from St Neots, who had been with the 2nd Bedfordshires from February 1910 until wounded in November 1914. Returning to the front and joining the 1st Battalion in May 1915, he had won his Military Medal on the Somme but was injured by shrapnel in his left knee and right shin.

Although Albert survived, his brother Thomas did not, having being killed in April 1917 during the 4th Bedfordshires' assault on Gavrelle.

Great Bramingham was a small hamlet in 1917, later swallowed up by urban sprawl and now a suburb of Luton, where *'one hears very little of what happens there, because normally, very little does happen'*. With so few homes and families making up the hamlet, sons lost in the war naturally made an impact, but none quite like the losses suffered by the Brightman and Horsler families. Herbert Brightman was one of five brothers and among those killed in the 1st Battalion on 25 October. His parents had already had the news of Alfred's death in the 2nd Bedfordshires during the First Battle of Ypres of 1914, with another son, Frank, going missing two years later in the same battalion, never to be heard from again. Learning of Herbert's death would have shocked the hamlet to the core but just days later Richard was mortally wounded in the 4th Bedfordshires, dying at Étaples twelve days later. Just one son was left, recovering from an illness, and *'when it was anticipated that he would have to go overseas again, appeals were made by the vicar of Streatley and others to the authorities ... and as a result he was released from the Army on compassionate grounds'*. Curiously, all four sons had been killed in October. These losses were further compounded by the Horsler family who lived two doors away. George Horsler was fatally injured on 30 October 1917, the same day and in the same battalion as Richard Brightman's mortal wound, with two more of George's brothers falling during the war.[117]

The Second Battle of Passchendaele started at 5.20 a.m. on 26 October and initial reports from around 5.40 a.m. told of the 13th Brigade taking the hard-fought chateau, but as the morning wore on, it became clear that German counter-attacks were in full swing and by noon the brigade were back at their jumping-off positions. The stubborn German defence was a difficult enough obstacle to overcome but the attackers could not physically move as they were weighed down by so much cloying mud, their rifles and machine guns inoperable for the same reasons.

The King's Own Scottish Borderers were ordered in to support the beleaguered 13th Brigade and at 1.30 p.m. the Bedfordshires also were pushed in to support the Scottish troops. By 4.30 p.m. the battalion had advanced through the German protective barrage and dug in east of Veldhoek; an hour later came the order for them to take over the front line from the surviving elements of the 13th Brigade.

As the night wore on, the Norfolks arrived on the Bedfords' right flank and half of the Warwickshires took over on their left, the Bedfordshires finally settling into the central position between the Reutelbeek and Scherriabeek streams. Brigade orders specified that *'the situation will be cleared up and patrolling will be energetically carried out'* but by daybreak the chateau was still firmly in German hands, although No Man's Land was, once more, dominated by British troops.

The 27th was a day of hard physical work, all the while under shell fire. By linking up shell holes, a complete new section of line was dug on the brigade front, including communications and support trenches, while the stretcher-bearers continued their work under sniper and shell fire, retrieving the wounded from the previous day's attack. Lieutenant Herbert Hutchinson was injured in the left shoulder during the day, being evacuated to Étaples to recover.

After another hard day's work on the 28th, the Bedfordshires were relieved that evening, the entire brigade being replaced by the 95th Brigade, the Bedfordshires remaining in tents and dugouts in Ridge Wood for several days.

Some 101 men and 2 officers from the battalion had been lost during the few days they had spent in the line, despite them having not been engaged in any direct offensive or defensive actions.

During their time opposite Polderhoek Chateau that October, the 15th Brigade's losses were 51 officers and 1,318 other ranks, with 13 officers and 247 men coming from the Bedfordshires. Yet the brigade was the least touched by the division's involvement in the Third Battle of Ypres, with both of their sister brigades losing over 2,000 men each.

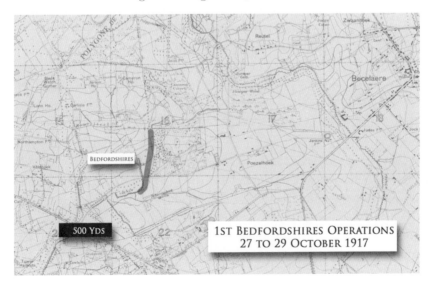

500 YDS

1ST BEDFORDSHIRES OPERATIONS
27 TO 29 OCTOBER 1917

And the chateau was still in German hands.

Second Lieutenant John Dalton had survived the fighting and came away with a Military Cross, but ten days of living in soaking-wet trenches took its toll on his system and he was evacuated to the field ambulance on 31 October, suffering from a temperature, headaches and nausea. He would not return to the battalion again but, being in the UK, John was able to attend Buckingham Palace on 19 December 1917 to receive his Military Cross from the King and would spend the rest of his war in non-combatant roles. Born to British parents in Dresden, Germany, John ironically found himself interred in Germany from December 1941, but lived to the ripe old age of 94, dying in Hove, Sussex, in 1984.

Sergeant Alfred Sale of Shefford[118] was awarded the Military Medal, his local paper attributing it to *'a stunt near Ypres, for keeping up communications under heavy shell fire'*. With nine years' service behind him, Sergeant Sale had come through every battle since Mons intact and would go on to add an Italian medal to his collection in 1919, for *'services whilst in Italy'*.

While the Third Battle of Gaza flared up thousands of miles to their south, on 1 November, the battalion moved into divisional reserve, half of the men being held in tunnels at Tor Top, the balance at Stirling Castle. Shelling was still a significant problem despite being in reserve, and gas precautions were in full effect while the men set to their fatigue duties, moving a vast array of supplies forward for those battalions on the front. Second Lieutenant Alfred Charles Williams was slightly wounded on 3 November, and the battalion worked tirelessly in support of the continuing offensives further east, enjoying the unusual experience of a three-day spell without a drop of rain from 3 to 5 November.

From 5 to 11 November, the Bedfordshires were based in Ridge Wood, from where they continued fetching, carrying, fixing and building, while the final phase of the Third Battle of Ypres was fought to their east, with the 95th Brigade being chosen for the final attempt to capture the chateau. In a repeat of all previous attempts, small gains were made at huge cost to the attacking brigade, who made it to within 50 metres of the structure and captured one large pillbox in the south-western corner of the grounds.

The chateau would remain in German hands until August 1918, when it was given up without a shot being fired during the German retreat.

On 6 November, Second Lieutenant Frederick Garwood was gassed but remained at duty for four days before having to admit defeat and return to England for treatment. The former sergeant with thirteen years in the regiment was passed fit again the following spring and served in the Royal Air Force before returning to the 1st Bedfordshires in October 1919, finally being released from the Reserve of Officers once he reached the age limit in 1937.

The Third Battle of Ypres finally ground to a bloody halt when the Canadian Corps took the village of Passchendaele (Passendale) on 6 November, the line having been moved forward across some 8km of the most heavily fortified ground in the world since the first shots were fired in July. Casualty figures for the entire battle are disputed, with both sides' estimates ranging from 200,000 to 450,000. Whatever the true numerical cost, the atrocious conditions had stretched the British and Commonwealth forces to their limits of endurance and no real breakthrough had been achieved.

## A last tour of duty in Belgium: 10 November to 11 December 1917

On 10 November, officers from the Bedfordshires and Cheshires reconnoitred the new section of the front they were about to take over, and the next day the battalion relieved the 10th Yorkshires in support positions. B and D Companies were based at Clapham Junction, with A and C Companies at the railway dugouts, Zillebeke, which were familiar to those still in the battalion from their time on Hill 60 in the spring of 1915.

Moving north-east on the 12th, they took over the right subsector of the 62nd Brigade lines around 1km north of Polderhoek Chateau, relieving the 12th and 13th Northumberland Fusiliers. Once the Cheshires arrived on their left and the Warwickshires on their right, the Bedfords

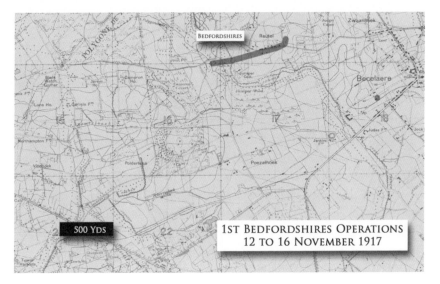

500 YDS

1ST BEDFORDSHIRES OPERATIONS
12 TO 16 NOVEMBER 1917

became the centre-front battalion of the brigade, manning trenches facing south-east, which ran from 200 metres east of Reutel to Polygonebeek.

During the relief, Sergeant James Sinclair of Wisbech was killed. The winner of a Distinguished Conduct Medal and two Military Medals, James had survived some of the battalion's most costly assaults, only to be mortally wounded by a chance shell. Although buried where he fell at the time, today he lies in the Hooge Crater cemetery.

Other than a German barrage, the 13th was quiet and work continued on drainage and improvements to their lines. A Prussian unteroffizier was captured after midnight, during a brief clash between patrols in No Man's Land, but the following day was generally peaceful, with work continuing on improving the lines. That night another Prussian patrol approached the Bedfordshires' lines, one being killed in the exchange of fire, the other being captured.

On the night of 15 November, the Bedfordshires were relieved. After an initial march of around 2km, they were bemused to be greeted by the sight of a fleet of buses, being the telltale sign that they were being sent back into the reserve areas and out of range of German artillery. The buses lumbered their way west to rendezvous with waiting troop trains at Ouderdom, the men still caked in the Ypres mud and exhausted after their tour in the line. Alighting some 50km due west at Lumbres, a 5km march west to Coulomby was rewarded with a well-earned rest in the British rear areas, 25km from Calais and Boulogne-sur-Mer.

The Battle of Cambrai was yet to be fought, but the 1st Bedfordshires and their division had completed their own offensives operations for the year, although they were not immediately aware of that fact.

Five more men from the battalion were mentioned in Sir Douglas Haig's despatches of December, for gallantry shown during the Third Battle of Ypres: Captain Allan Beale, who would also be awarded with the Belgian Croix de Guerre; Lieutenants Arthur James Fyson and Wilfred Hobbs; Sergeant James Bush from Bishop's Stortford, who was killed on 8 October;[119] and Corporal Arthur Francis, who was wounded during the autumn and would be discharged in October 1918.[120]

Two pre-war veterans won the Belgian Croix de Guerre for gallantry shown during the autumn operations, namely Company Quartermaster Sergeant Howard Bourn[121] and Private Leonard Ball.[122]

The date of 17 November was filled with cleaning up, inspections and making good their deficiencies, with training being planned immediately. Second Lieutenants William Martin Stantan and Noel Harry Wilkins joined that day, both having recovered from wounds received at Arras, Stantan's while in the 1st Bedfordshires and Wilkins's in the 6th Bedfordshires. Bombing and rifle ranges were set up for morning training, with football and boxing tournaments filling the afternoons, a routine that continued until the 24th.

Orders arrived late on the 23rd for a move early the next day and a 10km march due south took the battalion to billets in Merck-Saint-Liévin, followed the day after by a 20km trek south-east to Fontaine-lès-Boulans. In the cold but peaceful winter's countryside, the division would remain for two weeks, out of range of artillery fire and hostile air raids, a welcomed break following the draining conditions around Ypres.

Refitting and daily training became their staple diet of activities, punctuated with passes into the surrounding towns, parades and Sunday church services.

During a training exercise on the 29th, when D Company assaulted a 'strongpoint' using smoke grenades, one of the grenades failed to explode. Second Lieutenant Frederick Ray, who had been with the battalion since the summer, rushed forward to check the way was clear for his men to continue their advance and, when three paces from the grenade, was engulfed in an explosion. He came stumbling back out of the smoke with his clothes on fire, his face, both hands and left knee badly burned. Once he had been extinguished, the officer's language was certainly blue, although Second Lieutenant Vivian Farr was polite enough to remark to the board of inquiry that *'he used an expression to the effect that he was annoyed at the accident, because he wished to remain with his battalion'*.

On 30 November the battalion marched 3km west, to baths in Lisbourg, the same baths being made available to them again five days later.

The entire division noticed how the preparations were different to those normally effected before returning to the front and rumours started to circulate that a major move was imminent. All deficiencies were made good, artillery that was still bogged down in the Ypres salient was simply replaced and all leave to the UK was cancelled, with a series of small drafts arriving piecemeal.

Several second lieutenants joined during the rest, with the newly commissioned Ernest Charles Herberg transferring from his previous post as Warrant Officer in 176 Machine Gun Company on the 26th. Herbert William John Powell and Arthur Thomas Franklin arrived for their first tour with the battalion the following day, along with Basil Williams who was rejoining for his third tour with them, although still suffering noticeably from the effects of shell shock and several other ailments that had assailed his system over the previous fourteen months.

Second Lieutenant William Pottle, a former 1st Bedfordshires CSM and veteran of twenty-three years, rejoined the battalion on the 8th, although he would leave again on 29 December suffering from pneumonia.

Another rowdy rugby match between the officers and men saw the men even the honours on the 10th with a win, and the afternoon was spent gathering equipment and preparing for a major move. After a busy evening and short night's rest, the battalion marched 5km south to Anvin on 11 December and boarded trains bound for the north-east corner of Italy.

Chapter 5

# The Italian Front: December 1917 to April 1918

*'What a vast change I have experienced since I last wrote you!'*

The year 1917 had been one of military deadlock, but also one of political and social change, with internal and external pressures growing on all sides. Food shortages were starting to bite and, with over three years of unrelenting warfare, civil unhappiness was rising in all belligerent nations, with neither side appearing to have a clear advantage.

On 18 June 1917, Russia had launched a fresh assault against the German lines, which failed disastrously. Unrest had spread rapidly and, coupled with the return from exile of Vladimir Lenin in April, the Russian Provisional Government had lost its fragile grip on power. On 7 November Lenin's forces overthrew the Government and effectively ensured Russia's retirement from the Alliance and the war. This in turn would see the release of dozens of veteran, battle-hardened German divisions from the Eastern Front and enable Germany to take the initiative on the Western Front with the intention of ending the war before America's might could be brought to bear in Europe.

French morale had improved throughout 1917 after their near mutiny in May, and American forces were slowly building up in Europe, but the British and Commonwealth armies had borne the brunt of another costly year. Discussions were under way before the year ended that would see the British army reorganise to a smaller force in response to the growing lack of combat-fit men. Although the adjutant general's return of the numbers of British troops in Europe in January 1918 showed a 303,000 increase when compared to January 1917, the reality was that noncombatants made up the increase, with fighting troops actually reduced by almost 95,000; a significant drop of 8 per cent in real terms and in spite of conscription having been introduced in 1916. General Haig's divisions in Europe were suffering from a shortfall of 75,000 men against their ideal complement, with no apparent way to make good the deficiencies.

Italy had joined the hostilities on the Allied side when it had declared war on the Austro-Hungarian Empire on 23 May 1915, but ideas about expanding their territory had come crashing down once the realities of modern mountain warfare became apparent, the terrain always favouring the defender. Other than minor gains, each battle had resulted in the defender being victorious, until October 1917, when the Central Powers won a stunning victory at the Battle of Caporetto. The Italian army lost almost 300,000 men and were pushed back 100km to new battle lines along the Piave River. In response, Britain and France sent eleven infantry divisions to reinforce the shaky lines in north-east Italy.

However, the Axis powers were not having it all their own way. On the Turkish front, British and Commonwealth forces captured Gaza in November and the political prize of Jerusalem would fall before Christmas; the British and Empire forces were finally overcoming their Ottoman adversaries. In southern Europe, the Austro-Hungarian forces on the Italian front were weakening and needed the support of German divisions being released from the Eastern Front, in spite of the victory at Caporetto.

So as the 5th Division trundled their way south-east across the Alps, the uncertain future could easily have seen victory or defeat for any of the overstretched nations at war, in any of the theatres of conflict.

## The Bedfordshires arrive in Italy

After a three-day train ride, on 16 December the 1st Bedfordshires arrived in an area 40km north-west of Padova, 10km north-east of Vicenza. Following a short rest in San Giorgio de Brenta, B and D Companies moved on, making way for A and C Companies who billeted there overnight. The battalion concentrated the next day and moved to San Giorgio delle Pertiche, remaining in the area until 23 January 1918.

Training, route marches and sports kept the men warm and busy while the division concentrated, with an emphasis on lectures and instruction to adapt to the new style of warfare to which they were about to be subjected. Initially, passes were monitored carefully, the curious men eager to explore the delights of a country most of them had never considered visiting.

Several more small drafts arrived while they prepared, including seventeen-year veteran Edward Johnson, who joined on 18 December, assuming the role as Acting RSM.[123] Second Lieutenant Stuart Daniel Harrower[124] arrived on the 20th, having been a company sergeant major in the 4th Bedfordshires until being commissioned in the field for gallantry.

On Christmas Eve, ten officers visited the reserve lines near Rubio to prepare for the coming move, but Second Lieutenant Basil Williams was transferred to hospital, still suffering from the persistent shell shock that had plagued him since Falfemont Farm in September 1916. His system having been bombarded with a series of illnesses and ailments, Basil stuck to his duty but was frequently reported as being ill and thus delivering an *'ineffective and unsatisfactory performance'*.[125] His time on the front line came to an end as he was transferred to England and retired on account of his ill health within a few months, dying in 1947 aged just 53.

The entire division's post in and out had been heavily restricted for over a month and was still catching up with their move, so none of the men had anything in the way of comforts or personal messages from home for Christmas. Nevertheless, on Christmas Day a church service was followed by a cross-country relay race, after which the men had a delivery from the Bedford Comforts Fund to share between them. Divisional funds also provided for their dinners, with enough to procure some *'seductive vino rosso'* or the more *'villainous local cognac'*,[126] ensuring the festivities were as enjoyable as possible. That afternoon, the 'Bedford Boys' laid on two performances for the battalion, who were split in half so all could fit into the rooms allocated to them, before the men settled into a restful evening, sharing out what food and drink was available between each squad and platoon.

From Boxing Day training resumed, broken by a series of ceremonial parades and an inspection from Brigadier General Oldman, the brigade's commanding officer.

Signaller H. Bowker had worked at the *St Neots Advertiser* before enlisting and wrote home about their relocation:[127]

*What a vast change I have experienced since I last wrote you! Our journey from France to Italy, extending over five days and five nights, although tedious at times seeing that cattle trucks are not near so comfortable as G.N.R. corridors, had its bright spots. The part of the battalion I travelled with were unfortunate enough to pass through most of the famous large towns and cities en route during night time; yet probably we were recompensed by a daylight tour through the Alps. Although it was fast approaching Winter, the weather during the day was simply glorious. A bright sun and cloudless sky of Reckitt's blue hue gave the mountains (with their snow capped peaks) an added beauty. Bitterly cold moonlit nights made the surroundings look both grim and fascinating. Altogether it was a charming sight, one ever to be remembered.*

*On our arrival in Italy we had a nine days' tramp, tramp, tramp, to our first settled destination. Each day we halted and stayed the night in some strange town or village. During the whole of this period, the weather was grand, and, but for the fact of being penniless, fagless, and almost wholly existing on bully and biscuits, we should have made the journey more of a holiday trip than anything else. Nevertheless, we took advantage of opportunities offered and scraped a few coppers together and had raids on Italian bakeries and fruit stalls. Talk about sugar queues in Blighty, our queues beat them hollow.*

*For three weeks we were unable to write and let our relations and friends know we were in the land of the living and for a like period received no post or news from the outside world. Quite unique for us, who daily strain our necks when 'post up' is called. Right up to the present period, post has been a very disappointing factor in our Italian Rendezvous, especially during Christmas when parcels were almost unknown, our latest letters only being dated 15th Dec.*

*The people and customs here came very strange at first, but we gradually gained a smattering of their language and a knowledge of their ways, and now our procedure is much the same as in France. We freely mix with Italian soldiers and have had several games of football with them.*

*Christmas passed off quietly, but we enjoyed the day, and last night we celebrated New Year's Eve by a private supper off [sic] roast pork and vegetables.*

Private Robert Rockliffe Lambert was one of Signaller Bowker's comrades who had also worked at the *St Neots Advertiser* before the war. He added:[128]

*As you can imagine, we thoroughly enjoyed our journey here. We were a week in the train, and never shall I forget the beauty of those watering places on the Mediterranean. Coming to us as it did, after the unspeakable horrors and 'eternal' mud of Flanders, it seemed paradise itself. The cloudless sky, brilliant sunshine and warmth, the palms, the pretty houses, chateaux and hotels dotted here and there close to the sea, or perched high among the towering rocks, the gaily dressed visitors and their enthusiastic reception of us as we passed through the several stations – all these and many other unaccustomed scenes vividly imprinted a picture on our minds which will never be eradicated. But all good things come to an end, and when we awoke the following morning, it was to see the whole landscape covered slightly in snow, and the temperature down alarmingly. It seemed incredible that such a few hours could separate such an opposite, and we ardently wished ourselves back in the Riviera again.*

*We are fairly well settled down in our billets in a little northern village, with the Alps in the background. On a clear, early morning, the mountains, with their snow covered sides, and their crests tinted a delicate pink in the reflection of the rising sun (another picture to be remembered) appear to be only a very short distance away, but as the sun rises and the atmosphere thickens they gradually recede, until one can hardly make out their forms at all. They are, in reality, several miles away.*

*We have never been in one place so long before, and we are thoroughly appreciating it. The people are very hospitable. We are having glorious weather just now – brilliant sunshine, but very cold in the shade, sharp frosts and roads coated with ice.*

The arrival of New Year's Day brought with it a large ceremonial parade, during which General Plumer, Commander-in-Chief of the British forces in Italy, presented gallantry medals to men from the brigade. Of the Bedfordshires' medallists, two Military Cross and eight Military Medal ribbons were presented.

Captain James McKay, RAMC, attached to the 1st Bedfordshires, and Second Lieutenant Harold Loe both received their MC decorations. MM honours went to Acting Regimental Sergeant Major Edward Johnson, a veteran with seventeen years in the regiment behind him who was to be commissioned in the field on 16 January, remaining with the 1st Bedfordshires; and Lance Sergeant Hugh Johnson of Epsom.[129] Privates awarded the MM were Alfred Askew from Yaxley;[130] John Boxall of Petworth in Sussex;[131] Joe Clark of Buntingford,[132] who had been with the battalion since April 1915; Ernest Humbles,[133] who had enlisted in September 1914, winning his medal in the 2nd Bedfordshires; Richard Hoar,[134] a stretcher-bearer from Hemel Hempstead who had won his MM at La Coulotte; and Leonard King,[135] a stretcher-bearer from Diddington, who had gained his at Oppy Wood.

Parchment certificates for bravery were also presented to Acting RSM Johnson and Private James Sellers,[136] with RSM Johnson adding the Belgian Croix de Guerre (Belgian War Cross) to his impressive collection in April 1918.

Lieutenant Colonel Worrall was mentioned in despatches and awarded the Distinguished Service Order in the New Year's honours, to go with his Military Cross.

As the days turned into weeks, the men adapted to local customs and language, as soldiers on campaign invariably do. In no time at all, a

collection of anglicised local words were established and mutually understood by both the locals and the British troops. When mixed with sign
language, it ensured that there were not many Tommies who could not
buy bread, wine, or find ways to flirt with the local maidens. As the weeks
passed, other subtle differences emerged as French and Belgian locals grew
used to billeting large bodies of soldiers, and the troops in their turn
became accustomed to how things worked when dealing with them. In
contrast, the Bedfordshires found themselves in a part of the world that
had not needed to adapt to the presence of bodies of foreign soldiers, a
fact that was apparent in even the smallest of ways.

On 19 January, Private F.W. Richardson from Eynesbury, a former
Hunts Cyclist who had transferred into the Bedfordshires in 1916, wrote
home about the differences he and his comrades were coming to terms
with:[137]

*Am pleased to tell you that being out here is not like being in some parts of France, it*
*would be much better out here these cold nights if we could get some coals, but I don't*
*think they have ever seen any. They make a bit of fire on the hearth with wood, and*
*at night time the peasants take their sewing or knitting to the nearest cow shed for*
*warmth. They grow Indian corn in large quantities, what they don't sell they have*
*ground up into meal, and this is their chief food, and black coffee without sugar. It*
*looks quite different from our country, teams of oxen at the plough, also their funny*
*little waggons [sic].*

The Central Powers had been maintaining pressure on the defensive line
established in northern Italy although, since their arrival, XI Corps had
been held at the ready away from the front lines. Alongside one French
and one Italian corps, they provided the counter-attack force intended to
hold any Austro-German breakthrough between the Astico and Piave
Rivers, north of Venice.

While retaining their posture, expeditions were sent into the hills to
their north to prepare for an expected move to a pre-sited defensive line
among the rocky ridges. Meanwhile, the engineers worked continuously,
making the route as navigable as possible. When frosty, the British 3-tonne
trucks could just about use the local roads, but once the thaw set in and
the roads turned to a liquid slush, many of them came to grief and found
themselves in ditches, surrounded by groups of cold Tommies who could
do little but stare incredulously at yet another broken axle.

With these activities keeping the transport and pioneer sections extremely busy, the bulk of the Bedfordshires continued with their training, based from San Giorgio delle Pertiche, until late in January. Church services, leave into town, entertainment and occasional inspections punctuated their daily routines.

Throughout January, the division rebuilt following their ordeal around Ypres the previous autumn and several small drafts joined the Bedford-shires, although by the end of the month the battalion was still far from being at full strength. On 2 January Second Lieutenant Claud Gilbert Wilkins brought thirty-nine men with him, and three officers joined on 7 January, being Lieutenants George McMaster Betty, William Thomas Morris and Second Lieutenant Leonard Jack Hobson, who was return-ing after being wounded in October. Second Lieutenant Frank Herbert Fox arrived with nine men on 14 January, having recovered from wounds received while in the 7th Bedfordshires.

With a raft of new officers, those long overdue a spell of leave were issued orders to return to the UK, including the battalion quartermaster and honorary major Alfred Peirce. With no less than thirty years of regimental service to his credit, the veteran of the Isazia Field Force of 1892, the Chitral Relief Force of 1895 and the early battles of the war from Mons onwards, would not return to the battalion courtesy of an operation while back in the UK. Serving in administrative roles for the remainder of the war, Alfred retired on account of ill health in May 1919, dying in 1941 aged 70.

Although some of the reinforcements were conscripted men new to the firing line, most were tried and tested soldiers, such as George Drury of Letchworth,[138] who had served in the 1st Hertfordshires since 1914. His experience included their involvement in the Battles of Festubert and Loos in 1915 and the Somme in 1916, where he had been wounded. Returning to the front after over a year, his war was far from over and he was among those whose gallantry would stand out in the coming months.

The brigade boxing tournament on 15 January saw several of the Bedfordshires compete. Private Fanaday[139] conceded his middleweight semi-final round to Sergeant Auker of the Norfolks, and Private Williams lost his welterweight quarter-final to Private Artley of the Norfolks, who went on to win the weight class. In the lightweights, Mons veteran Private James Bagnall[140] and Private Batten made it to the quarter-finals, but both were beaten by opponents from the Norfolks. In the feather-weights, Private Harris lost his qualifier to Private Anderson of the Argylls, who was the eventual runner-up of the competition, and although Private Horne progressed to the semi-final, he was defeated by Bombardier Varlon of the RFA, who went on to win the class. Lance Corporal Kingsman, despite being a stone lighter than Private Davies of the East Surreys, lost in a 'Special Contest' arranged for those under the traditional featherweight requirements.

The battalion left their billets on 23 January and started a move that would take them to Villorba, 8km north-east of Paese and 5km north of Treviso, en route to the front lines. Overnight rests in Settimo on the 23rd and Paese on the 24th led to them entering Villorba on 25 January. A week of training and preparing for a tour in the front line followed, with staggered, daily reconnaissance trips by all officers and senior NCOs.

While training, news arrived that two of their Old Contemptibles had been awarded the Military Medal. George Hynard of Hadleigh[141] and Arthur King from Bedford,[142] with fourteen and thirteen years of service respectively, had been out since Mons, and Arthur had been among the wounded from the retirement from Le Cateau in August 1914.

### The Piave River sector: 27 January to 3 April 1918

On 27 January, the 5th Division started to relieve two Italian divisions in the line, although not in the north as expected, but on the line of the Piave River. Their new line ran from Nervesa della Battaglia in the north, to just below Salletuol, a stretch of around 13km. In their sector, the river varied between 300 metres and 1km wide, with flat, open plains on either bank, and the line being organised with two brigades behind the river and the third in reserve. Each brigade held two battalions in the front, with two in support, ensuring only a very limited time was spent in the front trenches per battalion.

During the first spell on the front, the 15th Brigade were in divisional reserve and courtesy of how the rotation of each battalion through the positions worked, it ensured a week was spent in the front, a week in support and a week in reserve. While in reserve, the brigade's qualifying games for the Divisional Senior Cup football competition were held, the Bedfordshires losing 3–0 to the Norfolks in the brigade final.

Lieutenant Herbert Powell rejoined from hospital on 31 January, in the midst of another sports tournament. After many knockout rounds, the final of the brigade's Junior Cup was won by C Company, 1st Norfolks, on 1 February, with none of the Bedfordshires' teams making it past the quarter-finals. The brigade's Association Football League came to a close at the same time, with the Bedfords holding fourth position from nine teams involved.

With the bulk of the battalion engaged in training, working fatigues and distracted by the football tournament on the 1st, a small group of officers scouted the next day's route as the following evening saw the Bedfordshires move into positions in support of the front line for their first tour since arriving in Italy.

Their brigade occupied the northern half of the divisional sector, the front line running along the Piave River between Rotondo and Bidasio, 8km due north of Villorba. In their sector, No Man's Land was so wide that sniping and machine-gun fire against troops in the trenches was infrequent. Artillery was also sporadic and relatively quiet compared to the levels the Bedfordshires had become accustomed to on the Western Front, but nightly aerial bombing raids from the active German squadrons became a regular hazard. However, their efforts were diverted to a disused Italian airfield, which they were deceptively encouraged to visit, ensuring the damage they caused in inhabited areas was limited.

The British army were relentless night-time patrollers and, although the front lines were far apart, this practice continued rigorously. Shingle islands broke the flow of the river and frequent meetings between patrols at night occasionally escalated into small skirmishes. On the occasions that neither patrol would concede their position, machine guns and artillery fire from both sides flared up in support of their own troops. With both adversaries firing blindly in the darkness, these clashes would fade away as quickly as they had escalated, with neither side losing any men.

The quieter spell allowed for selected periods of leave, Second Lieutenant Harrower being one of the dozens who were granted passes back to the UK. Stewart Harrower certainly had a unique career in the regiment, initially enlisting into the ranks in June 1906, aged 19. Serving in the 2nd Bedfordshires at home, on Gibraltar and Bermuda, he had disappeared from his tropical post in July 1911, being registered as a deserter. Four years later he had surfaced again while serving twelve months' hard labour for multiple counts of fraud in Glasgow, being handed over to the regiment to serve twenty-eight days for his desertion once released in April 1916. Remarkably, Stewart had been re-enlisted on release and joined the 4th Bedfordshires in France a year later. Within six months he had been promoted to Acting CSM for repeated bravery, the highly respected Lieutenant Colonel Collings-Wells[143] recommending him for a field commission. Even more remarkably for the social standards of the time, and apparently unaware of his past, the army council approved his promotion and the newly gazetted subaltern had been posted to Italy to join the 1st Bedfordshires in December. Still suffering from the effects of gas from the previous October, Stewart reported to the medical board while on leave and would not return to the 1st Bedfordshires until November 1919, having 'gained his wings' and been posted to lead the RAF Sports Council's football team in the interim.

A series of dishonoured cheques and bankruptcy in 1919 caused a furore within the Air Ministry and army, internal memos flying back and forth, with the senior staff split between him being a 'gallant scoundrel' and simply 'disgraceful'. Being thrust into a hitherto unknown financial life-style and expected to maintain an outwardly appropriate appearance in keeping with his fellow officers, he had moved between hotels during his service, as was the norm for officers at the time. However, the RAF had not been as quick in paying him as he had been in spending his income, and the difference between his allowances and expenditure soon became telling, the official receiver remarking he had been 'wickedly extrava-gant' while commanding the football team. His past came to light during the investigation, along with other cases of unpaid debts, which resulted in the call for his resignation instead of a dishonourable discharge, given that his 'services from a fighting point of view' had been 'satisfactory', not to mention his impressive, meteoric rise from private to com-missioned officer in just six months. Sadly, in 1924 he was sentenced to another year's hard labour for further counts of unpaid debts, his father, a famous football referee, even remarking in open court how he knew of hundreds of cases of his son's borrowings from all over the country.[144]

Back in Italy, two men were wounded during shelling on 3 February, as the battalion were kept busy with fatigues, staggered throughout the day and night. During another day of repairing trenches and general fatigue duties, Major Walter Allason, Second Lieutenant James Christopher Meade and nineteen men joined the battalion.

Lieutenant Colonel Percy Worrall, who had commanded the battalion since April 1917, was transferred to the 1st Devonshires on 5 February, with Lieutenant Colonel Edward Ivan de Sausmarez Thorpe assuming the role of commanding officer. Edward Thorpe's war had already been eventful. Having been among the pre-war officer corps of the 1st Bed-fordshires, he had fought from Mons until wounded at La Bassée, return-ing to the 2nd Bedfordshires months later. Commanding battalions of Borders and Lancashire Fusiliers in the interim, Lieutenant Colonel Thorpe had returned to the 2nd Bedfordshires late in 1917 before completing the circle by rejoining the 1st Battalion as they enjoyed their quiet tour in Italy.

On 6 February Second Lieutenant Frank Hughes retired to the field ambulance sick and the following day saw the first of the battalion's two combat deaths from their tour in Italy, when Private Bertie Warwick[145] from St Albans was killed during an exchange of artillery fire while attached to the 15th Trench Mortar Battery.

Several more relatively quiet days followed, with just light shelling interrupting their daily fatigues, until the battalion moved into the front lines again on 10 February. Meanwhile, on the Western Front the British army was busily reorganising itself into a new, smaller structure to account for its deficiencies in manpower. Although this reorganisation saw divisions reduced from their twelve-battalion structure down to nine, the Bedfordshires' division would not be affected by this change, remaining at full strength.

Four very quiet days passed until late on the 14th, when one advanced post was disturbed by the sound of approaching men from the Austrian lines. Waiting until the last moment, they determined the unseen party were not British so bombed them. Advancing towards the cries of alarm, they soon learned that two wounded Italian soldiers had escaped from their Austrian captors and had fumbled their way west in the darkness. Both men were lightly wounded and were treated in the field ambulance. As day broke on the 15th, another advanced post reported in that a large board had appeared on the Austrian side of the river overnight, bearing the inscription '*Eviva Pace Russo*', which was later translated by brigade officers into '*Long live the peace with Russia*'.

Other than sporadic enemy artillery fire and the arrival of officers from the East Surreys who reconnoitred the lines in preparation for their coming tour, trench life continued uninterrupted for the rest of their spell on the front. Although the riflemen of the battalion were immersed in their fatigues and routines, one group of Bedfordshires were busying themselves with solving the problem of how to cross the river effectively under combat conditions.

An operation was planned for early March to support an Italian attack further south, with the 15th Brigade being selected to conduct the assault between Nervesa and Bidasio, capture the northern bank and hold it for forty-eight hours. Preparations and training went ahead, the entire brigade seemingly buoyed up by the prospect of operations once more.

Pioneer Sergeant Richard Wheeler[146] and his fellow pioneers were always an active group who worked tirelessly under fire and looked for innovative ways to overcome obstacles faced by their battalion, and this operation was no different. After several doomed attempts to overcome the strong river current, the muscular, six-foot-tall Sergeant Wheeler, a carpenter by trade, designed and built a craft that could cope with the eddies. He was spotted while launching it but continued the test under heavy machine-gun fire, the trial proving a complete success.

The brigade were relieved on 18 February, the Bedfordshires moving into billets in Visnadello, 5km south along the road towards Villorba, where training got under way for the coming operation. Other than a German air raid on the 24th, and a lively evening provided by the 'Bedford Boys' on the 25th, training was uninterrupted until orders moved them into support positions at Bidasio on 27 February.

The plan was kept relatively straightforward, given the difficulties associated with a river crossing under fire. On the left flank one battalion was to be ferried across the channel and establish their bridgehead, which would allow two supporting battalions to move in behind them and deploy to their south, as far as the bridges at Bidasio. The right-hand battalion, being the Bedfordshires, were to make their way across, *'some on boards, some on broken pieces'* and form a bridgehead for the remainder of their men to follow behind them. To their south, the 13th Brigade was to make a demonstration against their counterparts and exploit any potential opportunity if it arose. Sailors from HMS *The Earl of Peterborough* and some gondoliers from Venice were even brought into the line to ferry the infantry across.

On 28 February, the Bedfordshires were busied repairing their trenches, providing carrying parties and on general fatigue duties, keeping them occupied in the run-up to their assault, while the evening saw a marked increase in counter battery shelling from British heavy artillery further back. Everything was in place by 1 March but the Italians asked for a twenty-four hour postponement of the planned 2 March operation. By the following morning, heavy rain had swelled the river by eighteen inches, forcing the operation to be called off. Although a revised plan was considered and prepared for, the entire operation was eventually cancelled, to the annoyance of the restless troops.

February had been another very quiet month, with the brigade reporting the loss of a remarkably light fourteen officers and men, three of them being Bedfordshires.

Lieutenant Sidney Allport was among those granted leave to the UK during the calm period, heading home on 3 March. Although he returned on the 17th, he was posted to the GHQ Sniping School as an instructor and struck off the battalion strength, going on to serve as commandant of two POW camps well into 1919.

The usual carrying and working parties continued while in support at Rotonda, until the Bedfordshires returned to the front on 4 March, resuming their position holding the right subsector. A Company in the centre held the bridges at Ponte della Priula, on the north side of the river from Bidasio, with C Company to their right, B to their left and D in close support. Several days of patrolling and relative inactivity followed, broken only by active artillery from both sides. Counter battery fire dominated the first few days until a heavy bombardment fell on the Bedfordshires on 9 March, severely wounding Second Lieutenant Perham, who died the next day in the 13th Field Ambulance at Arcade.[147]

William Perham, a Somerset-based carpenter by trade, had served as a pioneer sergeant in the Devonshire Regiment from October 1914. He had been wounded in March 1916 and healed quickly, only to be among the 57,000 British casualties from the infamous opening day of the Battle of the Somme a few months later. Once recovered, a third tour had ended in March 1917 when he was recommended for officer training, joining the 1st Bedfordshires over the winter of 1917. Revealing the grief rarely seen in the 'business as usual' society of the time, a letter to the War Office from a family friend in March begged, *'Please let Mrs Perham have a few details as soon as possible, or she will be in an asylum. Being her only child, she is quite overcome by grief and heart broken.'*

On the 11th, the Bedfordshires moved into brigade reserve at Arcade, a deserted and ruined village that hosted the 13th Field Ambulance, 2km south of Bidasio. Unbeknown to them, they were not to return to the front lines again as the tide of the war was about to change. Rumours and speculation about German preparations for a mass offensive on the Western Front had found a welcome home among the British forces in Italy, fuelled by news that the 41st Division had been moved back to France days earlier. In the event, the rumours would prove accurate over the coming days and weeks, although the battalion were blissfully unaware of that as they retired into reserve.

On 12 March Pioneer Sergeant Wheeler was granted leave to the UK until the end of the month, the first since marrying Elsie Chandler in December 1916. *'An excellent man in every way'*[148] and a veteran of ten years with the battalion, he was mentioned in Douglas Haig's despatches and would be awarded with the Distinguished Conduct Medal in March 1920, in recognition of his continuous courage, devotion and innovative thought throughout the war. Despite being six-foot tall and with a muscular frame that made him a noticeable target on a battlefield, he could always be seen laying cable under fire, or otherwise keeping operations moving forward by working tirelessly in the background. Remarkably, given the hazardous nature of his job and constantly exposing himself to danger, Richard survived the war without a single wound, having been on the front lines since Mons in 1914.

Working parties repaired roads, built dugouts and generally improved the reserve area away from the attentions of hostile artillery over the coming days, but on 14 March, Austrian gunners targeted a heavy British gun battery just behind the huts and buildings the Bedfordshires were billeted in. The heavy-calibre shells fell short, demolishing one wing of the battalion's billets, which had housed an entire company before they had left to watch a musketry competition earlier that day. Remarkably, no one was hurt, the damage was repaired and life went on as if nothing had happened.

Several more days providing working parties followed and, on the 16th, the battalion had one man wounded during heavy shelling of the village that afternoon.

That day, the Bedfordshires' adjutant, Captain Allan Beale, was assigned to Brigade HQ to assume duties as acting staff captain once again and the battalion spent 17 March preparing for a night move, which took them to Santa Andrea (Santandra), 4km south of Arcade. By midnight, the entire brigade was out of the line as the 48th Italian Division had taken over from the 5th Division entirely. The next day another march moved them to Castagnola, 6km south of Santa Andrea where they were billeted for several days.

In General Sir Herbert Plumer's despatch from Italy in June, several of the battalion were mentioned for services and bravery: Acting Major Eric Loder, Acting Captains Sidney Draper and Geoffrey Millais, Lieutenant John Kingdon, Honorary Captain and Quartermaster Alfred Peirce, Sergeant John Cordell,[149] Corporals John Bass,[150] Algernon Breed[151] and H. Lee, and Privates Sydney Rawlings[152] and James Smith.[153]

Orders arrived warning of the plan to move into the mountains and train for mountain warfare, but fragments of disturbing news started filtering down to the battalion of a massive German offensive launched in France, and on 23 March the battalion were on the move again, billeting for two days in Le Pitocche, 1km south-east of Loreggia, midway between Castagnole and Vigodarzere.

Resuming the move, the Bedfordshires lodged at Vigodarzere on the 24th, 4km north-west of Padova (Padua), where orders arrived at divisional level to prepare for a move to the Western Front. By the time the battalion reached Creola, 10km south-west of Vigodarzere, the next day, the news of their departure back to France had spread throughout the division, but it would take a week to concentrate and make ready. So, with preparations at full swing, the Bedfordshires spent one last peaceful spell on the banks of the Bacchiglione River, billeted among the inhabitants of Creola.

Training started in earnest, with time on the hastily constructed ranges, fitness training and lectures interspersed with sporting events, and passes into Padova for a final look around before returning to the rigours of warfare in France.

As the battalion waited, Private George William Weston[154] of Norfolk died, being the only British soldier buried in Creola cemetery. In spite of George's death, March's casualty list had again been thankfully light, with just one officer killed and four men wounded from the entire brigade's casualties of twenty-one officers and men.

But that was about to change as their four-month tour of Italy came to a close.

Chapter 6

# The German Spring Offensives: March and April 1918

*'With our backs to the wall, and believing in the justice of our cause, each one of us might fight on to the end.'*

With the collapse of the Eastern Front late in 1917, dozens of battle-hardened, veteran German divisions were released and the balance of power on the Western Front shifted noticeably. Allied generals knew a German attack was imminent, fully understanding that they needed to hold on as America's military weight would not be a significant factor until late summer. Of the options open to them, German planners chose to focus on the British army, intent on knocking it out of the war and thereby gaining victory over the French who would be unable to continue against such odds.

The German spring offensives of 1918 opened with 'Operation Michael' on 21 March 1918. An unprecedented, meticulously planned and superbly executed German bombardment from almost 6,500 guns and 3,500 mortars fell on General Gough's overstretched, undermanned Fifth Army lines at 4.40 a.m. Heavily armed German storm troopers followed behind and infiltrated what remained of the British lines, before massed infantry advanced under cover of the engulfing fog to mop up pockets of resistance. Their attack was a stunning success with many British battalions reduced to nothing more than a cadre and even entire divisions unable to raise more than a few hundred men. The opening day alone saw close to 40,000 British casualties, but German losses were slightly higher, with many of them being from their elite storm trooper units which they could barely afford to lose. A series of localised battles and fiercely contested rearguard actions developed over the next fortnight, with the Germans outstripping their supply lines before the offensive ground to a halt on 5 April and their focus moved to another part of the Western Front.

Within a week of the German attack being unleashed, British losses forced a change in military service age to make the badly needed reinforcements available to the overstretched front line. At the younger end of the age range, the lower limit was changed from 19 years to 18¹/₂, providing the soldier had received his six months of basic training. These 18-year-old 'A4s' as they were nicknamed, courtesy of their medical categorisation, would find themselves on the front lines and facing highly trained, well-motivated German veterans within days of being mobilised. At the upper end of the range, all able-bodied men up to 50 years old were deemed to have enlisted, with the limit extending to 56 if fitness and other circumstances allowed. Local papers reported how the new act *'seems to bring in nearly everyone, including grandfathers'* and how a steady stream of local men were making the journey to Bedford for their medical examinations. Not all cases were clear-cut, with reports noting how *'one gentleman of 65 years of age was called up for the colours'*.[155]

The battle marked a dark time for the British army whose remarkable tenacity enabled them to hold their lines in the face of an incredibly well-executed offensive that almost brought the war to a close. The German army captured over 3,000km² of territory but paid a terrible cost for their gains. Close to a quarter of a million men from each side were killed, wounded, missing or captured during the opening fortnight and the German strategic objectives had not been achieved.

It was under the shadow of these desperate events unfolding in France that the 5th Division started to entrain for France on April Fool's Day, the Bedfordshires leaving Creola on 2 April and marching 11km north-west to Longare, where they rested overnight. Preparations for the journey took up the entire day on 3 April, the weather dismal, cold and wet as the men organised themselves to leave the relatively blissful Italian sector and head into the unknown conditions that awaited them in France.

The battalion moved to Tavernelle, 7km south-west of Vicenza, where A and C Companies under Lieutenant Colonel Thorpe embarked for France at 10.10 p.m. on the 4th, with B and D Companies under Major Halford following them on a second train at 6.15 a.m. the following day. Their 1,200km journey took them through Modane, 150km east-south-east of Lyon, past Fontainbleau, 50km south-south-east of Paris, and through Doullens, 30km due north of Amiens, before arriving at Frévent on 8 April, 35km west of Arras. On arrival, Lieutenant John Kingdon was sent to hospital suffering from illness, debility and diarrhoea that would keep him away from the battalion until late May, and the detachments detrained independently and concentrated in billets at Neuvillette, 8km to the south. In accordance with divisional orders to move into the line south of Arras, the Bedfordshires left the village at 7 a.m. and marched 13km west to Sombrin on the 10th, where they were held in readiness to move at 30 minutes' notice in response to the fluid nature of events unfolding to the north. The forward units of the 5th Division were on their way to relieve the 2nd Canadians when urgent orders arrived to cancel the relief and redeploy further north, in response to a new German attack in the Lys valley.

## The Battle of the Lys: 9 to 29 April 1918

Following the cessation of Operation Michael, focus then moved north to the Flanders hills between Ypres and Béthune, where a series of battles collectively called the Battle of the Lys was fought. Opening on 9 April, the Battle of Estaires saw German forces attack on a 17km frontage, between the La Bassée canal and Bois-Grenier, 5km south of Armentières. Employing the same tactics that proved so effective during Operation Michael a few weeks earlier, an enormous bombardment decimated the front lines, storm troopers infiltrated what was left of the defences and massed infantry followed up under the cover of creeping barrages and yet more thick fog.

By the end of the first day, they had advanced a remarkable 6km west, destroyed the two Portuguese divisions within the opening few hours, and left many British units in their path a shell of their former selves; ironically many of the British divisions who faced the onslaught had been moved to this historically quiet sector to rest and rebuild after their ordeals during the offensives weeks earlier, with some of them not even remotely close to their paper strength. However, German troops were unable to prise the stubborn and well-prepared 55th Division from Festubert, Givenchy or the La Bassée canal on the southern flank and, in spite of the continued efforts of three assault divisions, supported by a further six in reserve over the coming days, would not overcome the territorial division who had a point to prove following criticism levelled at them after their part in the Cambrai defeat months earlier.

On the second day, the assault continued in the southern sector and advanced the German lines a further 1km between Vielle-Chapelle and

Estaires, but a new assault was unleashed on the already worn British troops further north, later entitled the Battle of Messines. The fighting front was extended a further 15km to the north between Bois-Grenier and Hollebeke, just 6km south-east of the prize of Ypres. In the centre of the assault, stunning advances of around 10km were made, although German progress was limited to around 1km at the northern extremity of the line.

Another thick fog shrouded the battlefield when a further massed assault hit the already exhausted British troops on 11 April, who faced a force three times their number, were hugely outgunned in terms of artillery and had no prepared defensive positions from which to repel attacks. Most British brigades could barely muster a battalion's worth of men and by the end of the day many had shrunk to company-sized units. The front lines, such as they were, saw troops as far apart as 20 yards with little or no reserve available to plug the inevitable gaps that would develop. Every available man who could be gathered was rushed into the line, with cooks, blacksmiths and regimental police being thrown forward, as British reserves were swiftly brought from other sectors towards the hard-pressed divisions.

Plans to retire back to a shortened line directly in front of Ypres and in doing so relinquish the ground so hard won in 1917 were put into action, thus releasing more badly needed units from the salient, and General Haig's famous Order of the Day was issued that evening: *There is no other course of action open to us but to fight it out; every position must be held to the last man; there must be no retirement. With our backs to the wall, and believing in the justice of our cause, each one of us might fight on to the end.*

On reading the order, *'at least one unit, knowing it was the last line of defence with little behind it bar the sea, asked "What ******* wall?"'*[156]

## The defence of Nieppe Forest: 12 to 27 April 1918

To the west of Arras, on 11 April, orders hurried the Bedfordshires 4km south-west to Saulty, where they boarded trains and were sped 50km north, detraining at Aire-sur-la-Lys before marching 3km south to Lambres and once again coming under the orders of XI Corps. Being so far inside what had traditionally been the reserve area of the British army, the companies were surprised to be given orders to establish an outpost line to the north of the village that evening, the 15th and 95th Brigades collectively extending east of Aire-sur-la-Lys and towards the Forêt de Nieppe (Nieppe Forest).

As dawn arrived on the 12th, it became clear that Merville had fallen overnight and reports told of there being no British troops in front of the division so, with the 13th Brigade on the right of the divisional line and the 95th Brigade on the left, orders were issued to retake Merville, with the 15th Brigade in support north of Saint Venant. At the last minute orders were cancelled but the division had already advanced through sporadic resistance to take up a line several hundred metres east of the forest, consolidating their position within hours. Several localised German attacks from Merville were broken up and the battalions had settled into a defensible line by evening. With the mauled 61st Division to their south across the canal and the 4th (Guards) Brigade to their north, a continuous line was formed and any German thoughts of maintaining the attack faded as their troops enjoyed the contents of the cellars in Merville.

As events unfolded to their north and east, the 15th Brigade were 'stood to' all morning, ready to move at an hour's notice, as the new phase of fighting later called the Battle of Hazebrouck, opened. The brigade finally moved east around 1 p.m., passing through Isbergues, Guarbecque, Saint-Venant, and Haverskerque, before halting in divisional reserve at the village of Croix-Marraisse, 1km north of Haverskerque, where the Bedfordshires billeted overnight.

The focus on the fighting on the 13th was a few kilometres to the north, as the German assaults tried to wrestle the high ground either side of Bailleul from the worn, tired but still resolute British troops. Just to the north of the 5th Division a heavy bombardment was followed by a series of German onslaughts against the Guards Brigade, who were holding an overextended frontage and were extremely weak after enduring days of fighting. Having resisted encirclement all day but refusing to give ground, the few remaining Guards retired through the Australians behind them, who had linked up in a continuous line with the 5th Division to their south. With the Australians in the north and the fresh, veteran 5th Division south of them, the sector was secure and many exhausted British units were rested and re-formed away from enemy observation to the west.

The following day Captain Allan Beale rejoined from his brigade staff posting as the entire brigade dug the divisional (support) line parallel with the north–south road through Haverskerque, running from Croix Marraisse to La Maladerie, 1km south of Haverskerque. The Bedfordshires prepared a line stretching from the north-east corner of Haverskerque to a stream 1.5km north-east, in the middle of the Bois Moyen, with the Warwickshires similarly engaged to their south and

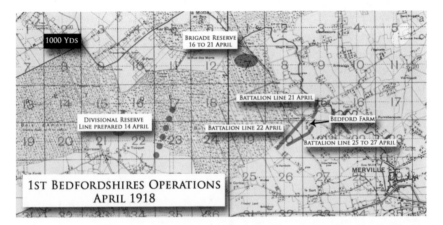

1ST BEDFORDSHIRES OPERATIONS APRIL 1918

Norfolks to their north. Battalion transport and details were moved to Tannay given that the division were expecting a German assault to come their way, the remaining fighting strength of around 750 Bedfordshires being among those preparing the defensive line. During their fatigues, British aeroplanes were reported as strafing the brigade, apparently not realising they were British troops initially, until the matter was resolved by Brigade HQ making their feelings clear to the local RFC squadron liaison.

German artillery and aeroplanes found the brigade and the 14th saw the Bedfordshires take their first casualties for some time, William Spicer from Great Hormead in Hertfordshire[157] being killed in action and a further five of his comrades being wounded.

Another heavy German assault developed against the northern half of the 5th Division, raging for five hours without a pause, but was repulsed with very heavy losses to the German troops through the concentrated artillery barrage from the guns of two divisions and accurate, withering rifle and machine-gun fire. On the southern sector of the line further attacks were driven back, the divisional line holding firm in spite of the German army's best efforts.

The Battles of Hazebrouck and Bailleul continued throughout the morning with localised operations for tactical positions ironing out kinks in the lines on both sides, but by the time the day came to a close on 15 April the entire battlefield calmed down significantly as the assaults petered out. In the wood, the Bedfordshires carried on with their fatigues, Harry Lowe from St Albans[158] being killed during the sporadic shelling, and four of his comrades being wounded in their relatively eventless day.

Dawn broke quietly on the 16th, without either the distant, thunderous bombardment or the crackling of massed rifle fire. The day would prove to be peaceful across the entire battlefield for the first time since 9 April as both armies drew breath and reorganised in readiness for the next phase of the battle. That day, the 15th Brigade relieved the 95th Brigade on the left of the divisional line, with the Cheshires moving into the left sector, the Norfolks into the right, the Warwickshires in support and the Bedfordshires in brigade reserve, remaining in the thin stretch of wood just east of the appealingly named La Rue des Morts, 4km along the road running north-west out of Merville. Once in position, Lieutenant Colonel Edward Thorpe left the battalion to command the decimated 152nd Brigade further north, Major Montague Walter Halford assuming command of the 1st Bedfordshires.

That night, the routine of harassment resumed, with constant nightly patrols spooking their opponent's lines, snipers targeting any troops foolish enough to show themselves, and artillery probing known enemy positions. German attempts to advance against the unshaken divisional front stopped for several days and stretcher-bearers dressed in field grey were hard at work throughout the day and night, clearing survivors from among the carnage in the open fields. In spite of being the strongest British division currently on the battlefield, they had not come through the battle unscathed, losing over 120 officers and 1,200 men, including a brigadier general and many staff officers.

In an attempt to pinch out the Ypres salient, on the 17th the Germans launched an operation called Tannenberg against Belgian forces 45km to the north-east of the Bedfordshires, which was bloodily repulsed, and the First Battle of Kemmel flared up 20km north-east of the battalion.

Back in their brigade support positions, the Bedfordshires continued with their duties, losing Harry Cotton from St Albans[159] to hostile shell fire and a further three men wounded. Another unrecorded casualty was Lieutenant Edgar Francis Kirkman Graham, who had recovered from his gunshot wound in October 1917 and was on his way to the re-inforcement camp in Calais before heading out to rejoin the battalion. On the night of 17 April he fell out of the moving vehicle, courtesy of the lack of rails to keep passengers inside the carriage, injuring his left ribs badly. Despite having served through the South African wars and surviving the Great War during hazardous service above and below the ground, even winning a Military Medal along the way, the innocuous accident ensured Edgar's active service was over. He continued serving in an administrative capacity until 1921, even rejoining the RASC as a private between 1921 and 1923.

Some 15km south-east of the Bedfordshires' positions on the 18th, the Battle of Béthune was fought as another quiet day digging and building passed, four men being caught by sporadic shelling in the wood. A further man was wounded the following day, with two more being caught by shells on the 20th. A draft of thirty-one men joined as the work went on, with building breastworks and wiring their lines taking the entire battalion's efforts between providing carrying fatigues for the battalions on the front lines.

The Bedfordshires relieved the 1st Norfolks in the advanced lines in front of the wood between the road running north-west out of Merville and the stream 600 metres to the north on the evening of 21 April but, although the relief was quiet, British artillery fired short overnight causing several casualties and a heavy gas and trench mortar bombardment swamped the forest and surrounding posts, with one man killed and a further four wounded during the night.

The next day, the battalion also relieved the 12th Gloucestershires' portion of the line and extended their own lines an additional 1km further south-west, to a point opposite Le Vertbois farm, lining the eastern edge of the wood around 150 metres into the open ground. Soon after the relief was complete, a bombardment of twenty trench mortar rounds pounded their positions opposite Le Vertbois, causing damage and casualties before they could familiarise themselves with their surroundings. By the day's end, two more men had lost their lives and a further nine were wounded.

Of those injured during the shelling, Private William Gray of Royston,[160] a well-known local gardener before enlisting in June 1917, died from his wounds. The 27-year-old was the second brother killed during the war, having been with the battalion since October 1917.

That day the brigade lines were flown over by large formations of British spotting aeroplanes, which were heavily shelled by German AA guns, intent on keeping their activities and preparations from the prying British airmen.

The reason for the Germans' wishes to keep British aircraft from seeing their support areas became clear on the 23rd, when a large body of German infantry were seen advancing on the centre company. An instant artillery barrage and hail of rifle and machine-gun fire dispersed the attempt to attack before it could develop, with the rest of the day being broken by the usual probing artillery fire. Second Lieutenant Harry

Wilkins, a bank clerk before the war, was hit during the day's shelling, being severely wounded in his right hand and left leg, the latter being amputated while still in France. Lieutenant Edward Johnson was evacuated to the field ambulance and Second Lieutenant Herbert Hutchinson rejoined the battalion in the day, having recovered from his wound from October 1917.

As darkness fell, large wiring parties busied themselves in front of their posts and strongholds while aggressive patrols went into No Man's Land. One of the patrols near the Merville to La Motte road took two artillery spotters prisoner who were attached to the 8th German Division and had become separated while making their way to the front to observe, wounding one in the exchange of fire. Another patrol further north investigated the farm and enclosure just south-east of Les Lauriers, finding it garrisoned with German infantry and machine gunners before retiring unmolested.

Overnight, very heavy gas and high-explosive shelling was directed against the woods, catching the Cheshires unexpectedly and causing over 100 casualties among them before the gas alert could even be sounded.

In light of the information gathered during their patrol against the farm opposite Les Lauriers, A Company spent the 24th preparing for a localised operation to move the brigade lines 250 metres further forward, capturing the farm and enclosure in the process. Elsewhere in the battalion lines, trench life continued, with three men being wounded by shell fire. An officer patrol that evening approached a farm at the northern edge of their lines but were fired on and kept from learning anything other than the fact that it was garrisoned.

The Second Battle of Kemmel to the north-east of the division's position was launched on 25 April but the Bedfordshires' front was quiet all day other than occasional shelling and aircraft patrolling overhead.

The rotation of troops returning to the front after recovering from wounds continued with the arrival of three officers that day. Lieutenant Alexander Herbert Oliver Riddell joined from the 2nd Bedfordshires and Lieutenant Edgar Nailer reappeared after recuperating from his wounds during the Third Battle of Ypres. Second Lieutenant Frederick Lee Ray also rejoined, having recovered from the accidental injury sustained on the practice ground the previous November.

As darkness fell that evening, the assaulting units from the Bedfordshires and Gloucestershires moved into position, ready for their operation. At 9.15 p.m. A Company and one platoon from B Company braced themselves for their assault and fifteen minutes later the British barrage opened, the Bedfordshires advancing behind its protective screen. Several shrapnel shells fell short, landing among the right platoon of the advancing waves and causing a dozen casualties, including the raid commander, Captain Frederick Hague. Regardless of his injuries, Captain Hague insisted on continuing and led his men forward to the position, the men from the supporting platoon replacing their casualties according to the plan. Eight minutes after their push forward had commenced, a red rocket pierced the sky, signalling the farm was in their hands. Seeing the Bedfordshires advancing with bayonets fixed, the defenders had offered little resistance and at 10.35 p.m. a runner from A Company reported to Battalion HQ in Les Lauriers that the entire position was secure and clear of German troops. At 11 p.m. and having physically visited each section of men himself, Captain Hague limped into Battalion HQ and reported that the entire line was secure and had linked up with C Company to the north and the Gloucestershires to the south. However, the wound to his thigh was found to be getting worse, so he was sent back to the field ambulance suffering from his second wound since joining the battalion. On arrival, he collapsed and was returned to England to recover, being presented with the Military Cross by the King on 11 September 1918 and serving into the Second World War with the Bedfordshire and Hertfordshire Regiment.

The operation had advanced the brigade lines around 250 metres, the Gloucestershires capturing La Vertbois and another farm to the south in conjunction with the Bedfords' assault, with the two new posts being named Bedford Farm and Gloster Farm. Twelve German prisoners and one machine gun were captured by the Bedfordshires, for the loss of Captain Hague wounded, one man killed and a further twenty injured, many being lost to the British barrage falling short during their advance.

Letchworth resident Corporal George Drury[161] had seen much since joining the territorial Hertfordshire Regiment at the outbreak of war, aged 17. Serving on the Western Front from 1914, he had fought alongside the British Guards throughout the 1915 campaigns until wounded on the Somme. Arriving with the 1st Bedfordshires in January 1918, he had been busy in the preliminary operations against the farm and during the raid itself, winning the Distinguished Conduct Medal for his gallantry, the citation reading: *'For conspicuous gallantry and devotion to duty during operations in patrolling the enemy's line and bringing back valuable information. During the attack he led a patrol party through, and, on reaching the objective, pushed on to the enemy's main line and reported their position to his platoon commander. The success of the operation and the covering of the consolidation were greatly due to his courage and skill. He captured a machine gun and made the enemy personnel carry it back.'*

The 26th was a quiet day but on the 27th a German counter-attack was launched. At 4 a.m. around 200 troops advanced towards Bedford Farm under the protective screen of a creeping barrage and with the added aid of morning mist. Initially firing blind into the white curtain, the Bedfords could see shapes advancing towards them at around 100 metres and opened a withering fire. The British defensive artillery barrage was adjusted and, coupled with the machine-gun barrage, a Lewis-gun post enfilading the attack from the south, as well as continuous rifle fire, the attack was completely broken up before the forward elements had come within 60 metres of the farm.

The intense shelling accounted for twenty Bedfords, with 20-year-old stockbroker's son Second Lieutenant Ambrose Peel being killed by a shell[162] and a further eight men losing their lives. Private Henry Clarke,[163] a 27-year-old resident of Finsbury Park, was among those killed; he had been with the battalion since January 1907 and had fought with it since Mons.

Acting Captain William White had been in charge of A Company since Captain Hague's wound days earlier, but the farm was to prove unlucky for company commanders, as William was also wounded during the shelling, along with ten of his men.

The rest of the day was spent repairing the damage under sporadic shell fire and that night the brigade was relieved by the 13th Brigade, with the covering patrols sent into No Man's Land discovering dozens of dead German troops from the earlier fighting.

On the 29th, the Battle of Scherpenberg brought the series of battles in the Lys valley to a close, the fighting fizzling out by midday. Although the German army had achieved some stunning successes, overall their strategic objectives had not been achieved. Furthermore, the British army had been badly mauled but just managed to hold their lines. In return, the German losses were heavy, many of them being from their elite assault units that they could not afford to lose.

Many British units had suffered such heavy losses that they were reduced to administrative units while being rebuilt, but the 15th Brigade had lost a relatively light 18 officers and 390 men since their return to the Western Front, with 4 officers and almost 90 men being from the Bedfordshires.

Among the wounded was 19-year-old Albert Peacock from Letchworth, who was reported in his local paper as returning home on leave after his recovery *'wearing three blue service chevrons and three wound stripes'*.[164] He had enlisted aged just 16 and had already seen two and a half years of active service, originally in the 8th Bedfordshires, and had been injured at Vermelles and Loos. Albert was badly wounded in his left leg and gassed, but recovered and would be back among his comrades sporting a fourth overseas service stripe before the end of the war.

As May 1918 opened, British generals were oblivious, but the main German threat had come to a close on their front and, against the odds, the thin ranks of the British and Commonwealth forces had come through in one piece.

Chapter 7

# Summer in Nieppe Forest: May to August 1918

*'Trees, heat and Yellow Cross mustard gas.'*

In May the British army reorganised once more, adjusting to a smaller structure following their losses in the German spring offensives. Among the reductions, the 6th and 7th Battalions of the Bedfordshire Regiment were amalgamated into the more senior regimental units, although none of the drafts from either battalion would be sent to the 1st Bedfordshires, who were still in relatively good shape compared to their sister battalions.

That summer, the 5th Division would settle into three months of trench warfare with offensive activities over and above those typically associated with time on the front lines limited to tactical improvements in the local area. However, this period was not spent in countryside representative of the trench warfare previously experienced, the ground having been farmland until recently, with defensive trench lines still in the process of being established on both sides.

During their tour around the forest, the divisional sector was split in half, with two brigades being in the front line at any given time and the third being in support. The northern part, called the Arrewage sector, ran from a line connecting the villages of Vierouck (Vierhouck) and Caudescure (which extended west to the edge of the wood and then north-west towards La Motte-au-Bois), to the road running north-west out of Merville, towards La Motte-au-Bois. From there, the southern area – the Le Sart sector – continued to the Nord Pas-de-Calais canal (Canal d'Aire). Although the brigade dividing line shifted from time to time and localised gains moved their front lines forward during the summer, this was to be the home of the division until the Allied armies went back on to the offensive in August.

Gas would be a constant problem all summer, especially the use of what was labelled Yellow Cross mustard gas, which was very hard to see or smell, extremely persistent, and did not always take hold of its victim immediately, by which time it was too late. RAMC gas patrols were set up throughout the forest to identify lingering clouds and warn local or passing troops accordingly, but pockets of mustard gas still caught divisional troops out from time to time.

### The Le Sart brigade sector: 28 April to 28 May 1918

The Bedfordshires spent six days based in the Nieppe Forest Camp, making good deficiencies, cleaning up, and then providing large parties for working on the divisional support line once again, in response to the warnings to expect a German attack.

At 11 a.m. on 29 April, the corps' commander, General Haking, presented company colours to each of the sixteen companies in the brigade. The company commander, CSM or CQMS and eight men from each company paraded to accept the colours, which were attributed to being the work of Lady Haking.

The following day Sergeant Charles Vowles from Taunton[165] was commissioned from the ranks, being transferred home for officer training and returning to join the 2nd Bedfordshires in October.

After the initial two days of reorganising themselves, Battalion HQ moved to L'Epinette on the edge of the wood, 500 metres north of Croix Marraisse, as fatigues picked up pace.

A move into support positions inside the Bois Moyen followed on 3 May with the transport, two officers and a cadre of 128 men being left in Tannay. The Bedfordshires would spend a week in this position, the battalion being employed on making a trackway to the front line, in addition to wiring and improving their support line.

Overnight on the 4th and 5th, the battalion came under heavy shell fire, losing eight more men. Ernest Forster from Lowestoft was killed instantly, with five of the seven wounded Bedfords dying over the coming days. Of those mortally wounded was 19-year-old Private Harry Byatt[166] of Eynesbury. Days later his parents received the news in a letter from Chaplain G. Provis, who wrote how *'he was out with a wiring party when he was badly wounded by a shell late on the evening of the 4th, and died of wounds early on the 5th. He is buried in a little cemetery behind the line.'* Harry had enlisted into the Hunts Cyclists aged just 16 and was the second brother to be lost on the Western Front, Martin, his older reservist sibling, being killed in the 2nd Bedfordshires in 1915.

On 9 May the Bedfordshires moved back into the front lines in the left subsector of the Le Sart brigade front, from north of the railway line to around Le Vertbois, with the 16th Warwickshires on their right. By this time, the defensive works had been improved but were still far from complete, with the main line of resistance still a disconnected series of trench works, screened by a collection of forward posts designed to delay any enemy assault while those holding the main line were organised. Over the coming days and weeks, relentless efforts would see the disjointed defences come together, but for the time being, the division were still in a far from ideal situation.

Overnight on the 9th and again throughout the 10th, their positions were shelled, with the garrisons in Bedford Farm and Les Lauriers being especially targeted by over 100 shells. Around 4 p.m. on the 10th, a battalion Lewis-gun team engaged a German scout aircraft, hitting it but not bringing it down.

Three more men were wounded on 11 May as the battalion continued their activities of repairing damage created, patrolling and looking for opportunities to harass those opposite them. Bedford Farm was heavily shelled at 10 a.m. and again at 2.30 p.m. on the 11th, with more attention being paid early the next morning, the many direct hits accounting for five dead and four wounded over the two days. In retaliation, a concentrated, five-minute artillery and machine-gun barrage was levelled at an identified German post at 10.30 p.m. on 13 May.

Late on the 15th, to cover the relief taking place behind them, a Bedford patrol approached known German positions in the enclosure south of the track between Le Vertbois and Le Sart. Discovered to be a machine-gun post once fire was directed against them, it forced their quick retirement. Soon afterwards a firefight erupted in the dark night to their south bringing the line to attention, the Warwickshires repelling an assault against one of their Lewis-gun posts.

During the relief early on the 16th, which saw the entire brigade moved into divisional reserve, Second Lieutenant Frederick Lee Ray and one of his squad were killed instantly by a trench mortar shell. The 24-year-old former haulier from Bedford had only returned to the battalion a few weeks earlier, having recovered from injuries sustained during an accidental bomb explosion while training the previous winter.

A cricket match between officers and sergeants at the Ampthill Depot on 20 June 1916. Several of the officers joined the 1st Bedfordshires in a draft on 18 September 1916.

Standing: CSM Clark; Second Lieutenant Carl Henry Zeuner Piercy; Sergeant Reginald Charles Humphries MC, who was commissioned after service in the 1st Battalion from late 1916; Second Lieutenant William Martin Stantan, who was wounded in the 1st Battalion at La Coulotte in April 1917 and again at Achiet in August 1918; Second Lieutenant Gordon; Sergeant Cooper; Second Lieutenant Arthur William Matson, who saw service with the 1st Bedfordshires before transferring into the Royal Flying Corps; Captain Tanqueray; Second Lieutenant John Titcombe Ryde, who served with the battalion from 1916 but was killed in May 1917 while attached to the Gloucestershires; Second Lieutenant Robert Guthrie Forbes, who joined the battalion with John Ryde in 1916 and was accidentally wounded on a bombing range in March 1917; Second Lieutenant Henry Leigh Farnell, later of the Army Intelligence Corps, who served in the Army of the Rhine and became a well-known actor.

Middle row: Second Lieutenant Algernon Smee Lockhart; Second Lieutenant Thomas Murray Kilpin Fletcher, who joined the battalion in September 1916 and wrote a farewell note from the battlefield at La Coulotte as he lay dying; Sergeant Samm; Sergeant Allen; Major and Adjutant Albert Edward Nelson; Colour Sergeant Pegg; Dr Garner; CSM Peck; CQMS Sadler.

Seated: Sergeant Jeffs; Sergeant Quartermaine; Sergeant Bell; Sergeant John Hughes.
(Ceinwen Hughes)

**Major John Moyse, who died from wounds 8 February 1917.** (Doug Moyse)

**The grave of Major John Moyse, in the Béthune town cemetery.** (Steven Fuller)

**Percival Hart and his final resting place, taken after the war.** (Steven Fuller, David Sankey)

Private 3/6448 Sidney Wilson, MM, who was killed 2 July 1917. (Julie Day)

Below: Sidney's final resting place, Roclincourt cemetery. (Julie Day)

Above: Second Lieutenant Paul Christie while an officer cadet at RMC Sandhurst, 1917. (Steven Fuller)

Above, right: A selection of the battalion's dead from the 2,345 British soldiers interred in the Hooge Crater cemetery, Belgium. (Steven Fuller)

Right: Second Lieutenant Frederick Halsey, formerly CQMS 6756, killed 10 August 1917. (Steven Fuller)

Above, left: Lance Corporal 3/7450 George Henry Bland, MM, killed 4 October 1917. (Steven Fuller)

Above, right: Sergeant 28207 James Sinclair DCM, MM and Bar, killed 12 November 1917. (Steven Fuller)

Left: Second Lieutenant Harold Henry Reynolds, killed 4 October 1917. (Steven Fuller)

A collection of the battalion's gallantry medal winners taken in 1917; includes Captain Chirnside (MC and Bar) and John Stapleton (DCM). (Imperial War Museum, reference IWM 388)

CSM 7623 Sidney 'Spot' Chamberlain, killed 25 October 1917. (Steven Fuller)

Private 29549 Samuel Thomas Spicer, killed 25 October 1917. (Derek Lawman)

The Giavera British cemetery, Arcade, northern Italy. (Pierluigi Sanzovo)

Private 15568 Bertie Warwick's grave, the first of only two Bedfords killed during their tour in Italy. (Steven Fuller)

The grave of Second Lieutenant William Francis George Perham, who died from wounds received during a bombardment and who was initially interred in the Arcade communal cemetery. (Steven Fuller)

**Eight of the battalion killed while holding Nieppe Forest in April 1918, facing Merville.**
(Steven Fuller)

**The final resting place of Second Lieutenant Frederick Ray and Private Len Gray, killed by the same trench mortar shell on 16 May 1916.** (Steven Fuller)

**Second Lieutenant Frederick Lee Ray, who was killed alongside his runner Len Gray.** (Chris Ray)

Temporary Major Frederick Ray, father of Second Lieutenant Frederick Lee Ray, seated front centre, outside the Rushey Ford Farm, Kempston. He is surrounded by officers from either the 1st Bedfordshire Volunteer Corps or the Bedfordshire Motor Volunteer Corps. (Chris Ray)

Above: Captain Geoffrey de Carteret Millais, died of wounds 21 August 1918. (Steven Fuller)

Right: Lieutenant Colonel Hugh Courtenay, DSO, MC, killed 23 August 1918. (Penny Maitland-Stuart)

LIEUTENANT COLONEL
H. COURTENAY DSO MC.
BEDFORDSHIRE REGIMENT
23RD AUGUST 1918

**The final resting place of Lieutenant Colonel Hugh Courtenay, DSO, MC, in the Bagneux British cemetery, Gézaincourt.** (Steven Fuller)

Harold McHugh, MM, and some of his chums from the battalion. Harold is seated front centre and sports an array of overseas and wound stripes in addition to his MM ribbon and sergeant's chevrons, as do most of those around him. (Paddy McHugh and John Law)

Harold McHugh and his wife Ivy, in more relaxed conditions. (Paddy McHugh and John Law)

Three of the battalion who were killed fighting around Beugny, 2 September 1918, and who now lie in the Red Cross Corner cemetery, Beugny: Private 7170 Edward Davis, whose service with the regiment went back to 1902 and who had been on the front for over four years; Private 269463 Arthur Nevard, formerly of the Hertfordshire Regiment; and 35-year-old Londoner Corporal 42403 George Togwell who had originally served on Gallipoli before joining the regiment late in 1917. (Steven Fuller)

Three of the battalion's NCOs killed during their assault on Beaucamp village, 27 September 1918: Corporals Alexander William Fuller, William Read and Arthur Parkes. (Steven Fuller)

Private 16750 Owen Brown's grave, who died of wounds 5 November 1918. Owen's is the only CWGC grave in the Jolimetz communal cemetery. (Steven Fuller)

Sergeant 10052 George Neale's grave; died of wounds 6 November 1918. (Steven Fuller)

Private 47366 William Walter Jones's grave, the last member of the battalion to be killed in action on 6 November 1918. (Steven Fuller)

Pre-war regular and bandsman 10241 Thomas Haynes, who survived wounds at Hill 60, Faffemont Farm and the battalion's final offensive in November 1918, going on to serve in the battalion until 1925. (David Downes)

'Return of the Bedfords': a cadre of the 1st Battalion march through Bedford centre on their arrival home, 28 April 1919. (Steven Fuller)

The sergeants' mess at Colchester, August 1922. All hold the rank of sergeant unless otherwise stated. Back Row: P. Connolly; 8851 Harry Arthur Hoar; Lance Sergeant S.H. Thrussell; Lance Sergeant A. Sales; Lance Sergeant 10201 Daniel Goodchild. Fourth row: 10292 Anthony Davidson; 10244 Cecil G. Warner; Lance Sergeant J. Carmody; Stephen Norton; L/Sgt A.E. Conquest; F. Cutler; 9056 and 43969 Alfred George Poulter; Julius J. Shelley; 45454 Robert William Tharle. Third Row: 7459 Harry Allison, MM; Lance Sergeant 5943864 H. Williams; 9502 Alfred J. Sale, MM; A. Childerhouse; 22367 Stanley Mackrory; Lance Sergeant 10188 George Oliver Stringer; John (Jack) Wheble; 7601, later 5942037 Harry Coe; H. Lamble: A. Austin. Second row: CSMIM H. Brown, MM; 9778 Frederick Thomas Coe; 8271 Stuart Franks; 10242 Leonard Harper; 10264, later 5942344 William James Chambers; CQMS J. Cannon; CQMS 10027, later 5943970 William Newbound; CQMS 8309 Howard Bourne; CQMS 8755 William Murrell; P.W. Armstrong; Band Sergeant 5942168 P. Humphrey; Sergeant Drummer E. Goddard. Front row: CSM 8966, later 5942077 Sydney Unthank; CSM 9221, later 542090 Charles Mansfield; ORQMS 7116 Hugh Robin Box; RSM 7171 Walter Headland, MC; Lieutenant Colonel William Roland Harris Dann, DSO (second in command); Lieutenant Colonel Walter Allason, DSO (commanding officer); Lieutenant and Adjutant Geoffrey Arthur Anstee, MC, Bandmaster J.E.S. Vince; RQMS 16488 Cyril Walter; Arthur Keen; CSM 9465, later 7811773 Percival J. Hunt, DCM; CSM J. Finn. (Ron West)

Above: Retired RSM William Newbound, DCM, waiting to meet the honorary Colonel-in-Chief, Queen Elizabeth the Queen Mother, in June 1965. (Ron West)

Below: RSM Newbound and the Old Contemptibles amuse themselves while waiting to meet Queen Elizabeth the Queen Mother in June 1965. (Ron West)

The hip flask of Captain (later Lieutenant Colonel) Geoffrey Anstee, OBE, MC, DL, who served throughout both world wars, including as a deputy to the Lord Lieutenant of Bedfordshire after retirement. (Steven Fuller)

**The Mons Drum, within the Escort to the Colours, 2nd Royal Anglians.** (Mike Bates)

The 19-year-old Private Len Gray of Biggleswade was killed next to his officer. He was the second of two sons to lose his life in the 1st Bedfordshires: William Gray had been a regular soldier since the summer of 1913 but was still only 18 when he was killed during the battalion's costly defence of Ypres on 7 November 1914. Len Gray had enlisted aged just 16 when the regimental recruiting march had passed through his home town in 1914 and had already recovered from a wound received during the Third Battle of Ypres in 1917, before returning to the battalion while based in Italy.[167]

Once out of the front line, the tired battalion marched to one of the rest camps in the divisional area, all being named after Italian villages they had resided in. Several days were spent based from Villorba Camp, which was sited just inside the wood, north-west of Croix Marraisse. A day of cleaning up, replacing deficiencies and even being given a complete change of uniforms, was followed by three-hour fatigue duties digging the divisional reserve lines in the woods. That day, Lieutenant Vivian Farr was granted leave to England, but would not be seen again, as medical boards and hospital visits for an eye injury from 1901 kept him from the firing line for the rest of the year.

On the 19th, half of the battalion moved to billets in Tannay, the remainder lodging in Thiennes, 9km behind the front lines. Working parties were broken up with training over the coming days, which included familiarising themselves with the use of the Popham Panel, designed to enable communication with spotting aircraft during operations. Baths at Neufre mid-morning rounded off their duties on the 21st, the battalion then making their way back to billets and preparing for another move that afternoon.

A week in Spresiano Camp, just to the north-west of Villorba Camp inside the Bois d'Amont, followed, as the brigade proceeded into the left Arrewage sector of the divisional front and the Bedfordshires spent the first spell of their tour in brigade reserve. Training was continued between fatigues to improve the divisional line, all conducted with the ever-present threat created by the liberal use of the nasty, often undetectable, Yellow Cross gas shells that swamped the wood.

Five reinforcements joined on the 24th, the only casualties from the period being two men wounded on the 27th, and Private Frank Simpson dying from wounds the same day, while the Battle of the Aisne opened much further south.

News also arrived that one of the battalion's stalwart, often unsung, ever reliable heroes that everyone knew for one reason or another had been recognised and awarded the Distinguished Conduct Medal. Master Cook Bertie Washington[168] had been serving in the regiment for twenty years, including in India and on home soil before landing in France with the battalion in August 1914. Surviving the battalion's trials and tribulations alongside them, he had always been there in the background, supporting the battalion through thick and thin. His citation read: *'For conspicuous gallantry and devotion to duty since the beginning of the war as master cook. On all occasions when the battalion has been in action he has shown great personal courage and coolness cooking tea and food for men in the front line under great difficulties and at considerable risk. Twice his cookhouse has been knocked out by direct hits from hostile guns.'*

## The Arrewage brigade sector: 29 May to 4 June 1918

At 9 p.m. on 29 May, the Bedfordshires' latest tour of the front began as they moved into the right subsector of the Arrewage brigade sector, the front lines running from just south-west of Arrewage to Les Lauriers. Although the northern section of their lines was predominantly open ground, the southern section between Les Lauriers and the river was a complex of copses, houses and hedges, which attracted regular enemy shelling. Natural and man-made enclosures as well as sporadic buildings were littered across the ground facing them, all of which would be patrolled during their tour.

While the bulk of the battalion settled into this new area, patrols from both the Bedfordshires and the Warwickshires to their left were sent out immediately. Lieutenant Herberg took two men on a reconnaissance patrol for an hour from 2.15 a.m., coming across a two-man German listening post; the enemy ran off into the darkness when they saw them.

Throughout the 30th, a heavy gas bombardment plastered their area, but good gas precautions resulted in just one man being wounded from the Bedfordshires. Captain Harry Willans, attached to brigade as staff captain, was gassed during the day and evacuated to the Casualty Clearing Station at Thiennes, and Captain Beale left to take over his duties.

At midnight Corporal Boston[169] took a two-man patrol out to scout houses alongside the road north of the river, finding several evacuated posts and a previously unseen trench system.

Daylight brought intermittent but heavy salvos of shells, especially directed against the houses, orchards and enclosures on the southern portion of their lines, south of the river. The right-hand company were also smothered with a sustained gas bombardment, Second Lieutenant Herberg and three men being wounded by the day's end. Private Josiah Swain from Hitchin died as a result of his wounds that day, bringing their casualty count for the month to one officer and fifty-two men.

From 6 a.m. on 1 June the crossroads between Les Lauriers and the river was heavily shelled for two and a half hours and the barn at Roussel Farm, 1km north of Les Lauriers, was set on fire by persistent attention from German gunners later that morning. A further bombardment fell on the crossroads again at 1.15 p.m., gas being mixed in with the explosives, leading to an uncomfortable day during which three men lost their lives. Second Lieutenant Frank Hughes and one other rank were wounded, the lieutenant suffering from a severe injury to his right forearm that saw the end of his active service. Lance Corporal Edward Rolph from Kentish Town was among those who died of wounds as a result of the shelling, having enlisted into the 7th Bedfordshires in September 1914 and being presented with the Military Medal in November 1917.[170]

Patrolling continued, including Lieutenant Hayes and two men scouting the German lines midway between the river and Arrewage, returning to verify that the entire line was held and giving their gunners some confirmed targets for the morning.

Two more days of heavy gas shelling followed but no casualties occurred until overnight on 2/3 June, when German artillery retaliated against a localised tactical assault from the Warwickshires, who moved the lines forward around 100 metres, capturing the remaining houses and enclosures in and around Arrewage. The entire line of Bedfordshires were subjected to intense high-explosive and gas shelling, with Les Lauriers catching fire under sustained direct hits, a garrisoned house midway between Les Lauriers and the river being pounded by over thirty shells and the orchard west of Arrewage seemingly disappearing in a gas cloud. Five of the battalion were killed during the bombardment, with Lieutenant Horace Everett and four men being wounded.

### Return to Le Sart: 5 June to 5 July 1918

At 10 p.m. on 4 June the brigade was relieved and moved into divisional reserve, the Bedfordshires being billeted in Steenbecque, west of the forest. After a day of cleaning up and reorganising, a week of training followed, telling the experienced soldiers that they were being prepared for an assault in the coming weeks. Baths at Arcade Camp were postponed on the 6th, courtesy of heavy shelling, and transferred to Neufre the next day.

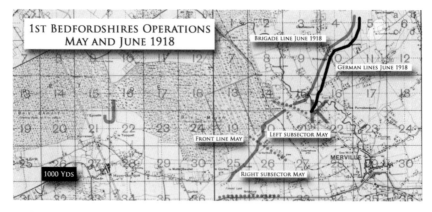

Corporal Tom Connolly[171] had been with the battalion for almost eleven years and had been at the front with them since Mons in 1914. On 7 June he was granted a well-deserved field commission, remaining with the battalion to continue his service.

Two reinforcement drafts joined during their time in reserve, twenty-one men arriving on the 9th, and fourteen on the 11th, just in time for the battalion being warned to prepare for a return to the front.

Training over, the 15th Brigade relieved the 95th on 12 June, in the southern Le Sart sector, opposite Merville. Between 12 and 18 June the Bedfordshires found themselves holding the support lines, which were now 100 metres east of the edge of the wood, anticipating being thrown into a new offensive at any moment.

The sporadic and dangerous side of trench life aside, early summer had been relatively pleasant in and around the forest since German attacks had drawn to a close, but as the heat increased alongside the gas shelling, the wood became a stuffy, uncomfortable place to move through, let alone work in. Nevertheless, fatigues continued within the dubious cover of the wood during daylight and out in front of the British front trenches overnight, fetching and carrying, or wiring parties taking up much of the battalion's time.

From 9 a.m. on 12 June, ninety minutes of heavy shelling pinned most of the Bedfordshires into their trenches, the German gunners paying particular attention to the wood north-west of Le Vertbois and causing casualties among the working parties. Less intense bombardments harassed the battalion throughout the day and just after midnight another heavy barrage fell on the wood, which was supplemented with a liberal dose of gas at 3.45 a.m. By daylight eleven men had been wounded, with two dying during the day, and the 14th saw the shelling continue.

An increase in the artillery bombardment on the 15th resulted in re-quests for retaliatory strikes, which neutralised the German batteries, but not before two more Bedfords had been killed and another five injured.

Sergeant Alfred Page of Baldock[172] was one of those who lost his life that day while attached to the brigade's Trench Mortar Battery. A reservist when hostilities started, Alf had been wounded twice, gassed and had returned to the battalion a year earlier. The 26-year-old was severely in-jured during the artillery duel and died at the Casualty Clearing Station in Aire-sur-la-Lys, leaving a young widow and distraught parents who had lost another of their three sons just six months earlier.

On a day of enemy aircraft spotting patrols and sporadic shelling, two more of the battalion were wounded on 16 June, one dying later that day. A more intense bombardment hit their lines between 10 p.m. and mid-night, with the hours of darkness being filled with carrying fatigues and a practice 'stand to'. Aerial activity continued over the next two days, as did the shelling, with Second Lieutenant Claud Gilbert Wilkins being wounded but remaining on duty and two other ranks evacuated with shrapnel lacerations. Some forty reinforcements arrived on the 17th, and Major Hugh Courtenay returned to take command of the battalion the next day, having already seen an extremely busy war since leaving the battalion in September 1914 suffering from a facial wound that had taken his eyesight in one eye.

Hugh Courtenay had been in a comfortable staff post for around two years but, on joining his old battalion for Christmas dinner in Italy months earlier, had remarked to Lieutenant Colonel Worrall that 'I want to come back as your second in command.' Lieutenant Colonel Worrall later wrote: *'G. H. Q refused it for 2 months, he applied a second time and was appointed after I had left. I know the feeling that prompted him, a human love to share the priva-tions and danger of the men of his old Battalion and the call was irresistible and he left his post on the staff because he felt it his duty to be a leader of men.'*[173]

When the Bedfordshires took over the left subsector of the Le Sart brigade sector early on 19 June, they learned that their lines had been ex-tended north to the River Bourre days earlier as a result of a local tactical operation carried out by the Cheshires. Between 1.30 and 3 p.m. the recently added northern portion of their lines between Les Lauriers and the river was heavily shelled, five men being wounded.

British aircraft were active all day and a large formation flew over the brigade lines in the evening, the battalion having a ringside seat as they brought down a German observation balloon in addition to a German scout plane that crashed close to the southern flank of the Bedfordshires' sector.

Divisional intelligence was warned of the strong possibility of a German offensive against their lines and preparations were made for a defiant resistance. Although in hindsight it came to nothing, patrols were increased and sent out to identify all previously unknown posts, while watching for anything that would warn them of an impending attack.

At 11.15 p.m. CSM Davis took a patrol out due east of Les Lauriers, finding an entrenched machine-gun post that would be subjected to British artillery fire overnight, while Second Lieutenant Robson's patrol 250 metres to their north identified a similar post on the south bank of the River Bourre.

The next day was very quiet, but B Company's 21-year-old Lance Corporal Fred Richards of Bedford[174] was mortally wounded by a German sniper, dying at the Casualty Clearing Station at Aire-sur-la-Lys the following day from his injuries.

That night Corporal Swift took a four-man patrol towards the German lines; they came across several working parties cutting corn, patrols moving along a prearranged route and protective posts, so learning their locations. On their return, a heavy burst of rifle and machine-gun fire was directed towards the areas known to contain troops and the coordinates were fed back to artillery observers, who obliged by sending a volley of shells in their direction.

The 21st June was quiet and was passed digging a new communications trench, as well as repairing damage to their existing trenches and wire. Captain William Barnett, who had rejoined the battalion days earlier from a staff post as railway transport officer in Italy, became the second in command and was promoted to acting major. Second Lieutenants Archibald Douglas Farnsworth Sheldrake and Henry Manwood Blakeney arrived during the day, while the night saw the battalion shuffle into a shortened line, covered by listening posts pushed out into No Man's Land to guard against intrusion for the duration of the move.

Their last three days in the front line were fairly quiet, with sporadic shelling and nightly patrols breaking the routines of preparing their lines in case the anticipated German attack materialised. Captain James McKay, the battalion's long-serving medical officer, left for duties at a base hospital and was replaced by Lieutenant Edward Digby Kinsey of the RAMC.

At 5.30 a.m. on 23 June Corporal Drury, winner of the DCM two months earlier, and two men set out on patrol, finding the post they were sent to investigate unoccupied, and returning again at midday to find it still vacant. At 3 p.m. and again at 10.15 p.m. CSM Davis and Corporal Drury scouted a German sniper post, finding sign of habitation but no sniper both times. Sergeant William Felstead,[175] a veteran with fourteen years' service in the regiment who had been out since Mons, also took four men out to investigate machine-gun posts along the Merville road, both patrols coming back to report that they were unoccupied.

Scarcely had Corporal Drury returned from patrol when Second Lieutenant Hayes took him and seven men on another patrol at 11.15 p.m. headed for the junction of two gullies 600 metres east of Le Vertbois, some 100 metres in front of their own lines. Their orders were to engage any post with a view to identifying the unit opposing them. The protective cover provided by the withering crops stopped abruptly near the junction so, with a bright moon illuminating the landscape, the patrol turned north-east in search of a suitable target on the southern embankment of the railway line. A post was identified en route, which they engaged, only to be swamped with rifle fire and hand grenades from unseen positions on either flank. After a one-sided skirmish that left Corporal Drury and three other Bedfordshires wounded, they withdrew, having killed two German sentries and scoring direct hits on the enemy trench with two Mills bombs. It was later established by aerial reconnaissance that they had identified a well-concealed defensive trench line with a strong garrison and supporting machine-gun post, hidden within the cornfield.

Harry Drury's time with the 1st Bedfordshires had come to an end and he was evacuated to England. Two months later he was among the British contingent sent to take part in an Allied North Russia Intervention force, and was reported missing on 26 March 1919. The holder of a Distinguished Conduct Medal and veteran of battlefields all along the British-held sector of the Western Front, Corporal Drury was later presumed to have been killed, aged just 21.

Late on 24 June, the Bedfordshires were relieved and marched back to Villorba Camp after a day of heavy gas shelling, especially around Croix Marraisse. Brigadier General Oldman was gassed, as was Captain Allan Beale of the Bedfordshires, who was acting as brigade staff captain. He was evacuated to England, never to return to the battalion. Resuming duties at home once he had recovered in October, Captain Beale went on to serve in north Russia and Constantinople before resigning his commission in 1922.

Five days in Villorba Camp followed, a variety of fatigues in and around the woods being broken by training and absorbing the thirty-nine-strong draft that arrived on 29 June. By the end of June, the temperature was steadily rising and troops inside the forest worked in increasingly stuffy conditions, plagued by mosquitoes and under the constant threat of lingering, invisible mustard gas. Malaria did not surface but localised incidents of PUO increased noticeably, being labelled 'Merville Fever'.[176] Fortunately, the first wave of the infamous 'Spanish flu' that was taking its toll on so many European countries by now also failed to make an impact on the divisional area.

Ten men were evacuated to hospital on the 25th, suffering from the effects of the lingering gas that had enveloped the wood a day earlier, and Lance Sergeant William Dighton of Godmanchester[177] was killed on the 27th, having joined the battalion in the draft from the Huntingdon-shire Cyclists Battalion in July 1916. That day Lieutenant John Kingdon arrived after recovering from illness and completing a senior officers' course, just as two officers and fifty men left on attachment to the 13th Brigade as stretcher-bearers, the brigade preparing for an assault the next day.

In cooperation with the main thrust from the 31st Division to their north, elements of the 5th Division conducted an operation intended to move their lines away from the forest, later named the 'Action of Le Becque'. Ironically, it fell on the anniversary of the assault against Oppy Wood exactly a year earlier and involved the same two divisions. As with Oppy Wood, the operation was a great success and, given that it was the year's first significant offensive exercise, congratulations poured in. As some of the Bedfordshires were engaged in the hazardous task of stretcher-bearing during the attack, it is surprising that the only battalion casualty during the operation was Lieutenant Colonel Courtenay's horse, who was hit by a shell fragment while in camp and far from the intense fighting.

Once darkness came on 30 June, the Bedfordshires moved back into the front trenches, taking over the left subsector of the Le Sart sector again, the Warwickshires to their right. Since their last visit, the Cheshires had moved the line forward, the new front line at the northern end of their subsector being 500 metres east of Les Lauriers, with the river being their northern boundary. B Company held the left with C in support, while D Company was on the right and A in support of them. Persistent artillery and machine-gun fire was being directed towards their lines from the moment they arrived, the edge of the woods being smothered with gas, while the houses, enclosures and tracks were hit by concentrated machine-gun and high-explosive barrages. By midday on 1 July, Private George Sparrow[178] had been killed, Major William Barnett had been severely wounded and a further ten men were injured and evacuated.

Major Barnett had already been wounded with the battalion at Falfemont Farm on the Somme and again with the 4th Bedfordshires in February 1917, but this one was to ensure the end of the 42-year-old's military career and he would die suddenly from a blood clot in 1936, being attributed to the head wounds received in 1918.

Patrols were set in motion immediately, with one leaving at 6 p.m. to lie out in front of the German wire and learn what they could about their new positions and opponents. The officer and four men explored the ground 1km south-east of Les Lauriers, in the open area north of the railway, discovering two hidden machine-gun emplacements before being driven off by machine-gun fire.

Four days of sporadic artillery bombardments, repairing trenches and patrols followed, with daily casualties despite their opponent's reluctance to engage with their fighting patrols. By the time relief arrived in the form of the 95th Brigade late on the 5th, one officer had been wounded, seven other ranks killed and a further twenty-three men injured.

### Last tour of the Arrewage sector: 12 to 22 July

After the initial period of cleaning up, baths and refitting, six days in divisional reserve at Arcade Camp were spent training and marching, with the brigade swimming carnival and aquatic sports competitions at Pont-des-Thiennes providing distraction and amusement between 3 and 6 p.m. on 9 July. Every race was won by men from the Bedfordshires, but the same could not be said of the boxing that was interrupted by heavy rain the next day.

Major William Stuart Chirnside rejoined to replace the wounded Major Barnett on the 8th, assuming the role of second in command, and on the 12th, the brigade took over the Arrewage sector of the line, the Bedfordshires moving into support.

That day also saw the arrival of Second Lieutenant David Lydle from the 2nd Bedfordshires, who had already been heavily engaged during the war and was suffering from the effects of prolonged exposure to combat conditions. Originally a pre-war private in the 2nd Battalion, David had been wounded at Ypres in 1914 before fighting in all of his battalion's actions in 1915. Shrapnel in the chest at Trônes Wood in July 1916 had sent him to England for treatment, after which he was thrust into a commissioned position with no training early in 1917. An illness, coupled with the obvious signs of neurasthenia, shredded his confidence and strengthened his commanding officer's scathing opinion of his leadership abilities. This in turn led to him being moved into an administrative role after he had come through the battalion's intensive defensive battles of March and April 1918, after which he was transferred into the 1st Battalion, under report. After so much fighting, Second Lieutenant Lydle was simply one of thousands of men who were 'war worn', but carried on to the best of his abilities and in spite of a collection of nervous behaviours and symptoms of shell shock.[179]

The division had assumed an aggressive stance since its arrival in the area and the next fortnight was to be no different. Divisional artillery was very busy in engaging enemy batteries and aggressive patrolling was continued to try and draw the Germans into skirmishes, but the brigade war diary reports that their enemies remained 'abnormally quiet' throughout the tour, contenting themselves with heavy anti-aircraft fire and extensive wiring parties.

In support until the 17th, the Bedfordshires were busy with fatigues, wiring and working parties. Just two men were wounded and a draft of sixteen other ranks joined on the 13th, along with Second Lieutenant Ernest Howlett,[180] who had started his war as a private in the 1st Bedfordshires before being commissioned as an officer.

Second Lieutenant Arthur Thomas Franklin from Brixton was given two weeks' leave to England from 17 July. A former Royal Navy able seaman, Arthur had served through the Gallipoli campaign before being taken ill with malaria and dysentery, which would resurface while at home and ensure his combat service was over.

On St Swithen's day, 250km south-east of the Bedfordshires, the German army launched the Second Battle of the Marne around Reims which, although unknown at the time, would become their last, unsuccessful attempt to win the war.

Late on the 17th, the Bedfordshires relieved the Norfolks in the right subsector, A Company on the left with D in support and C Company on the right with B in position behind them. Once daylight had faded, the need to establish what was happening around them led to several patrols being organised.

At 10.30 p.m. on the 18th, a fighting patrol of twelve men and a Lewis-gun team under Lieutenant Cornelius scouted the area from 500 metres due south of Arrewage to the river. Some 100 metres north of the foot-bridge, a retiring German party was spotted 25 metres away but the Bedfordshires were unable to engage them in time, so the patrol continued. Soon afterwards, Lieutenant Cornelius's revolver was accidentally snagged and went off, bringing the entire patrol to an abrupt halt. Having given their position away and encouraged the likelihood of a German counter-attack, the patrol retired back to their own lines with no casualties.

At 12.30 a.m. on the 19th, Second Lieutenant Arnholz and two men moved out to examine the German wire, posts and layout of defences around the railway and road 500 metres south of the river, to ensure no enfilade fire could be brought to bear on their lines. Only one of the several posts they explored showed any signs of occupation, the patrol destroying the position and removing the ammunition they found. On resuming the patrol, two sentries spotted them and retired into a house, machine-gun fire following soon afterwards and drawing their activities to a close.

Second Lieutenant Melvill also took a small patrol out to gather information, finding a well-concealed machine-gun post before returning to the British lines at 2.45 a.m.

Leave passes continued to be issued, Second Lieutenant Herbert Powell being among those who left for Blighty that day. The battalion would not see him again as he reported ill to his local hospital after his fortnight at home in Cardiff, not being passed medically fit again until 1919, when he joined the Bedfordshire Brigade in the Army of the Rhine.

After a day of relative inactivity, the highlight of which was when the men watched two German aircraft being brought down overhead, the night saw the resumption of patrols, in readiness for a planned raid.

At 10 p.m. Second Lieutenant Leonard Hobson, two sergeants and five men ventured out to secure a prisoner but came across an impenetrable line of wire, were spotted and retired from the heavy machine-gun and hand grenade salvos that followed. Sergeant Rowley and one man went on a separate patrol into the 400-metre stretch of No Man's Land just north of the intended raid area, the sergeant bringing down one retreating German soldier in a brief exchange of fire, before returning to their lines unscathed.

Midnight on 20 July was zero hour for a local, tactical operation to eliminate a triangular sector still held by German troops between the

Bourre River and Platebecque streams. The raiders' objective was to secure a line north of the river, running just west of the Platebecque stream, 150 metres west of the road between Merville and Arrewage. In addition to moving their line forward, prisoners were to be taken, the brigade operational order remarking how *'the raid will be carried out with the utmost rapidity and vigour'*.[181]

A Company conducted the raid, organising themselves so that two platoons advanced in two waves split into four rifle sections, with two Lewis-gun sections in the second wave. Each wave was led by a single officer, Second Lieutenant Cornelius in the first and Second Lieutenant Blakeney with the Lewis gunners. A third platoon was held ready in support in the British front trenches, with the fourth in reserve, prepared to move forward as needed.

Assembly was complete by 11.40 p.m. but as soon as the bombardment opened, the German troops retreated across the footbridge 100 metres along the stream, north of the river. Even with their quick advance, by the time the Bedfordshires reached the German lines, they had set up their defensive line in a trench on the opposite bank from where they strafed and bombed the raiders, causing several casualties. Despite searching the entire bank, no prisoners could be found, although the objective of pushing the German line back across the stream was secured. A heavy German trench mortar barrage was also laid down on the raiders, bringing any thoughts of advancing across the stream to a halt.

The officer leading the first wave, Second Lieutenant Herbert Walter Cornelius, was killed, aged 25. Herbert, a civil servant from West Ealing, had been with the battalion since September 1917 and left a young widow.

Seven other ranks were also killed, including CSM Reginald Lansbury, a Mons veteran who had survived many of the battalion's costly battles, winning the Distinguished Conduct Medal and Military Medal in the process; his demise came in a relatively small operation during the last few months of the war.

Second Lieutenant Blakeney, who had only joined the battalion a month earlier, was also wounded, along with another eight men. Henry Blakeney, the son of a grammar school headmaster, had enlisted in May 1915 and, following a long series of operations to cure eye and inner ear problems, had become a member of the 1st Bedfordshires just a month earlier. His very first action had left him with multiple injuries caused by an explosion to his right foot as well as his left hand, leg and foot. Following eight gruelling operations to save it, the lower third of his right leg was amputated, although Henry lived until 1983, dying in Norwich aged 87.

Throughout the 21st, artillery on both sides was busy and the forward posts of the Bedfordshires engaged a German working party at 10 a.m., who seemed to be unaware they were visible to their opponents. A German sniper was killed, falling from his tree over 500 metres east of the new section of lines taken over the previous night. A 'remarkably quiet' day on the 22nd finished their tour, with just small patrols led by CSM Stanley and Sergeant Felstead venturing out that night to identify the new lines taken up by German troops since the raid and to cover the relief taking place behind them.

As the battalion marched quietly west and entrained on to carriages on the light railway in the wood, they were unaware that they had just completed their last spell on the front in the Nieppe Forest region. The brigade moved into divisional reserve once more, with the Bedfordshires billeting in La Lacque Camp next to the Canal D'Aire, midway between Isbergues and Aire-sur-la-Lys.

### Final spell around Nieppe Forest: 23 July to 20 August 1918

The usual routine of cleaning up, refitting and bathing between training resumed until 25 July, with the 'Bedford Boys' entertaining the battalion in the camp theatre that evening. Training became specific once more, in preparation for what was labelled 'Operation Partridge', although it would be handed over to the 61st Division when they relieved the 5th Division on 7 August. Heavy rain hindered their progress over the 26th and 27th, with concerts on both evenings being laid on to divert the men.

A church parade on 28 July was attended by both the divisional commander and the band. Between 3 and 5 p.m., the brigade boxing tournament resumed, the finals being held the following afternoon when five of the winners were Warwickshires, the other two titles going to men from the Cheshires. In the 'Whizzbang Hut', Thiennes, at 5.30 p.m. the battalion officers and NCOs were lectured by Lieutenant Colonel Thomas Walter Carthew (Bedfordshire Regiment attached to the RAF) about the Royal Air Force and its role in the continually refined 'All Arms' tactics being practised.

A last day of training and an evening concert from the 'Bedford Boys' rounded off their break in reserve before the brigade returned to the Le Sart sector on 30 July, the Bedfordshires moving into brigade reserve at Villorba Camp that afternoon. Until 6 August, the battalion were engaged in constant working parties, repairing damage caused by the repeated shelling of the camp and improving the reserve areas through the wood.

Divisional artillery was busily engaging every identifiable German battery, ammunition dump and garrison building leading to retaliatory gas and high-explosive bombardments against the woods. Five men were gassed on the 5th, but none were killed throughout the tour, despite the attention paid to their camp and working areas.

Blenheim Day was celebrated earlier than usual, with a remembrance service being held on 4 August as intelligence advised that it would not be possible for the battalion to do so on 13 August, as regimental tradition demanded. After the service, Lieutenant John Kingdon left the battalion for a post as an instructor in the Fifth Army School, while Captain and Adjutant Alexander Riddell and Lieutenant Edgar Nailer were granted local leave.

The date of 5 August was spent preparing for a permanent move away from the area, which started the following evening with the Bedfordshires returning to billets in La Lacque Camp as the division started the process of handing over their area and concentrating in readiness for a major relocation.

On 7 August the battalion moved 7km to a camp north of Blaringhem, where they remained until the 13th. Route marches, training, inspections and sporting diversions made up their routines, while two major Allied offensives were launched around Amiens and Montdidier.

Second Lieutenant Arthur William Rope had contracted jaundice while in the woods, which removed him from the battalion on 13 August. Service in the 2nd Garrison Battalion in India beckoned once his health returned, his service coming to a close in January 1920.

D Company marched 10km west to Wizernes on the 13th, with orders to prepare as the battalion's loading party, being followed by the rest of the Bedfordshires the next day. Boarding trains at Wizernes station, the battalion were moved 50km south to Doullens, marching into billets 6km north-west at Outrebois on arrival.

As the rest of the division arrived and concentrated in their GHQ Reserve position, speculation was rife as to where they would be posted, coming under the Third Army as they now did and with news of the remarkably successful offensives now filtering through to them. Preparing and organising themselves for the expected offensive operations, on the 16th the Bedfordshires moved into new billets at Remaisnil, 3km north, where training resumed.

Orders to operate under a veil of complete secrecy arrived, with no outdoors movement permitted during daylight and marches being conducted under cover of darkness. Another march 14km south-east, through Doullens where transport and details were left behind, took them on to billets in Orville on 18 August. During the trek, word travelled along the column that the division were to prepare for an attack on 21 August, the gossip arriving many hours before written orders confirmed the plans. By the end of their next leg of the journey that took them a further 14km due east to the ruins of Sailly-au-Bois the next morning, the entire brigade were soaked, having marched through persistent rain all night. On what would be their last move before battle, the Bedfordshires arrived west of the German-held town of Bucquoy midway through 20 August, where they were greeted by written orders for the following day's plan of attack.

After a brief pause to make final battle preparations, the battalion set off to their assembly positions at 8.55 p.m., bound for their first major offensive action for ten months.

Chapter 8

# The Second Battle of the Somme (1918): 21 August to 3 September 1918

*'The enemy made best use of these trenches with his machine guns while we were held up, but directly we came to grips with him he surrendered freely.'*

Over the summer it became clear that the German army had exhausted the last of its resources on their spring offensives and, with the build-up of men and materiel on the Allied side, the balance of power had shifted. Planning, training and preparation, all conducted in the utmost secrecy, came to a head early in August when what would later be labelled the 'Hundred Days Offensives' began.

The first wave of the American Expeditionary Force had arrived in France in June 1917, 14,000 strong. Early in 1918 elements had been deployed alongside British and French divisions in quiet sectors to gain experience in trench warfare. By May 1918 there were over one million American troops stationed in Europe, although they were yet to be committed as a unified force. The Battles of Cantigny (28 May) and Belleau Wood (6 June) had seen their first taste of offensive action and by the end of the month fresh American 'Doughboys' were arriving at the rate of 10,000 per day, magnifying the definite shift in power.

The Battle of Amiens, alongside the French Battle of Montdidier to the south, opened on 8 August 1918. Careful preparation and almost faultless implementation resulted in complete surprise being achieved and a stunning victory. On the opening day alone, 30,000 German casualties compared favourably against the 6,500 Allied losses, and a 24km gap was opened in the opponent's defences. German General Ludendorff dubbed the day as *'the black day of the German army'*.

By the end of 10 August, almost 20km of territory had been captured and the German forces began to pull out of the salient created from their victory during the spring offensives, retiring back to the formidable Hindenburg Line once more.

Further offensives kept the pressure on the retiring enemy forces and Haig resisted Foch's insistence to continue with the Amiens offensives as he recognised the German resistance had stiffened. Accordingly, Haig planned and issued orders for a fresh offensive further north.

In what would become the opening action of the Second Battle of the Somme (1918), General Byng's Third Army, holding a 24km line north of Albert and supported by 200 tanks, was ordered to advance on Bapaume, break into the German lines and turn their flanks.

### The Battle of Albert (1918): 21 and 22 August 1918

After their heavy losses in the spring, many British divisions were rebuilt using 18-year-olds and men who had previously been held in training posts, as well as those from regimental depots and other supporting roles. The 5th Division had not suffered anywhere near as badly during the fighting so were still comprised of largely seasoned troops, even if there were very few of the original pre-war veterans left. As a result, they were certainly counted among those divisions classified as experienced and highly motivated, which would show in the difficult battles to follow.

Overnight on 20/21 August, the 15th Brigade marched across unfamiliar ground, in darkness and shrouded in mist, but arrived in their correct jumping-off positions west of Bucquoy on time. By zero hour, 4.55 a.m., a thick fog smothered the battlefield, favouring the assembling British troops who were able to gather unseen.

The IV Corps' line-up boasted a collection of experienced divisions with well-earned reputations, who performed as expected. The 37th and New Zealand Divisions took the initial objectives of the original German front lines, with the 5th and 63rd Divisions passing through them to carry the line forward even further. On the 5th Division front, the 15th Brigade held the left sector, the 95th Brigade held the right, and the 13th were in reserve, the final objective being the ridge south-east of Achiet-le-Petit, incorporating the village of Irles. The 15th Brigade followed in the wake of the 37th Division, assembling just south-east of Bucquoy and halting for an hour while the 37th secured the ridge between Bucquoy and Achiet-le-Petit.

With the 63rd Division to their left and the New Zealanders to their right, at 6.25 a.m. the advance continued, with the 15th Brigade attacking

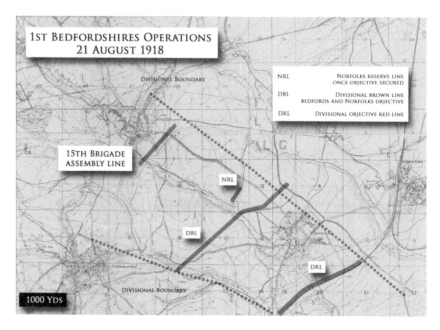

in a south-easterly direction towards Achiet-le-Petit. The Bedfordshires advanced on the right and the Norfolks on the left, passing through the 37th Division and taking their objective line just north-west of Achiet-le-Petit with only light casualties, an advance of 2km. Once the line was secured, the Norfolks retired into a reserve line around 600 metres north-west of Achiet-le-Petit, leaving the Bedfords to extend and take over the entire line, consolidating it in readiness for a defensive action.

The flow of battle was unfamiliar to many of the British Tommies, with those left from the 1914 campaigns likening it to the open warfare of the early battles. With few firm lines of resistance to overcome and engulfed in shifting fog, some squads spent the entire battle advancing without meeting any enemy troops, in spite of the unnerving, muffled sounds of battle all around them, whereas others would find themselves under fire from unexpected directions once disjointed bodies of soldiers stumbled across one another.

By now the fog had become even thicker, but at 7.37 a.m. the Warwickshires and Cheshires continued the brigade advance, passing through the Bedfordshires and Norfolks, headed for the ridge south of Achiet-le-Grand. The units were already mixed up and maintaining direction became difficult, the advancing battalions being broken up by a mixture of pockets of resistance, the fog isolating each group from their neighbours and reliance on compasses instead of eyesight.

Progressing in a south-easterly direction with the Achiet to Bucquoy road on their left flank, the Cheshires initially met stiff resistance in Achiet-le-Petit before pushing on towards the ridge south-east of the railway line in the face of heavy machine-gun fire, even gaining a footing on the ridge with around one hundred men. Unknown to the brigade, the 63rd Division to their left had been held up north of Achiet-le-Petit, and at 9.30 a.m. a counter-attack hit the badly exposed Cheshires on the ridge. With the fog obscuring what was unfolding, the Norfolks to their rear were oblivious of the plight of the group of Cheshires, who were forced back across the railway line and even partially through Achiet-le-Petit. A Cheshire counter-attack was organised against the advancing German troops, throwing them back in their turn and establishing a line south-east of the village by 10.30 a.m. The Norfolks arrived soon after and that afternoon the Cheshires were retired to cover the exposed northern flank of the brigade, leaving the Norfolks in command of the new front line.

On the right, the Warwickshires had also pushed on to their objective south-east of the railway embankment, but to their south, the 95th Brigade were held up before reaching the railway and had settled for a line 150 metres in front of the embankment, in turn leaving the isolated groups of around 150 Warwickshires south-east of the railway line. The German counter-attack not only threw the Cheshires from the ridge, but carried the Warwickshires with them, who were also forced back across the railway, leaving the brigade just short of their final objective and having outrun their artillery protection and tank support.

As the fog thickened, the tank drivers and commanders' task also became more difficult. Not only had many of them lost the infantry following them, but as they manoeuvred their way over the bleak battlefield several reported how they came across unidentifiable groups of infantry running towards them and only avoided firing on the British troops they encountered by keeping their nerve and waiting until the last possible minute before committing to engage them. Within a few hours, all of the tanks had broken down, become lost in the fog and returned to their assembly area, or had been destroyed by anti-tank guns covering the railway crossings. None had made it beyond the railway line, leaving the infantry who had, exposed and unsupported.

Elements of one of the 63rd Division battalions from around 1km north, believed to be the Hawke Battalion, even arrived in the Warwickshires' lines mid-morning, illustrating just how problematic finding their way through the fog had become.

Around midday, Brigadier General Oldman, commander of the 15th Brigade, visited the front lines and saw that '*no good purpose could have been served by attacking the ridge a second time until the division on the left had made more ground to its front*'.[182] So, after a long night of marching, followed by a difficult day of advancing in thick fog, IV Corps set about consolidating their lines.

After their march to assembly positions south-east of Bucquoy the previous night, the division had advanced almost 3km with remarkably light casualties compared to previous engagements. They had captured over 500 prisoners in addition to two German artillery batteries, with hundreds more prisoners being taken by patrols overnight.

Although still just 21 years old, Acting Major Geoffrey de Carteret Millais had been through many battles and raids during his two years with the battalion, and had been recommended for a Military Cross at Arras. He was mortally wounded during the attack, dying that day in the 14th Field Ambulance.

Captain Herbert John West was also fatally hit during the battle, having rejoined the battalion that spring after recovering from his second wound. A series of injuries that day, including a serious compound fracture to his right arm, overcame him at 11 p.m. the following day, while being treated at No. 3 Casualty Clearing Station. He died just days before his 30th birthday and was buried within feet of his lieutenant colonel.

Forty-six men were also killed or wounded during the advance, having been picked off by snipers, caught in the sporadic bombardments that plagued their advance, or during the brief encounters with enemy posts they came across while moving forward through the fog.

Among the day's honours, the Distinguished Conduct Medal was awarded to Private Herbert Creighton from Peckham,[183] his citation reading: '*Since February 1918, he has acted as runner to his company commanders. When his company commander was hit during the operations north-west of Bapaume on 21st August 1918, he bound him up and carried him to a place of safety, subsequently returning to the line and joining in the assault on the enemy's position.*'

The Bedfordshires remained in their support line under heavy gas and shell fire throughout 22 August, consolidating the position and preparing for the next advance. Second Lieutenant Harry Maw was killed during the day's shelling, having joined the battalion over the summer. Harry had served in the ranks on Gallipoli and in Egypt before being commissioned into the Bedfordshires a year earlier and spending time in the

7th Bedfordshires. The 25-year-old farmer from Lincolnshire was buried alongside his comrades in a makeshift cemetery 200 metres east of Achiet-le-Petit, being moved to the Adanac military cemetery in Miraumont after the war.

Among those gassed that day was Frederick Cook of Stagsden. Aged 17, Frederick had initially enlisted into the 5th Bedfordshires in January 1915 and had been kept on home service until he was old enough to go abroad. Joining the 1st Battalion on New Year's Eve 1916, the 5-foot 2-inch tall private had already survived several major battles despite being gassed twice; he remained at his post and came through the final series of battles, surviving the war. Sadly, in July 1921, pulmonary tuber-culosis claimed his life, being a direct result of the gassing his system had endured, as was the case with thousands of servicemen after the war.

Lieutenant William Martin Stantan was also wounded while attached to the Trench Mortar Battery. William had already been injured in the battalion's assaults on the Somme, and again at Arras, and was to be hit a third time when shrapnel caught him in the back of the neck, signalling the end of his active service.

The Third Army's assault was a complete success all along the line. Albert was captured and the French developed their offensives further south in the Battle of Noyon, with the British extending the battle front a further 11km north when they launched the Second Battle of Arras.

For the Bedfordshires, their part in this phase of the offensives was not over, as they were to be committed to a fresh phase of the assault against the ridge the following day.

## The Second Battle of Bapaume: 21 August to 3 September 1918

The Third Army and elements of the Fourth Army were ordered to ad-vance on a 50km front, which included the Bedfordshires' IV Corps sector. The New Zealand and British 5th Divisions assaulted the well-defended Le Transloy–Loupart trench system and strongpoints around Bapaume, with the 37th Division being rushed into the line to the north of the 5th Division at short notice.

Late at night on 22 August, orders arrived for the attack to continue the following morning, the brigade's objective being the hitherto elusive ridge facing them. With no time to prepare, the brigades already in position were used and with no German defences visible to British artillery spotters beyond the high ridge facing them, an arbitrary barrage was planned, hoping it would hit the German wire and trench systems. Adding to the concerns of the commanders was the fact that no tanks were allocated to the frontal assault as the ground was far too open and would have made the slow-moving hulks easy targets. So, with the plan of the infantry going in under cover of a heavy barrage that all hoped would find its target, they started hurriedly preparing for an attack in broad daylight.

At 5 a.m. the 500 Bedfordshires who comprised the assaulting element of the battalion relieved the Cheshires from the front line, with 450 Warwickshires lining up to their right. On their left, the 37th Division had been swiftly pushed in to replace the 63rd Division and the assaulting battalions settled into their assembly positions as best they could.

Zero hour came at 11 a.m., and with it the problems started. Before the infantry had even started to advance, it was clear that the barrage was landing too far ahead to cover their move forward. To compound the problem, unbeknown to the troops who started to climb the slopes between them and the ridge, the German trenches, wire and the unusually high concentration of machine-gun positions that faced them, were almost completely untouched. Regardless, the Bedfordshires and Warwickshires pressed on and were met immediately by a heavy barrage from over forty German machine guns spread along a trench system high above them. The Bedfordshires struggled up the 'glacis like slope' under constant fire, only to be greeted by three thick, intact belts of barbed wire in front of the railway line. Probing along the wall of wire for gaps created heavy

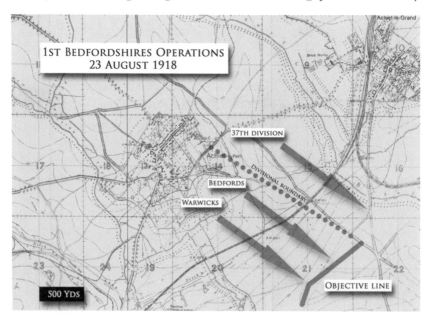

1ST BEDFORDSHIRES OPERATIONS
23 AUGUST 1918

37TH DIVISION

DIVISIONAL BOUNDARY

BEDFORDS

WARWICKS

500 YDS

OBJECTIVE LINE

casualties among the attacking waves of Bedfordshires and before long their advance was brought to a complete halt as they fought to try and prise a way through the obstacle. While the Warwickshires to their right progressed through the gaps in the wire facing them, the beleaguered Bedfordshires were helplessly pinned to the slope until two tanks that had reached the crest as part of the 37th Division's attack to their left started working their way along the trenches and cleared some of the German gunners from the Bedfordshires' front, freeing them up to continue the attack.

From slightly further back with the HQ Company, Lieutenant Colonel Hugh Courtenay saw the centre of the assault becoming disorganised once the heavy fire started to take its toll on his men. He rushed forward under fire and reorganised the attacking platoons until the deep, uncut layers of wire finally stopped movement altogether. Scanning the slope, it became clear that his left company were also under increasing pressure so Lieutenant Colonel Courtenay made his way to their position in person, under the constant scrutiny of the many German gunners facing them. Arriving to find the company were without any active officers, he stood tall despite the lethal machine-gun fire and personally rallied two platoons from in front of the wire, leading them forward in short rushes. As fire from the machine gunners above them dwindled, he led his first wave from the front, charging into the remaining German defenders, who fell to their bayonets and bombs, or surrendered.

Seeing the new movement on the left, Second Lieutenant Henry John Snashall collected his men and charged through the gap they had been cutting in the wire facing them. Despite already struggling as a result of a wound to his arm, the former company sergeant major's charge inspired those around him to follow in his wake and he led the determined band into the German trenches until wounded a second time. The momentum created was enough to see the battalion through the continuing hail of fire and Second Lieutenant Snashall received the Military Cross for his gallantry.

The ridge and trench line in their hands, Lieutenant Colonel Courtenay started organising his battalion and sent advanced posts out in front of the newly won trench system while the bulk of his men set about consolidating their gains. By the time the Bedfordshires started to set the position up for defence against the expected counter-attacks, almost a third of them had fallen, including over half of their officers.

While moving between his men just before 3 p.m., Lieutenant Colonel

Courtenay was severely wounded. His men immediately set about treating his wounds and transferring him to the care of medical staff further back, the battalion's chaplain being at the aid post when the litter carrying their colonel arrived: *'At about 3 o'clock he was brought in wounded at our aid post and some of his own men carried him on for another hour to the advanced dressing station in order to get the first motor ambulance. He was given morphine and some lemon juice at our Aid post and seemed to find it a help to hold the hand of someone he knew. When I left him at the ambulance he was very weak but did not complain of pain – his servant went down with him.'*

Two companies from the Norfolks were moved up to strengthen the brigade who were lining the ridge south of the railway line, their left flank having gained touch with the 37th Division at the sunken road junction south of Achiet-le-Grand.

With the process of consolidation under German artillery fire continuing at speed, the smaller but just as essential jobs also required attention, including finding water for the thirsty men who had scaled a steep hill under fire and while the August sun was at its hottest. Sergeant Harold McHugh, one of the battalion's Military Medallists, who also made regular appearances singing in their concerts, had been among those sent into No Man's Land to establish a forward defensive line.[184]

*The day was hot with sun pouring down on us to say nothing about the shells. After we had dug ourselves in and sort of connected up with one another, the officer in charge asked for volunteers who would risk creeping back to the German trench to try and scrounge something to drink as we had run short of water and were fairly gasping for the want of a drink. Myself and a couple of others volunteered. The dead Germans, of which there were many that had been horribly shattered by our artillery, lay about. Well, after helping ourselves to the dead Germans' water bottles, they seemed to have plenty, also coffee, as each had two, one water and the other coffee, we decided to get back to our trench when one of our chaps called Snowy, being inquisitive, said he thought he should like to have a look at a Gerrie who was sitting in an upright position with a sheet covering his head and shoulders. I told him not to be so daft, hadn't he seen enough horrible sights, as I fully expected the Gerrie had had his head shattered and a pal had thrown a sheet over him to hide the terrible sight from their gaze. Imagine my astonishment when Snowy came running up to me as white as a sheet to tell me he saw the Gerrie move his legs as he approached. I ask [sic] him what he had been drinking as I had passed the same Gerrie several times and didn't notice any movement but Snowy convinced me he was quite sober and I was quickly back and snatched the sheet from him. Imagine my surprise to find he had not been touched by the terrible bombardment but it had driven him stark mad and as hapless as a child.*

At 7.30 p.m. that evening, the right flank of the division conducted one last localised assault and cleared the village of Irles, thus capturing the last section of their objective along the ridge. With their flank secure against German counter-attacks from Miraumont, the division settled down for a well-earned overnight rest.

The 5th Division's attack was a remarkable success, given the ground they faced and that the final, staggering count of machine guns captured from the position that day came to over 150. Much to the annoyance of senior staff, every battalion commanding officer had become personally involved in their men's attacks, each understanding the importance of leading their men themselves in the face of such adversity.

The Bedfordshires suffered heavily as they were pinned in front of the wire belts. Of the 500 who went forward, 7 officers were killed and 2 injured, in addition to 129 men who were struck down or wounded.

Although he had been rushed back into the medical system, news filtered through to the battalion that evening that Lieutenant Colonel Courtenay had died from the wounds sustained leading his men up the slope in the face of heavy machine-gun fire. He had made it back to No. 3 Casualty Clearing Station but his injuries were too severe and he died there, the site at Gézaincourt now being the Bagneux British cemetery.

Among the letters Hugh's wife received after his death was one from fellow staff officer Harold Westley, who had served alongside him for two years, writing: *'I cannot help just telling you how fond we were of him. It is an expression I do not often use of any one but he was a thorough English gentleman, and as an officer he never thought of his own career only that of his regiment and the service as a whole. It is Hugh and a few others like him who have made this regiment what it is today. Someday if I survive the war I would like to come and talk to you about him, he often talked to me about you all.'*

Hugh's second in command, Major William Chirnside, added in his own thoughts in a letter to Hugh's parents and widow:

*There is no one in the Regiment I would have preferred to serve under as 2nd in command and his loss is equally felt not only by the few officers remaining with us, but by every N.C.O. and man in the Battalion. His conduct and personal example – for he went out with his men – is beyond any praise of mine and our success in the operation was mainly due to his bravery and coolness when our line was held up by intense machine gun and artillery fire. The attack was nearly over when he was hit and everything that could be done for him was done at once. I am unable to let you know at the moment where he was buried but he reached Casualty Clearing Station and will have been laid finally to rest in one of our Military Cemeteries in the back area. I hardly know what consolation I can offer you except that he died a soldier's death leading his battalion in a manner inflicting the highest credit both on himself and on the Regiment. We are all very proud of him indeed and feel deeply for you in your great loss.*[185]

For his gallantry and leadership, the well-known Old Contemptible who had arrived in France with the battalion in August 1914, was awarded a posthumous Distinguished Service Order to supplement his Military Cross and was mentioned in despatches in July 1919.

In addition to Lieutenant Colonel Courtenay, the 20-year-old company commander Lieutenant Robert Henry Preuss Arnholz was among the officers killed. After enlisting aged just 17, Robert had served as a Territorial officer in Mesopotamia until dysentery had sent him back to England. Once recovered, he had found himself posted to the 1st Bedfordshires, a letter from his father to the War Office after his death sharing *'the boy's pride in the fact that though only a Territorial officer, he was in command of a company of the 1st Battalion of a Regular Line Regiment'.*[186]

Lieutenant Edgar Ivan Fitzroy Nailer, the son of a colonial colonel who had been born in India, was killed, aged 27. Lieutenant George Abbott died aged 35, and 29-year-old Lieutenant Alexander Robert Charles Eaton also fell, as did 35-year-old Second Lieutenant William Thomas Paine.

Another 20-year-old killed on the slope was Second Lieutenant Frank Herbert Fox from Nottingham. The son of the Nottingham Deputy City Treasurer and a former private in his local regiment, Frank had enlisted in the 1st Bedfordshires less than a year earlier and joined his only brother on the country's roll of honour when he died in the Casualty Clearing Station at Achiet-le-Petit.

The 23-year-old Lieutenant Henry James Arthur Watson, who had been with the battalion since their return to France in April 1918, was hit by a machine gunner and never regained consciousness, dying before he could be moved to a Casualty Clearing Station.

As well as Henry Snashall, Second Lieutenant Frederick James Kelf from Ware was also hit during the assault. After joining Kitchener's New Armies in September 1915, Frederick had served in the ranks as well as in a Tunnelling Company until injured on the Somme in 1916. Being discharged to commission the following year, Frederick had been with the battalion only a matter of weeks before being wounded. X-rays would show that he had suffered considerable damage to his left shoulder, including a compound fracture of the scapula in addition to bone damage at the base of his spine. Although he survived, Frederick's war had come to an end and he would be medically discharged the following June.

From the 129 'other ranks' who were killed was Private Arthur Hackett of Great Staughton. His father, Tom, had already lost one son at Festubert in May 1915 while serving in the 2nd Bedfordshires, making Arthur his second son to fall in the regiment. The war had one final blow to deal him when just three weeks later, his third son died, leaving just one of the original four brothers standing.[187]

Algy Breed had been seriously wounded in the thigh and hand during the assault. Out since November 1914, Algy had been posted as killed on Hill 60 but later turned up *worth forty dead ones*, had picked up a knee injury on the Somme and survived Ypres in one piece, also managing a mention in despatches during the battalion's tour in Italy. Writing home from his hospital bed after the battle, Algy knew that he was *finished as far as fighting goes. I shall no doubt be here some time, then finish up by being discharged.*[188]

Southill resident CSM Harry Allison was awarded with the Military Medal and made it home for a short spell of leave in September, looking 'very fit' despite sixteen years with the battalion behind him and having been on the front almost continuously since August 1914.[189]

After the battle, Brigadier Oldman reported how *'the enemy made best use of these trenches with his machine guns while we were held up, but directly we came to grips with him he surrendered freely'*. Some 657 prisoners were taken by the brigade that day, along with around 60 of the machine guns that had been the cause of so many casualties as the British troops had forced their way up the slope towards them.

During the division's operations over the previous three days, over and above the defenders who had been killed during the fighting, 2,768 prisoners were captured. Also taken were 25 artillery pieces, over 350 machine guns, 37 trench mortars and a plethora of anti-tank rifles and stores, which, curiously, included 2 pigeons. However, the division had lost 70 officers and 1,600 men, including 4 battalion and 3 battery commanders.

**Pursuit to the Hindenburg Line: 24 August to 3 September 1918**
Major William Stuart Chirnside, who had already been awarded the

Military Cross twice, assumed command of the battalion on the news of Lieutenant Colonel Courtenay's death, and the small officer corps was reorganised until reinforcements arrived.

The 13th Brigade took over the front line in support of the New Zealanders, who were working on capturing Bapaume, giving the 15th and 95th Brigades a chance to re-form and refit. Accordingly, the following morning Acting Lieutenant Colonel Chirnside led his half-strength battalion into reserve, north-west of Achiet-le-Petit.

At 9 a.m. on 25 August the brigade were moved forward on the heels of the general advance, the Bedfordshires setting up for the day east of the recently captured ridge, south of Achiet-le-Grand. As the division prepared to take over the front line and village of Favreuil from the 37th Division in readiness for the continued assault north of Bapaume, orders were delayed, units became mixed up, and the dark, wet night did nothing to help the assembling troops. Nevertheless, Beugnâtre fell to the 13th Brigade as part of the scheme to envelope Bapaume that afternoon, and the Bedfordshires' brigade remained in reserve in the open fields south of Bihucourt for the next few days.

On 28 August the Bedfordshires received a draft of sixty-two men and moved east, closer to Bapaume. Orders arrived the following day preparing them to depart at a moment's notice, as the New Zealanders wrestled Bapaume from the Germans' occupation, in turn freeing up the entire sector to continue with its advance.

The 95th Brigade took over the front from the 13th overnight and assaulted the German line between Beugny and Ytres on the 30th, with the 15th Brigade shuffling along in close support to them, ready to exploit any significant gaps as they developed. The Norfolks provided the brigade's advanced guard, while the Bedfordshires and other units made the most of a relatively unmolested series of moves that saw them halt some 12km due east of Achiet-le-Petit that evening. The brigade spread out in close support behind the new front line and rested, the Bedfordshires making their shelters in the recently abandoned German trench system 1km north-north-west of Beugny, just north of the summit of Hill 120. All of the following day was spent in that position waiting for orders, cleaning, reorganising and resting as final plans were being drawn up that would conclude the Second Battle of Bapaume.

On the night of 1 September, the 15th Brigade took over the front with a view to maintaining the momentum in their divisional sector. The exposed landscape and the unavoidable need for the battalions to move across the open ground resulted in casualties from sporadic artillery while assembling, with one company of the Warwickshires being badly mauled by a German aircraft on a night bombing raid that caught them unawares, causing around eighty casualties in just moments.

In the larger picture, IV Corps' operations were intended to hold as many German units in place as possible while XVII Corps broke the German Drocourt–Quéant line. The 5th Division's specific objective was to take the German trenches in front of Beugny, as well as the village itself and the high ground to the east of it. South of the village and an integral part of the defensive position was the well-sited, fortified Delseaux Farm, which formed part of the natural feature called Chapel Spur that ran behind the village and faded into the landscape north of the Cambrai Road.

The Norfolks were to advance on the right of the brigade frontage, with the Cheshires to their left, the Warwickshires in support and the Bedfordshires in reserve. Four Mark IV tanks were allocated to the brigade, all of which would advance behind a heavy barrage.

Zero hour was set for 5.15 a.m. but overnight the division on the extreme south of the corps' frontage unexpectedly advanced their zero hour by eight minutes, and in doing so brought a massive counter-barrage down on the assembled troops, who had little option but to soak up the punishment. The Cheshires suffered especially badly, enduring a seven-minute bombardment and having nowhere to shelter throughout the entire ordeal.

When zero hour finally arrived, the brigade advanced on the heels of their own barrage, with the Norfolks to the south of Beugny slicing through the resistance they came across with light casualties while taking 250 prisoners.

Although the village itself was not seriously contested, the left flank of the Cheshires met with heavy machine-gun fire as they passed the northern outskirts of the village, with the entire flank having to seek shelter in the sunken road due north of Beugny. One of the tanks was hit in the village and set on fire, although a second passed clean through, out the other side and over the spur, returning some time later after it had run out of targets. Sadly, the remaining tanks did not make it to the fighting line, both failing as a result of all-too-familiar mechanical problems.

By 6 a.m. the brigade line ran from the sunken road north of Beugny, where contact had been made with the 62nd Division, through the village, on to the southern edge of the spur and past Delseaux Farm, where it connected to an isolated platoon of New Zealanders who had yet to make contact with the rest of their division. Advancing to the eastern edge of the village was not possible courtesy of the bank of German machine gunners engaging all movement on the spur, so a firm line of resistance was established amid the ruined piles of rubble.

All morning the Bedfordshires held their reserve positions outside Frémicourt under shell and machine-gun fire, and with little or no cover available in the open landscape. Around midday a German counter-attack was thrown at the weak southern flank, bringing one company of Bedfordshires forward to repel their attempts as the New Zealanders had yet to appear in strength.

On the northern flank, a British battery was repositioned to try and eliminate the German machine guns that had so effectively pinned down the Cheshires and 62nd Division troops. The entire battery was wiped out, forcing another gun to move forward, where it remained in the open for three hours, engaging the machine guns and any reserve German troops being pushed ahead to counter-attack assembly point.

That evening a decision was made to continue the onslaught the follow-ing morning, with two companies of the Bedfordshires, a meagre 120 men in all, being allocated to lead the assault, the remaining half of the battalion moving up behind them. In conjunction, a similarly sized party of the Warwickshires made a strike from the north-west of the village, forming a pincer movement intended to cut off, surround and capture the remaining defensive garrison. Following an effective, focused bombardment from three entire brigades of artillery, at 5.15 a.m., the infantry advanced on to the village, quickly learning the garrison had only left behind a rearguard, presumably having slipped away under cover of darkness.

In spite of the limited opposition, heavy artillery and machine-gun fire killed twelve Bedfordshires, including two veterans with sixteen years each in the regiment: Edward Davis of Luton[190] and Charles Meakins from Waddesdon.[191] Among those killed was Lance Sergeant John Bass from Kimbolton,[192] who had been mentioned in despatches for service in Italy and would be awarded with a posthumous Military Medal. Lieu-tenant Charles George Hayes and eighty-two men were also wounded, leaving the battalion at considerably less than 50 per cent strength once again.

Charles Hayes's injuries were categorised as 'very severe', machine-gun bullets having fractured both legs. His war was over and Charles would be demobilised a year later, but not before being awarded a Military Cross *'for conspicuous gallantry and good leadership in an attack. He led his company with marked coolness in an attack after all the other officers had become casualties, and himself fired a Lewis gun, whose team had been put out of action. He set a splendid example of initiative and skill.'* [193]

Although it was not known at local level immediately, the Canadians had broken the Drocourt–Quéant switch line south-east of Arras, forcing the German generals to retire back behind the formidable Hindenburg Line where they intended to make a firm stand. Overnight patrols on the Bedfordshires' front first suspected, then confirmed, that no German troops appeared to be facing the brigade. After consultation with his seniors, Brigadier Oldman ordered the brigade to prepare for a pursuit, which would be led by the battle-worn Bedfordshires and Warwickshires, each fielding around 330 men. Advanced guards were sent forward from each battalion, with B and D Companies leading the Bedfordshires' line ahead, the remaining companies moving in close support, and the rest of the brigade 1km further back.

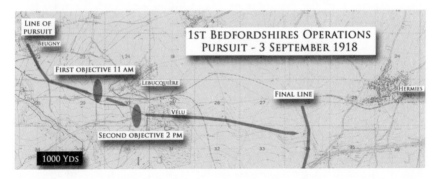

Planned as a series of bounds forward, the first objective of the high ground west of Lebucquière was reached at 11 a.m. by the advanced squads moving astride the railway line heading east. The second objective of the high ground west of Vélu was gained by 2 p.m., with a further, longer movement over the ridge and down into the valley stopping only when the advanced Bedfordshires and Warwickshires met with defensive fire from in front of Hermies, itself sited just west of the Canal du Nord.

The process of digging in started once it became clear they had identified the new German line of resistance and that evening the entire division was relieved by the 37th Division. The 320 remaining Bedfordshires retired to Lebucquière station to rest after their long day, where they were met by the transport and 'details' left out of the fighting, as well as the welcomed sight of the battalion cooking limbers.

That day alone, the divisional line had moved forward around 7km, the Bedfordshires losing nine wounded once they came under fire opposite Hermies and other battalions suffering similarly light casualties. Of the nine injured, another pre-war Old Contemptible was lost: 29-year-old Edward Jarvis from Essex,[194] who had been with the regiment since the summer of 1905 and had joined the 1st Bedfordshires with their first draft of reinforcements in August 1914.

The date of 3 September marked the end of the Second Battle of Bapaume, as well as the beginning of a short, well-earned spell of rest and reorganisation for the division, who had advanced the British line almost 25km since their secret arrival late on 20 August.

The division had overcome some difficult positions in the fortnight they had been in the line, but at the cost of 210 officers and over 4,000 men, which included no less than 8 commanding officers. Over and above those Germans killed during the fighting, close to 4,000 prisoners had been taken in addition to a wealth of equipment and munitions, but, more importantly, the German army's morale had been weakened as it had been sent reeling back across distances that can only be categorised as significant in terms of the Great War.

Given the fact that the Bedfordshires and other battalions in their division had been almost constantly in the line since their return to the Western Front, no time for training had been possible, yet it did not go unnoticed how well the troops performed under trying and often unaccustomed conditions. Open warfare such as that experienced over the past fortnight was unfamiliar to many, with even the Old Contempt-ibles straining their memories to go far enough back to recall the last time such styles of fighting had been seen.

In the twenty-seven days since the launch of the general Allied offensives, over 100,000 German prisoners had been taken, three-quarters of those by the British. The German High Command understood that the war was now over and tried to approach the Allies to agree a peace settle-ment. The terms were refused completely and, with their own allies warning they would be unable to continue the war beyond December, German leaders started to put together plans for armistice negotiations.

Even with the end in sight, the fighting would continue and some of the bloodiest battles of the war were still ahead as the Allies pressed their adversaries ever east. British 'All Arms' tactics were paying dividends but the German defence was as stout and tenacious as ever, even in the loom-ing face of defeat.

## Corps reserve: 4 to 26 September 1918

September would see fighting go on along the approaches to the Hindenburg Line, with strong German rearguard actions and unending counter-attacks swinging back and forth but never managing to hold the British troops back for long. A string of heavily contested towns, heights and other such fortified positions designed as outposts of the Hindenburg Line fell in turn, until the entire main line system was within reach of the British infantry.

Throughout these localised actions, the 1st Bedfordshires were kept in reserve, rebuilding, reorganising and refitting in readiness for the next phase of their war and the assault against the formidable, allegedly impregnable defensive position that faced the British army.

Between 4 and 15 September, the battalion rested in camp near Biefvillers-lès-Bapaume, 5km west-north-west of Bapaume. After an initial spell of cleaning up and making good their deficiencies, training started in spite of several days of bad weather and high, blustery winds.

On the 12th, a badly needed draft of nine second lieutenants arrived, comprised of William Robert Turner Brandreth, Frank Whateley-Knight, Stanley George Fisher, Keith William Pittman Harvey, Ernest Walter Pillis Robinson, Greville William Blackwell, Frederick Augustus Clarke, William Walter Humm and Lawrence George Cale.

On 15 September, the battalion moved 7km south-east, through Bapaume and Riencourt-lès-Bapaume, into divisional reserve at Villers-au-Flos, where they were greeted by the site of huts and dugouts to billet in. German night bombers had the site well mapped out but the battalion suffered no casualties during the sporadic bombing raids until their move five days later.

Another night march 7km east-south-east on the 20th took the battalion through Barastre and Bus, on to Ytres, where they remained until moved forward to take on the Hindenburg Line late on 26 September.

Although in camp and away from the firing line, the battalion were shelled by long-range, high-velocity German guns on 22 September, Second Lieutenant Reginald John Cropley being among those wounded. Other than a bout of colitis and suffering from the ever-present problem of trench feet while serving in the ranks of the Royal Fusiliers in 1916, Reginald had until now come through the war without a scratch and had joined the battalion as a newly commissioned officer over the summer. Although he was moved back to No. 34 Casualty Clearing Station at Grevillers, his wounds were too extensive and he died later that day, aged

21. Among the effects returned to his mother after his death were several personal grooming items that suited his pre-war occupation as a dentist, as well as a purse containing what were recorded as '10 lucky coins'.[195]

# Chapter 9

# The Battles of the Hindenburg Line: 12 September to 12 October 1918

*'Had the Boche not shown marked signs of deterioration during the past month, I should never have contemplated attacking the Hindenburg line.'*

Since breaking out from their position behind the Hindenburg Line in March 1918 and pushing west during the German spring offensives, the Germans had not been idle, and the defensive position facing the British troops was even more formidable than that in 1917. A mutually supportive outpost line made from a series of fortified redoubts and emplacements was the first obstacle faced by the attackers, which shielded the main Hindenburg system of defences. In itself, the main trench system was intimidating enough, yet a further Hindenburg support system was behind them, and the Hindenburg reserve system provided another serious line of resistance further east. Each line as an isolated trench system was impressive enough, but with the series of systems collectively forming a battle zone of around 6km in depth, the challenge facing British troops was daunting.

Portions of the German position were built into the partially completed St Quentin canal, which not only provided a solid defensive position but formed a significant physical obstacle. Some sections of the structure were almost 40 metres across, with great tracts of land around it being turned into a swampy quagmire by the ever-efficient German engineers who flooded approaches where possible.

All along the Hindenburg Line, thick, multiple belts of wire, all methodically covered by numerous machine-gun redoubts, reinforced concrete enclosures and mutually supportive trench lines, made the task of capturing it unenviable. General Rawlinson later wrote that *'had the Boche not shown marked signs of deterioration during the past month, I should never have contemplated attacking the Hindenburg line. Had it been defended by the Germans of two years ago, it would certainly have been impregnable.'*

To reduce the chance of German reserves being used en masse to blunt any successful penetration of their lines, a series of orchestrated attacks along half of the length of the Western Front were launched with the express intention of breaching the last significant, organised defensive line the German army had built.

The main assaults were launched from 26 September, with a joint French–American attack called the Meuse-Argonne offensive near Verdun being the opening phase at the southern end of the enormous battlefield, although the series of assaults failed to break the German defences until 17 October. Some 250km away in the northern sector of the Western Front, a Belgian–British–French offensive was launched around Ypres two days later, with the central British and Commonwealth offensives, collectively known as the Battles for the Hindenburg Line, starting on 27 September.

Part of the Hindenburg Line offensives, the objectives of the Battle of the Canal du Nord were to advance towards Cambrai and secure the northern flank of the British attack that would develop into the Battle of the St Quentin canal two days later. The British First Army spearheaded the assault, with the Third Army, of which the Bedfordshires were a part, taking the fight to the Germans further south.

In the Bedfordshires' IV Corps sector, the 5th Division lined up on the right, with the 42nd to their left and the 17th Division from V Corps to the south. Within the narrow 5th Divisional sector facing Beaucamps and Villers-Plouich, the 13th Brigade were in the line on the right, with the 15th on the left.

## The Battle of the Canal du Nord: 27 September to 1 October 1918

Late on 26 September, the Bedfordshires left Ytres and marched out in artillery formation, headed for their assembly area. They moved along Winchester Valley track, partially sheltered by the valley slopes immediately south of Metz-en-Couture, along the Quivering support and Quotient trenches that ran between the Havrincourt and Gouzeacourt Woods, to Bank Post. Following the line of another communications trench, they reached their assembly trenches north of Trig Post, which was sited 600 metres south-west of Beaucamps, 12km south-south-west of Cambrai. Beating the first slivers of dawn to the position, camouflage netting was

issued to the Bedfordshires and Warwickshires, concealing them from prying eyes as they crouched in their assembly trenches once daylight came.

Further north, at 5.20 a.m. the four assaulting divisions of the First Army
launched their attack from the darkness, achieving complete surprise and
capturing all of their objectives. In accordance with the prearranged plans,
divisions further south instigated a series of staggered assaults, which included the Bedfordshires' 5th Division.

With the familiar sounds of battle raging further north and out of their
field of sight, the battalion lined up with A Company on the right, C on
the left, D Company 100 metres behind in support and B Company 200
metres further back in reserve. The Bedfordshires left their assembly
trenches at 7.52 a.m., as burning oil drums were projected towards the
village, and advanced close behind the creeping barrage. German artillery
responded with an instant retaliatory bombardment, but both the Bedfordshires and Warwickshires advanced through the storm, arriving at
the first halt line 100 metres south-west of the village as per their time-
tables. After an eight-minute pause while the barrage pounded the garrison
in the village, the explosive curtain jumped forward 100 metres, followed
closely by the khaki line, each man being held back by the NCOs to avoid
running into their own creeping barrage.

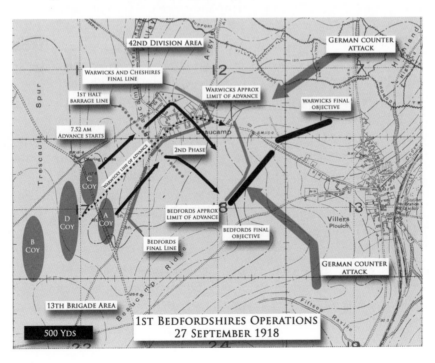

C Company advanced into the village, bombing and bayoneting their way through the shattered homes, while A Company moved forward in artillery formation along the open slopes, heading towards Villers-Plouich. D Company followed on the heels of C and took over the task of clearing hidden German posts and guarding dugout entrances until the tunnelling sections arrived to explore each dugout in turn. The tactics employed by the retiring soldiers since August saw all German prisoners being questioned to see where booby traps and mines had been laid, and explicit orders were issued not to touch anything, however tempting, under any conditions. Once D Company had arrived in the ruins in force, C Company resumed their advance, turning south-east for 250 metres towards Villers-Plouich, where they linked up with A Company who were almost on the final objective, being a line facing Villers-Plouich midway between the villages. Under shell fire, the men quickly started the process of digging in, while keeping a wary eye on the slopes and sunken road to their south.

As D Company were busying themselves with the mopping up, a company of Cheshires arrived to support their operations and the Warwickshires advanced through the Bedfordshires to take up position on the left of the line established by A Company. Now on the heels of the creeping barrage, the Warwickshires initially went unchecked, but they ran into trouble short of their objective when they met a German counter-attack coming from the north-east, where the 42nd Division was expected to be.

By 10 a.m. messages were sent back to brigade advising the objective had almost been taken and that B Company had moved in to close support of the village, which had been left in the hands of the Cheshires and tunnellers, with D Company in support behind the new front line. A section of tanks had been assigned to the brigade's advance, each with their own three-man team providing a smokescreen and giving the slow-moving mammoths a chance of reaching the battle lines intact. In the event, just one made it to the village, leaving the Warwickshires and Bedfordshires with no tank support and only able to field the equivalent of a company of men each.

By midday, the Warwickshires were having a difficult time. All four company commanders had been lost and the 42nd Division had failed to arrive and link up with them. As a result, they were isolated and being forced back by the large German counter-attack that had hit them from the space that was expected to be occupied by the 42nd Division.

Reports reached the already thin British line of Germans concentrating in Fifteen Ravine, 1,500 metres south-east of the village, and a large German bombing attack in the afternoon cut the line formed by the two brigades in half at Dunraven Trench south of Beaucamps. After a fierce close-quarters fight, the remaining Bedfordshires withdrew from the slopes facing Villers-Plouich and reorganised themselves along the sunken road south-west of Beaucamps, aligned with the 13th Brigade to their south and with the Warwickshires and Cheshires moving into the village and trying to link up with the 42nd Division, who were themselves still trying to break the stiff resistance they had run into.

By the end of the day's fighting, the village was secure but the brigade line had been pushed back 500 metres from its final objective. Some 250 German prisoners were taken by the brigade that day, with scores more being killed in the close-quarters fighting, but the brigade lost hundreds of men they could ill afford, given their already seriously undermanned condition. The Bedfordshires alone lost a further 8 officers and 136 men, leaving their trench strength the size of a company once more.

Captain Harold Charles Loe, who had won the Military Cross almost exactly a year earlier, was killed aged 27. A grocer before the war, he had enlisted into the ranks of the Black Watch at the outbreak of hostilities, quickly rising to CSM. Other than two bouts of sickness, his time in the ranks was free of wounds and he was commissioned into the Bedfordshires in May 1917, joining the 1st Battalion in August.

Second Lieutenant Herbert Hutchinson was also killed. The 23-year-old former grocer's assistant from Worcester had already served in the ranks through the atrocious conditions on the Gallipoli peninsular before joining the battalion eleven months earlier.

Second Lieutenant Joseph Thornton Laughton was mortally wounded, dying on 29 September, aged 22. Suffering from gunshot injuries to his right shoulder and left thigh, the thigh also being fractured, he died on the ambulance train before arriving at the No. 2 Red Cross hospital in Rouen. A farmer and auctioneer from Sutton Farm near St Albans, Joseph had enlisted as an officer cadet late in 1916 and joined the 1st Bedfordshires in July 1917. Among the effects returned to his widowed mother was his tunic which, noted in his service record as having the full array of buttons, badges and wound stripes, also carried the warning that it was 'damaged' and 'badly bloodstained'.[196]

Captain Robert Leslie Shaw was wounded, his brother having been killed in the 2nd Bedfordshires in August 1917. Robert had recovered from a fractured skull, and the ensuing headaches, vertigo and dizziness, after falling from his horse when a motorcycle despatch rider had collided with it in September 1916, returning to the battalion in July 1918. Although the shrapnel in his left knee did not stop Captain Shaw from attending a posting to the British Military Mission to train the United States army, he returned to the UK late in the year for further medical treatment, which was cut short after hearing of the death of his wife in America. Trips back and forth followed, before he retired on account of ill health and set off to make a new life in America late in 1919.

Captain and Adjutant Alexander Herbert Oliver Riddell was injured, having been with the battalion for six months after initially serving with the 2nd Bedfordshires throughout 1915 and 1916. He recovered and was awarded the Military Cross for gallantry the following June.

Lieutenant Frederick Henry Melvill had been a Stock Exchange clerk before enlisting in the ranks of the London Regiment in September 1914. Gazetted as an officer in the Hertfordshire Regiment in January 1917, he had been with the battalion a matter of weeks before a shell fragment had penetrated his helmet, leaving him dazed but conscious. Days later he was back in Blighty and would be medically discharged in February 1919, still suffering from the effects of his injury.

Second Lieutenant Greville William Blackwell had been in the battalion for just fifteen days before he was wounded.

Second Lieutenant William Thomas Morris was hit by a shell fragment in the right wrist and arm, his third wound of the war. After service in the ranks of the 1st Bedfordshires since June 1911, the former tailor had recovered from a bayonet injury at Givenchy in October 1914 and a bullet wound in the 2nd Battalion at Festubert in May 1915. Having recovered from the trio of mishaps, William would join the 52nd Bedfordshires in the Army of the Rhine in 1919 and return to life in Northampton in November of that year.

One of the Bedfordshires, Private Charles Kidby from Stratford,[197] had been with the battalion since April 1915, when he had arrived in a large draft as the battalion grimly held on to Hill 60. During the assault Charles was attached to the brigade's Trench Mortar Battery, positioned on the exposed Beaucamps Ridge in direct support of the brigade's attack. The senior men from his battery had all become casualties from the heavy counter battery fire that trench mortar teams tended to attract, so Private Kidby took over. Directing his battery while under continuous fire and arranging resupply, he displayed *'exceptional coolness and leadership'* throughout the battle, keeping his battery active. His bravery was rewarded with the Distinguished Conduct Medal.

Private Frank Burch from Aldbury was among those killed. He had enlisted in the Hertfordshire Regiment in March 1915 and had later served in the 7th Bedfordshires before being transferred into the 1st Battalion. Frank would be posthumously awarded the Military Medal the following March.[198]

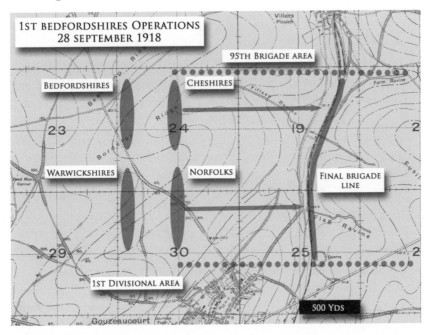

Sergeant William Papworth from Peterborough had arrived in the large draft from the Huntingdonshire Cyclists Battalion in September 1916 and had come through every engagement since unscathed. He was lightly wounded in the left arm but returned to his battalion soon afterwards and was awarded the Military Medal in 1919.[199]

After an evening of patrolling and keeping watch for German raids and counter-attacks, the 95th Brigade advanced through the 15th at 2.30 a.m. on 28 September, leaving the 15th Brigade to side-slip to their right and take over the 13th Brigade sector. Immediately, patrols were pushed out to establish whether the German garrisons had evacuated Gouzeacourt and by 9 a.m. the entire line was ready for another push forward. With the 95th Brigade to their north and the 21st Division to their south, the line advanced, maintaining the pressure of their adversaries. The 15th Brigade advanced from Borderer and Beaucamps Ridges to the railway line running between Gouzeacourt and Villers-Plouich, with the Cheshires on the left and the Norfolks to their right, supported by the Bed-fordshires behind the Cheshires, and the Warwickshires following in the wake of the Norfolks.

Lieutenant Claud Gilbert Wilkins from the 1st Bedfordshires was slightly wounded during the advance for the second time since joining the battalion in January, but remained at duty, one man being killed and three more injured.

Late that night orders arrived from Corps HQ to resume the advance at 3.30 a.m. on the 29th, but the inter-brigade relief was not completed as there simply was not enough time. Adapting the plans according to what was possible, the 12th Gloucestershires and 1st Duke of Cornwall's Light Infantry from the 95th Brigade advanced from the railway, with the plan being for the Bedfordshires and Warwickshires to follow behind and push on once the line had reached a sunken road running between Gonnelieu and La Vacquerie, some 1,600 metres to the east. The final, ambitious divisional objective was the line of the Canal de L'Escaut, 10km away.

At 3.30 a.m., with the New Zealand Division to their north and the 21st Division to the south, the battle-worn and somewhat disorganised division went over the top once more. The initial advance carried their lines forward some 800 metres before heavy machine-gun fire from both Gonnelieu and La Vacquerie stopped the front waves in their tracks. The British creeping barrage had moved on, leaving the advancing waves unprotected, and with flanking fire coming from both north and south, the 95th Brigade came to a halt.

The Bedfordshires and Warwickshires caught up with the sheltering troops but Lieutenant Colonel Chirnside and his counterpart in the Warwickshires chose to press on despite both brigades becoming extremely mixed up. The main body was soon stopped completely by the withering flanking fire, but Acting Captain Albert Henry Wakefield gathered a small party and took them on a flanking attack under heavy fire, capturing a section of the sunken road and around 130 prisoners. Captain Wakefield, who had joined the battalion a year and two days earlier, was awarded the Military Cross for bravery. He survived the rest of the war unscathed and would be presented with his medal by the King at Buckingham Palace on 12 May 1920, two days after his 34th birthday.

By the day's end, the garrison in La Vacquerie to the north had fallen, but Gonnelieu to the south was still in German hands, the 21st Division having been unable to break into the village. In the middle, the mixed force of 5th Division troops had taken their lines forward to the sunken

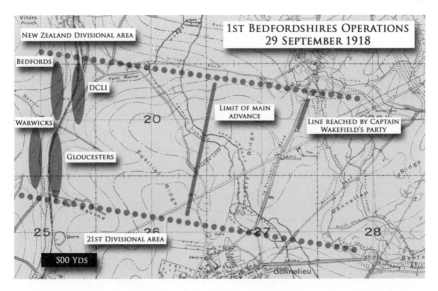

road, taking 200 prisoners and over 50 machine guns, although the bulk of their men had to wait until nightfall to join the advanced group under Captain Wakefield. All things considered, the Bedfordshires' casualty list was remarkably light, with three 'other ranks' killed, two officers and three men wounded and one reported as being missing.

Second Lieutenant Frank Whateley-Knight, a horticulturist before enlisting into the ranks of the Warwickshires, was slightly wounded but remained at duty. Described as a *'rugger player, nervous at times, with a retiring disposition'*,[200] Frank had joined the battalion just over a fortnight earlier and would survive the final battles, serving with the 52nd Bedfordshires in the Army of the Rhine before returning to civilian life.[201]

Second Lieutenant Robert Turner Brandreth was hit by a machine-gun bullet which, remarkably, passed through both ankles without touching any bones or vital arteries. The son of a gentleman who owned Houghton Hall in Bedfordshire, Robert had already served in the 5th Territorial Battalion between 1910 and 1913, before resigning his captaincy to concentrate on poultry farming. He had enlisted into the ranks under the Derby Scheme of December 1915 and, following his commission into the 5th Bedfordshires once again, sailed for France the day after his 30th birthday. Along with Frank Whateley-Knight, Robert had joined the battalion a fortnight previously. Fortunately, the bullet wound inflicted in this battle would heal completely by early 1919, although his service in this war was over. However, Robert was among those veterans who re-joined the colours two decades later, enlisting back into the ranks of the

6th Dorsets in August 1939.

The date of 30 September saw the advance continuing, the Cheshires taking over the front line, with the Norfolks in support. The dwindling numbers of exhausted Bedfordshires and Warwickshires were held in reserve, keeping to their lines in the sunken road they had taken the day before. The objective of the day was to break into and capture the main and support Hindenburg trench systems, 900 metres east, both heavily fortified and wired. Advancing behind an intensive creeping barrage at 3.30 a.m., the Cheshires and Norfolks took their objectives and by late morning held the high ground overlooking the Canal de L'Escaut. Although the New Zealanders to their north had moved forward, the 21st Division to the south was slower in coming into the newly won line, so the Warwickshires and Norfolks formed a defensive flank facing Gonnelieu, with the Bedfordshires moving into reserve at Flag Ravine, south of Villers-Plouich, while the Cheshires held the Hindenburg support system called Barrack Support trench.

By late afternoon the battlefield had quietened down and the brigade were well dug in. Some 272 prisoners, several field guns and dozens of machine guns had been captured in addition to those defenders killed during the barrage and subsequent fighting, with 200 of the prisoners being taken by the Norfolks alone.

That evening, the 37th Division relieved the exhausted 5th Division, the 111th Brigade coming into the line in place of the 15th. As the division gathered to move into reserve, the Bedfordshires rested in Dead Man's Corner, a star-shaped sunken crossroads 1.5km north-west of Gouzeacourt. Their last day of operations had cost them a further seven men, two of whom would die from their wounds later that day.

A year after, CQMS William Austin from Redbourn[202] would be awarded the Distinguished Conduct Medal for his part in the operations between August 1916 and September 1918, his citation reading: '*He has served continuously with the battalion since the Somme operations in August 1916, and in his capacity as CQMS has on several occasions shown great presence of mind and courage under shelling, as well as performing his duties in a most zealous and capable manner. During the operations at Nieppe Forest in April and May 1918, and the operations NW of Bapaume, in August and September 1918, he conducted ration parties to the outpost lines through heavy gas shelling and machine-gun fire, and personally distributed rations.*'

The Hindenburg Line had been breached along its entire length and, despite their determined efforts, the German defence was collapsing. The

Allied forces had enjoyed success in all three operational areas, and the German army was retiring all along the Western Front, with only open country behind them. Although they would fight on, it had become clear that they were only capable of delaying the inevitable Allied victory, having only the power to delay and disrupt their advance, but not to stop it.

On 29 September, Bulgaria signed an armistice, giving the Allied forces control over the Balkans. Germany's allies were in freefall, with Turkey retreating in the face of an unstoppable British and Commonwealth advance and Austria under intense pressure from the Allied forces in Italy and those moving up through the Balkans.

While German Quartermaster General Ludendorff, who had been under extreme stress for months, suffered from something akin to a breakdown and seems to have received psychiatric treatment,[203] the soldiers fighting on the ground were surrendering in their thousands, with over 250,000 Germans having been captured during 1918 alone.

The end of what had been, for some of the Bedfordshires, over four years of warfare, was most certainly in sight.

### Return to Le Cateau: 1 to 16 October 1918

Between 1 and 9 October, the 5th Division was held in corps reserve to rest, make good their deficiencies and reorganise, the Bedfordshires in huts at Neuville-Bourjonval, 7km west of Villers-Plouich. Not only were structures reformed at battalion level, but the entire division was shaken into a new shape when orders arrived that would reduce it to a nine-battalion unit, in line with the other British divisions. As a result, each brigade effectively lost one battalion from its strength, the 16th Warwickshires from the 15th Brigade being moved into the 13th Brigade, leaving just the Bedfordshires, Norfolks and Cheshires, who had been together since August 1914.

On their first day in reserve, a German high-velocity shell found its target, wreaking havoc among the transport section. Three horses were killed, with a further three being wounded, and Private Edward Strudwick from Stevenage was found to have been killed in the explosion.[204] Private Fred Breed of Potton was hit in the head, having already been injured several times during his three years of service, and he died as a result of his wounds on 10 October at a hospital in Rouen, aged 22.[205]

Over the next week, the battalion's officer corps was practically rebuilt, with sixteen replacements arriving. The first draft to join on 1 October included five officers: Captain Frederick William Ballance, who served in the 5th Bedfordshires on Gallipoli and the Middle East and would survive the war, going on to a career in the RAF during the Second World War; Lieutenant Arthur James Fyson, who had recovered from the wound received at La Coulotte eighteen months earlier; Lieutenant Bernard Lancelot Pavey; Second Lieutenant Frank Flavell, who was returning after being hit at Ypres a year earlier; and Second Lieutenant William Henry Thomas Cothill, who joined after recovering from gassing in the 4th Bedfordshires in mid-March 1918, which had happened just 8km north-east at Ribécourt-la-Tour. Three more arrived on the 6th: Captain Walter John Campion; Lieutenant Reginald Caldwell-Cook, who had recovered from wounds received in the 6th Bedfordshires fourteen months earlier; and Second Lieutenant William Ross Hope. On the 7th, the 6-foot 2-inch tall Second Lieutenant John Hollingshead joined, along with Claude Oliver Fowler and former 8th Bedfordshires Sergeant Robert Edward Collins. Two days later a final officer draft arrived, this time from the Gloucestershires: Lieutenant Arthur Conrad Holborow; Daniel John Roberts, who had recovered from an injury sustained at Ypres in 1917; and Second Lieutenants Bernard Lionel Walker, Frederick Charles Foote and A.E. Davis.

On 2 October the battalion were given a day to bathe, clean up and relax a little before six days of training resumed in readiness for their next offensive action. Second Lieutenant James Charles Abbott Birch went to the field ambulance ill on 6 October and news arrived two days later that Cambrai had fallen as the Allied advance pushed ever onwards.

News also arrived that Percy Appleby had won the Military Medal for bravery around the Nieppe Forest. Lutonian Percy had been with the battalion since 1916 but was among those wounded in the wood, losing an eye to shrapnel. Two months after his medal was awarded, he would receive his medical discharge papers, along with an army pension, and return to the civilian life he had left when enlisting in 1915.[206]

After their welcomed eight-day spell in reserve, orders came that saw the division moving into the line once more, the Bedfordshires starting a series of marches on the 9th that would take them 30km. Overnight rests at La Vacquerie on the 9th, Esnes on the 10th, and Ligny-en-Cambrésis on the 11th, were followed by a short hop to Caudry the next day, where they would billet in houses until 19 October.

The surviving Old Contemptibles who had arrived in France in August 1914 found themselves within 5km of the very ground they held during the Battle of Le Cateau over four years earlier, their war having taken them on a long, winding tour of northern France and Belgium in the interim.

Curiously to the eyes of those soldiers who were relatively new to the Western Front, Caudry was full of civilians who went about their daily lives, often rebuilding their homes regardless of the activities of the British troops around them. Over four years living behind the German front lines had taught them to simply get on with life, just as the woman who the battalion had watched milking her cow in the open fields during the Battle of Le Cateau had done, calmly ignoring the fighting raging around her.

In another twist, an old friend of the battalion, Lieutenant Colonel Charles Edward Gowran Shearman, rejoined to take over from William Chirnside on 14 October. Lieutenant Colonel Shearman had last been seen in the 1st Bedfordshires when wounded during the Battle of Mons in August 1914; he had served in several battalions in the interval, being mentioned in despatches many times in addition to winning the Distinguished Service Order. Now, at the very end of the war, he had returned to the fold.

Between the routines of fatigues, marches and intensive training that took their time over the next week, several distractions were arranged for the battalion. A church service was held on the 13th, with the usual suspects arranging the battalion concert the following evening. Recently arrived Lieutenant Daniel Roberts was sent home on leave on 18 October but would not return to the battalion again, and a ceremonial parade was arranged for 19 October, with the corps commander presenting medal ribbons to those whose gallantry awards from August and September had already been confirmed. After the parade, the battalion's transport and details were left in Caudry while the rest of the brigade moved off for the front lines once more, through a deluge of rain, resting overnight in Béthencourt, 2km north-east of Caudry.

With local papers at home publishing the growing casualty lists of a war that everyone knew was all but over, almost as many column inches throughout Bedfordshire were being devoted to the second influenza epidemic to spread through Europe in just four months.

Chapter 10

# The Final Advance in Picardy: 17 October to 11 November 1918

*'Their Divl. Commander [had] assured them that they would stay there till the whole Division could be fed from one cooker.'*

As the other major offensives to the north and south continued, the central sector was enjoying just as much success, the entire German line falling back in front of the series of superbly orchestrated and executed attacks. After Cambrai had fallen on 8 October, British and Commonwealth troops had harried the retreating German units until resistance stiffened once more around 20km east of Cambrai, along the River Selle. Co-incidentally, the advance came to a rest on the line of the 1914 retreat from Mons to Le Cateau, while Allied generals reorganised their battle-worn units in readiness for what would be the last series of encounters of the war, collectively known as the 'Final Advance in Picardy'.

On 17 October, the final advance opened with the Battle of the Selle. Rawlinson's Fourth Army attacked on a 13km frontage south of Le Cateau and after two days of heavy fighting had penetrated the German lines to a depth of 7km on the right flank. The assault was widened on 20 October as Horne's First Army and Byng's Third Army attacked north of Le Cateau, with the 5th Division (IV Corps, Third Army) being engaged in the fighting that day.

**The Battle of the Selle: 17 to 25 October 1918**
With the 21st Division to their south and the 42nd to the north, the 5th Division attacked German defensive positions set up on the banks of the Selle, east of Briastre. In heavy rain and through a thick mist, at 2 a.m., the 13th Brigade crossed the river and took up their objective line east of the

railway, with the 95th Brigade moving through and advancing the divisional line on to the ridge 500 metres further east. Fierce resistance
stopped the final bound of their move ahead but at 4 a.m. a fresh barrage
was laid down, enabling the infantry to make it to a line 2.5km east of
the railway line and capture the heights facing Ovillers and Beaurain. As
this was under way, the 15th Brigade shuffled forward into divisional
support, with the Bedfordshires taking up the most advanced brigade
positions in the quarry 1km north-west of Briastre. At 9 a.m. fresh orders
moved them through Briastre, across the river and to positions in direct
support of the 95th Brigade, midway between the railway and ridge.

That afternoon, the rest of the 15th Brigade started off, relieving the
13th Brigade and taking their positions in the villages west of the river,
leaving the 95th in command of the front line and the Bedfordshires in
support of them and temporarily under their orders.

Despite all the preparations for another assault in progress, and the
motivation of the troops being of paramount importance, army discipline still reigned. The date of 21 October saw Lieutenant Leonard
Hobson standing in front of a court martial for two counts of 'conduct
prejudicial to good order and military discipline'; the second count was dismissed
but Leonard was simply reprimanded for the first count and returned to
his company in time for their involvement in the forthcoming battle.[207]

After a wet but unmolested twenty-four hours hidden from German
artillery observers by a low ridge, the Bedfordshires moved forward through
thick mist to the front line at 9 p.m. on the 22nd in readiness for the re-
newed push the next day. Taking up positions along the ridge by 11 p.m.,
the Cheshires established themselves on their left and the Norfolks took

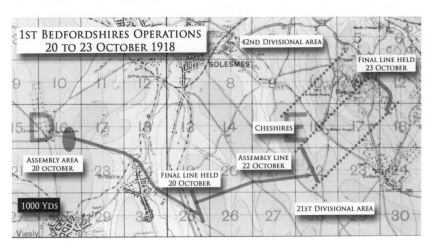

1ST BEDFORDSHIRES OPERATIONS
20 TO 23 OCTOBER 1918

42ND DIVISIONAL AREA

SOLESMES

FINAL LINE HELD
23 OCTOBER

CHESHIRES

ASSEMBLY AREA
20 OCTOBER

ASSEMBLY LINE
22 OCTOBER

FINAL LINE HELD
20 OCTOBER

1000 YDS

21ST DIVISIONAL AREA

over the Bedfordshires' original locations east of the railway line, the brigade's task being to capture Beaurain village as a part of the general advance.

Although not known until prisoners were interviewed after the battle, the German 25th Division had been mauled on 20 October and had been reinforced by the depleted 30th Division and 1st Guards Reserve Division. Significantly, their artillery had been heavily reinforced, the defenders being given explicit orders to hold at all costs and deny the British troops entry into Beaurain and the surrounding villages.

Typical of a growing number of combat veterans, since his arrival in July Second Lieutenant David Lydle had been fulfilling his duties despite suffering from shell shock and 'his nerves', even taking part in the battalion's actions since August. Reports showed that he was *not popular in the Mess but is trying to obtain confidence of the platoon* and interviews with his superiors made it clear that he *would go into action again if required*, even though he felt that he may break down if he did. In the absence of any other support or alternatives, Captain Loe, his company commander, simply said *just do your best* and posted him to the details that were being held back from their next assault. Several officers reported in sick at the last moment before moving forward, leaving Captain Loe with little option but to order Second Lieutenant Lydle forward to lead one of his platoons.[208]

Not long after midnight an SOS flare fizzed into the night sky, followed moments later by a heavy German counter-barrage. The storm hit the brigade's assembly area on the ridge as they were shaking themselves into shape, with both battalions losing a *considerable number of casualties*[209] before the battle had even started, despite having dug in. Forward posts placed by another regiment saw this as the sign of an imminent German counter-attack and sent their own SOS flares into the sky, calling the British barrage down in their defence. Unfortunately, it also hit the brigade's assembly area, leaving the Bedfordshires and Cheshires to soak up punishment from both sides before irate words reached the batteries advising them of their shells falling short. Nevertheless, by 1.15 a.m. both battalions were in position, if badly disorganised from the need to treat and move their casualties, redistribute the remaining officers and NCOs and shuffle men between platoons to balance out the formations.

Acting Captain George Betty had already been wounded while in the ranks of the Australian infantry on Gallipoli before being commissioned into the Bedfordshires. After also recovering from shell shock and an

injury received in the 8th Battalion at Arras, he was certainly accustomed to being under fire, which was to prove invaluable as the heavy deluge
of shells rained down on the waiting troops. Captain Betty had been
moving between the men in his company, reorganising them and calming
them continually, while battalion medical officer Captain Edward Kinsey
performed tirelessly dressing and conveying the wounded to safety from
the opening shots. Captain Kinsey worked in the open for over an hour,
under heavy shell fire himself, becoming the second consecutive medical
officer to win the Military Cross for bravery in such conditions.

At 1.20 a.m. a corps much further south started their own attack, which
brought yet another heavy German barrage down on to their assembly
positions. V Corps to their immediate south next advanced at 2 a.m., in
turn triggering yet another bombardment. In accordance with the
staggered timetable, and having spent most of the preceding hours taking
heavy casualties from artillery fire, the Bedfordshires and Cheshires went
over the top at 3.20 a.m., behind a heavy, rolling barrage of their own,
which started 200 metres in front of their assembly lines and moved forward 100 metres every six minutes.

A Company formed the right half of the battalion lines with C in
assistance, while B Company advanced on the left with D in support of
their attack. With the 7th Leicestershires in the darkness somewhere to
their south and Cheshires to the north, the brigade advanced towards the
ridge 400 metres south-west of Beaurain.

Unbeknown to them, no troops were on their flank and the southerly
companies came under heavy machine-gun fire around the sunken road
running between Solesmes and Ovillers, the German gunners having
a clear line of sight along the road and south-eastern edge of the ridge
and no targets to their front. Momentum on the right was halted and the
protective barrage lost, although the left-hand company continued its
progression towards the village and into the storm of shrapnel. At the
same time, the right company of Cheshires were also stopped by heavy
machine-gun fire from Beaurain, creating a two-pronged advance instead
of the continuous line intended.

Seeing the delay, Lieutenant Colonel Shearman immediately sent
urgent orders to A and C Companies to move forward, using the dubious
cover of the cabbage field they found themselves in and keeping one eye
to their south-east as there were still no British troops on their open right
flank. As they resumed their advance, the companies 200 metres to their
front were about to throw themselves into the second bound of their own

attack, aimed at the village itself.

After a twelve-minute delay to reorganise behind the protective shield of the British barrage, the curtain of shrapnel and high explosives started moving towards the village once more and D Company made their way through B Company into the village itself, with C Company rushing to catch up with them several hundred metres further back.

Company Sergeant Major Frank Mead from Dunstable[210] had already been very busy, as after holding his men together during the intense shelling earlier that morning, his company had been held up by a well-sited machine gun that was sweeping the entire frontage. Gathering a small team to him, he advanced against the position and single handedly knocked it out, thus freeing up his company and saving many casualties.

Of the four tanks assigned to support the attack, two had made it to the village, one working alongside each battalion in clearing stubborn positions. A mixed-up group of Bedfordshires and Cheshires found themselves with a particularly stubborn pocket garrisoning the Red House estaminet and set their minds on silencing the machine guns and rifles bristling from each window. Working their way forward in small groups until within bombing range, they attacked from several sides simultaneously, the entire garrison fighting to the last before being overwhelmed.

Lieutenant Archibald Sheldrake had already guided his company skilfully through the heavy defensive barrage and led them personally into the village itself. By 8 a.m., three muddled-up companies of the Bedfordshires and Cheshires, led by just a handful of officers, were in among the buildings, clearing the defenders with bombs and bayonets, Lieutenant Sheldrake being in the thick of the fighting. Despite the German division being given orders to hold the ground at all costs, they were overwhelmed by the initial waves. The remaining Bedfordshire platoons who had been held up on the right joined the fight around 8.15 a.m. and the Norfolks arrived in force around 8.30 a.m. to help mop up the remaining pockets of resistance. By 9 a.m. runners arrived back at Brigade HQ with the news that all objectives had been achieved.

Once content that his portion of the village was secure and no surprises were left for his men to deal with, Lieutenant Sheldrake made a *'daring reconnaissance when the situation was obscure and obtained valuable information'*, his actions throughout the assault being rewarded with the Military Cross.[211]

CSM Mead, once satisfied that the village defences were in place, also rigorously patrolled in front of the company lines and collected as much information as he could. Passing it back through a series of runners who relayed it to the brigade that were due to take the advance further forward, his reconnaissance enabled their advance to move on as unmolested as possible given the countryside and defences facing them. For his personal gallantry, leadership and the unwavering example of steadiness he displayed throughout the difficult day, Frank Mead was awarded the Distinguished Conduct Medal and, more importantly, survived the war. He had already been wounded twice on the Somme and had survived La Coulotte and Ypres in 1917 without a scratch, going on to serve as a regular warrant officer after hostilities ceased.

Acting Captain Walter Campion's company had been underneath the early morning bombardments, the citation accompanying his Military Cross explaining how '*by his cool courage and leadership he held his company together under very heavy fire. Later, upon the attack being held up, he reorganised the line and broke down the enemy resistance and successfully led the line to the final objective, capturing en route eighty prisoners.*' The 30-year-old former schoolmaster had already been wounded while in the ranks of the Cameron Highlanders at Loos in 1915 before serving in the 8th Bedfordshires once commissioned. He was among those noticeably shaken up by the intensity of the bombardment, but regardless of his own condition led his men through the fighting.

Meanwhile, the 111th Brigade of the 37th Division had moved through the village at 10 a.m. to attack Vendegies-au-Bois, thus taking over from the already exhausted 15th Brigade. The 42nd Division were on their objective to the north but there was no sign of friendly troops to the south, the supporting platoons of Bedfordshires setting up a defensive flank to meet any counter-attacks that might materialise from Ovillers until they arrived later that afternoon.

While occupying the village, standing orders prevailed, warning the British to leave all objects untouched in case of booby traps, and to question the captured garrison regarding the positions of mines and traps.

With the area secure, patrols continually checked the ground around the village, carrying parties were established, food and drink arranged and prisoners sent back to divisional cages for questioning, until orders arrived at 3.30 p.m. to retire to billets in Caudry once more.

Acting Captain George Betty had been in the thick of operations from the initial bombardments that had caused so many casualties, through the hasty reorganisation under fire, into the assault itself. Showing great coolness and devotion to duty, he ensured the attack had been successful and was awarded a Military Cross, receiving it from the King at Buckingham Palace on 5 March 1920.

In addition to the scores of Germans killed in the fighting, eighty-eight prisoners were taken by the Bedfordshires, including three officers. One 77mm gun, three trench-mortar pieces and twenty-four machine guns were also captured.

Interviews with German prisoners taken during the battle[212] gave the Allies an interesting insight into the overall condition of those facing them. Not only was it clear from the lack of rest being allocated to each division that there were no German reserves available, but supplies, rations and equipment were scarce, their horses being exhausted to the state of collapse. Infantrymen were complaining how their own gunners were firing short, the gunners responding that *'complaints are useless as the guns are worn out and unreliable'*. More than that, the disparity between the morale of the opposing armies was enormous. On arrival in the massed prisoner cages, the dishevelled German infantrymen would ask keenly whether it was true that their Kaiser's peace offer had been accepted by the Entente, and whether there was any truth to the explanation that their leave had been cancelled to facilitate the German army's withdrawal as part of the peace treaty.

Perhaps most telling of the remarks gathered from prisoners taken in Beaurain were those from men of the 1st Guard Reserve Division, considered among the elite of the German infantry, whose prowess and morale befitted their elevated status. They *'related with bitterness that, as punishment for retiring at Cambrai, they had been put back into the line in this sector, their Divl. Commander having assured them that they would stay there till the whole Division could be fed from one cooker'*. Their commander's wish had been granted.

Despite the already thinly spread 5th Division losing a further 80 officers and 1,300 men between 20 and 23 October, it was clear that rumours of their adversaries' imminent collapse were true in every respect, which provided an enormous morale boost to the exhausted troops.

The Bedfordshires, once again, suffered heavy casualties from their already badly depleted numbers, losing 10 officers and 134 men during the attack, half of the officers wounded having only joined the battalion in the last month.

Second Lieutenant William Henry Thomas Cothill from Hammersmith was killed, aged 23, having transferred to the battalion just three weeks earlier. With over four years of service behind him, William had suffered from blistered feet and a bout of gassing earlier that year, but the former bank clerk's luck ran out just two weeks before the end of hostilities.

Also killed was Second Lieutenant Claude Oliver Fowler, a former Royal Engineer sergeant who had come to the Bedfordshires days after William Cothill on 7 October.

After just a few days with his old battalion, Lieutenant Colonel Shearman was wounded and would spend the final weeks of the war in a Casualty Clearing Station before returning, leaving the soldiers temporarily in the hands of Major Chirnside once more.

Captain Frederick William Ballance was injured too, having also arrived two weeks earlier.

Second Lieutenant Henry Trasler, a thirteen-year veteran with the regiment and former acting RSM who had won the Distinguished Conduct Medal on Hill 60 in May 1915, was wounded. Henry had earned a commission in the field three months earlier and was hit by a shell fragment in the left thigh, which developed into sceptic arthritis in his knee joint. A year later Henry was retired on account of ill health caused by his injury and lived in Northampton until his death in 1968.

The 6-foot 2-inch tall Second Lieutenant John Hollingshead, who had arrived in the draft with Claud Fowler on 7 October, was *very severely wounded*,[213] suffering from a large shell trauma to his back as well as shell shock. After enlisting in September 1914 and service in the ranks of the 2nd and 4th Bedfordshires, the then Sergeant Hollingshead was commissioned into the 1st Battalion in June 1918. The gaping hole left in his back was severe enough to warrant wearing a supporting corset for the remainder of his life, but it did not seem to stop him too much as John married in 1922 and lived until 80 years old, still being classified as 70 per cent disabled when he passed away.

Second Lieutenant Bernard Lionel Walker had joined the battalion from the Gloucestershires on 9 October and sustained a severe fracture to his left elbow, leaving him 90 per cent disabled up to the time of his death. A former private in the Royal Fusiliers who had joined up in the Derby Scheme of December 1915, Bernard also went on to live a full life, dying the same year as John Hollingshead, aged 76.

Second Lieutenant Stanley George Fisher, a chartered accountant's clerk from St Albans, was also wounded in the left thigh but had recovered by early 1919 and was demobilised.

Second Lieutenant William Walter Humm from Walthamstow was injured, six days after his 22nd birthday.

Battalion chaplain, the Reverend John Bardsley Mayall, was among the casualties, suffering his second hit of the war. After recovering from a 'gutter wound' left by shrapnel at La Coulotte, Reverend Mayall rejoined the battalion in Italy, only to be 'very severely wounded' by a shell fragment.[214] He was attending to those injured by one of the heavy barrages early that morning when he was wounded himself, but carried on as best he could for as long as he could, until carried back from the chaos. John Mayall was the second battalion chaplain to be mentioned in despatches and awarded the Military Cross for bravery, but was demobilised on account of ill health caused by his wounds. The 29-year-old's right thigh, ankle and foot were badly damaged, but he also went on to marry thirteen months later and lived until 1965, dying at the age of 74.

Already suffering from shell shock, Second Lieutenant David Lydle was knocked unconscious and buried by a shell explosion during the assault, later being discovered by an officer from another regiment who helped him back to the field ambulance. After the action, his new company commander, Lieutenant Fyson, interviewed him. Despite making it clear that he was *feeling very war worn*' David was persuaded to remain with the company as *'his services were very valuable'*, although a letter from Lieutenant Colonel Shearman bluntly observed: *'I have now had an opportunity of seeing this officer in action and I consider he is unfitted to hold a commission owing to his total lack of control of men in action.'* Although obviously in a bad way, Second Lieutenant Lydle was one of many officers and men all along the Western Front who the army could simply not afford to lose, especially given how close they were to the final defeat of their enemy. While Second Lieutenant Lydle remained at duty, Second Lieutenant Bernard Lancelot Pavey was taken ill and evacuated.

Casualties among the other ranks reflected the structure of the battalion after four years of warfare. Although some of the Old Contemptibles were still among the ranks, many others had years of active service behind them and, although not pre-war regulars, were still seasoned soldiers nonetheless.

Reuben Jeffries[215] from Sandy had been with the battalion since 1905 and, a veteran of Mons, had already been badly injured. A spell in the 4th Bedfordshires during their assault on Gavrelle in April 1917 had seen Reuben wounded again but not before he had won a DCM by charging and wiping out a particularly dangerous machine-gun post in close combat. Returning to his comrades in the 1st Battalion, Reuben's third time as a casualty had not been lucky, as he was killed on 23 October, despite having come so close to making it through the war.

Herbert Dean,[216] also from Sandy, had been among the pre-war Territorial soldiers in the 5th Bedfordshires invalided from Gallipoli with dysentery and yellow jaundice before transferring to the Western Front in a large draft of former Territorials who had recovered from wounds or illness at the end of 1916. A member of the Sandy church choir, local football team and Sandy Boxing Club, he had been wounded twice by artillery fire in the shoulder, and later in his back. The third time was also not so lucky when a shell fragment hit him in the head, piercing his helmet and killing him instantly.

George Bellamy[217] of St Neots was also one of the fallen, aged 25. Alongside his two brothers George had enlisted in a large recruiting rally in September 1914 and, after training with the newly raised 8th Bedfordshires, had arrived on the Western Front in August 1915. He had been gassed and transferred to the 1st Battalion, only to be killed during the battalion's penultimate attack of the war.

One of the missing was 23-year-old Elstow resident Arthur Cox,[218] whose service went back to the first waves of Kitchener's volunteers in 1914, when he had enlisted into the 7th Bedfordshires. After being among the 57,000 casualties from the opening day of the Battle of the Somme in 1916, Arthur had joined the 1st Battalion and had been awarded a gallantry card for his work during the assault against Oppy Wood. Corporal Cox was among those wounded in the early morning barrages but was later hit a second time, this time fatally. Although initially lost in the darkness and chaos, his body was later found and now lies in the Romeries communal cemetery extension.

William Price was from Ferndale in South Wales and had only joined the battalion in a draft sent over from the Gloucestershires on 6 October. After almost three years of active service, predominantly in the Welsh Regiment, William was injured in the shoulder and found himself back in the UK for treatment on 31 October, his active service complete. He would be issued with a Military Medal in 1919 for gallantry shown during the battle.[219]

Although trying to hold together with impressive courage, the German army was all but broken and would be harassed further east by the pursuing Allied forces. A final German counter-attack in Belgium was repulsed on the 24th, and the Battle of the Selle ended the following day once the Allies had reached their objectives.

News of their imminent defeat spread throughout the German armed forces and the threat of mutiny became tangible. General Ludendorff and Admiral Scheer tried one final attempt to regain Germany's honour by launching a naval offensive without telling Prince Maximillian of Baden, who was provisionally in charge of the government, knowing that he would not countenance such a suicidal act. News of the plan spread, with the sailors refusing to take part and Ludendorff took the blame squarely on his shoulders.

The date of 26 October was the day that General Quartermaster Erich Ludendorff resigned under increasing pressure from Kaiser Wilhelm II, who was becoming desperate to reach an armistice with the Allied powers. With no reserves, food or oil and his entire military organisation on the verge of collapse, the outcome was undeniable and Kaiser Wilhelm II had no options left open to him.

Yet despite this the fighting still raged.

### The Battle of the Sambre: 4 November 1918

The 15th Brigade were relieved and rested, the Bedfordshires returning to billets in Caudry once more, where they remained until 3 November. Even though at rest and away from enemy guns, soldiers were still dying from seasonal illnesses, such as 32-year-old St Albans man George Thatcher,[220] a former Hertfordshire Yeomanry trooper, who died on 2 November from bronchial pneumonia.

After cleaning up, making good deficiencies and reorganising the companies to balance them out as much as was possible, offensive training resumed to improve their ability to operate in the style of open warfare now facing them. Baths, a church service and passes into town broke up their workload, with news arriving that the Ottoman Empire had signed an armistice with Allied forces in the Middle Eastern theatre on 30 October.

In what would be the last large-scale battle of the war, the British First, Third and Fourth Armies were allocated to the attack, with the French First Army in the line to their south also advancing. In the Third Army zone, the objective was a line running roughly from Bavay on the northern fringe, through Pont-sur-Sambre, on to Saint-Remy-Chaussée, some 11km east from their starting lines, much of which was covered by the thick Forêt-de-Mormal (Mormal Forest).

The 37th and New Zealand Divisions started the attack in IV Corps' sector on 4 November, capturing the intermediate line from north-west

of Gommegnies, to a point between Jolimetz and the western edge of
the forest, and continuing to Landrecies. Patrols were sent into the forest
to explore dispositions and defences in readiness for the continued attacks
the following morning, with prisoners captured revealing how a strong
defensive stand was intended in the Forêt-de-Mormal itself.

The Bedfordshires vacated their billets in Caudry on 3 November and
spent that night in Neuville-en-Avesnois, 14km north-east of Caudry.
Another march late on the afternoon of 4 November took them on to
Louvignies-Quesnoy, 6km north-east, where they paused and rested for
several hours. That night news arrived that Austria had joined the growing list of Axis powers to sign an armistice, leaving the German Empire
as the only aggressor facing the Allies.

Overnight, the 5th and 42nd Divisions relieved the 37th and New
Zealanders, the Bedfordshires leaving their billets at 2 a.m. and heading
for their concentration area in the centre of Jolimetz. Of the remaining
Old Contemptibles who took part in the retreat to Paris in August 1914,
the road passing between the village and the forest facing them would
have brought back memories, being the very route the small, tired army
had trudged along on a hot summer's day four years earlier.

The division were to move forward with the 15th Brigade on the left and
the 95th on the right. The East Surreys were furthest south, the Devons
next to them, with the Norfolks allocated to advance alone in the 600-
metre-wide 15th Brigade sector, closely supported by the Bedfordshires.

The beautiful early winter's day of 4 November was replaced with
torrential rain by the time zero hour arrived at 5.30 a.m. on 5 November.
Thirty minutes later the Norfolks passed through the 112th Brigade line,
around 1km inside the forest, while the Bedfordshires moved on to the
Bavay to Le Cateau road and marched north-east along the edge of the
dark, brooding shape of the Forêt-de-Mormal. Turning east, they joined
the mud road running from Herbignies, into the forest and eventually on
to Berlaimont some 9km further on. As they ventured through the 112th
Brigade lines, the battalion saw how extensively the Germans had been
felling trees during their occupation, as vast swathes of open ground and
undergrowth faced them where once there had been a thick forest.

The Norfolks reached their objective of the star-shaped intersection in
the middle of the forest with little sign of the enemy. Straddling the intersection, the Bedfordshires reorganised into open order, fixed bayonets, and
passed through the Norfolks for the next phase of their advance. Moving
in an east-south-east direction as dawn broke, they passed through one

intact section of dense forest 1,200 metres deep, crossed a track and a 200-metre stretch of undergrowth before reaching the eastern edge of the forest by 8 a.m. Once the Bedfordshires had disappeared into the wood, the Norfolks were immediately withdrawn into brigade reserve and just after 9 a.m. the Cheshires arrived in support of the Bedfordshires, taking up the line vacated by the Norfolks.

As they moved through the forest, groups of German soldiers put up sporadic resistance, including several machine-gun teams. D Company's Owen Brown of Letchworth[221] was in charge of a Lewis-gun team who were fired upon by an opposing team as they advanced. He brought his own gun to bear and while organising their assault, was severely wounded and rushed back to the dressing station in Jolimetz. Well known locally in football and hockey circles, Owen had enlisted in September 1914 and initially served in the 8th Bedfordshires. He died from his wounds, aged 24, within sight of the end of the war. Today he lies in the Jolimetz communal cemetery, the only British soldier interred there.

Reorganising on the perimeter of the forest, the Bedfordshires linked up with the DCLI to their south but there was no sign of the New Zealanders to the north. Nevertheless, the division resumed their advance but, after breaking from the cover of the trees and appearing in the open farmland to the east, came under heavy machine-gun fire from several buildings and one large concrete blockhouse. Moving forward by sections in short bursts, the Bedfordshires and DCLIs made it across the open ground with remarkably light casualties and overran the positions in their path, some thirty dead German troops being counted after the fighting had died down.

The Bedfordshires' objective, being the line between Embu Farm and La Porquerie, had still not been secured and with news arriving of the New Zealand Division's appearance to their north, Brigade HQ pushed the Cheshires in to turn the flank of the well-protected German gunners in their concrete enclosure. The Cheshires manoeuvred into a flanking position to the north of the Bedfordshires and, with both battalions rising, they reached their objective by 4 p.m.

The Cheshires then moved on to a further objective along the road between Pont-sur-Sambre and Bavay, pushing out patrols towards the river as the DCLI entered Pont-sur-Sambre itself, both coming under heavy shell and machine-gun fire. By 8 p.m. the divisional line had been secured and the infantry and artillery established their positions while the engineers eyed up their next task of crossing the well-defended river.

Other than dozens of prisoners taken by the Bedfordshires during their 9km advance through the forest and subsequent fighting, a six-inch naval gun was also captured, for the loss of seven men, which included pre-war regular Thomas Haynes. A plumber from Highgate, Thomas had enlisted into the regiment behind Henry Downes in June 1913, aged 18, the two becoming good friends until Henry's death on Hill 60 in 1915. Out since Mons, he had already been wounded in April 1915 and again at Falfemont Farm in September 1916, his final injury in the shoulder being mercifully light. Thomas married his old pal Henry's sister, Alice, on Christmas Day 1919 and continued serving as a regular soldier until moved into the reserves in June 1920, his time there coming to a close five years later.[222]

Throughout 6 November the Cheshires held the brigade front, with the Bedfordshires in support and providing carrying parties, while the Norfolks remained in reserve at La Haute Rue. The retreating Germans had destroyed every bridge and crossing, mining each railway or road junction as they came across it, and flooding roads and tracks at every opportunity, doing their best to delay the pursuing troops. All day German machine-gun and artillery fire swept the division's lines as they tried to build and deploy a pontoon bridge to cross the river, with the Bedfordshires' positions in La Porquerie being so heavily shelled that they were forced to retire from the hamlet twice during the day, losing thirteen men in the process.

The 24-year-old William Jones from Wolverhampton[223] was the last man in the battalion to be killed instantly, when he was hit during the heavy shelling.

Sidney Bryant from Pulborough in Sussex[224] had been among the 'A4s', conscripted into the army as soon as he reached 18. Sidney died from his wounds in hospital at Rouen that day, having been with the battalion only a matter of weeks.

Perhaps the most poignant of those lost in the closing days of the war was Watford resident George Neale,[225] who had been with the battalion since 1912 as a scout and had fought with them from the opening shots at Mons. Despite surviving the entire war and being awarded a gallantry card for bravery at Oppy Wood in 1917, Sergeant Neale was fatally injured during the last day of hostile fire his battalion were subjected to and was buried at the temporary dressing station at Fontaine-au-Bois.

The following day Arthur Newton from Norfolk[226] succumbed to his wounds at the Casualty Clearing Station in Caudry, and Edward

Lawson,[227] who had joined the battalion just a fortnight earlier, was also sent to the CCS feeling poorly. The following day the 19-year-old lad from Sandy died from the second rampant strain of influenza that was spreading throughout Europe, the news reaching his parents as the country celebrated Armistice Day.

On 7 November two companies of the Cheshires crossed the river north of Pont-sur-Sambre, with the entire Norfolk battalion following up in support of them, and the 95th Brigade passing through to take Fontaine. Although held on alert, the Bedfordshires remained in their positions as brigade support, were completely ignored by the German gunners, and were not called forward other than to provide working parties.

The next day saw the brigade relieved and moved into divisional reserve, with the 95th Brigade taking over the fighting front and resuming the pursuit across open countryside, followed a day later by the entire corps being replaced and transferred into army reserve. On the 10th, the Bedfordshires moved into billets in Jolimetz to make good deficiencies, clean up and do what they could to dry out their sodden clothes.

Given the difficulties faced by the brigade in the ground advanced over, and conducting a difficult river crossing under heavy fire, casualties were incredibly light during the four-day operation, less than one hundred officers and men being lost from the entire brigade.

In Douglas Haig's despatches the following July, four of the battalion were mentioned for gallantry shown in the final actions: Company Sergeant Major John Ryan;[228] Corporal James Tuckey from Irchester;[229] Alfred McDougall from Manchester, who had joined the battalion in July 1917 among a draft from the Essex Cyclists and was wounded in the chest and abdomen on 5 November;[230] and pre-war veteran Private 10346 James William Smith, who was also cited for the second time, the first being for service while in Italy.[231] Having been wounded at Le Cateau in August 1914, it was perhaps fitting that his war ended with a mention of gallantry almost within sight of where he was injured over four years earlier.

News also arrived that day of a German general on his way to Compiègne under a white flag, which created no more enthusiasm among the exhausted soldiers than a few grunts and some raised eyebrows.

# Chapter 11

# Armistice and beyond

*'May your pride in your achievements be as great as mine is in the recollection of having commanded the Army in which you have served.'*

After the loss of over six million casualties, with no allies left in the war and having exhausted every resource available to them other than their soldiers' courage, Germany sued for peace. Initial approaches to the American President Wilson had been made in the hope that more favourable terms of surrender could be reached than the unconditional surrender insisted by the French. In reply, Wilson demanded that Kaiser Wilhelm II abdicate. Philipp Scheidmann declared Germany the Weimar Republic on 9 November, the Kaiser fled to Holland and Imperial Germany was no more.

Two days later, in a railroad carriage in the forest of Compiègne, the armistice was signed. With effect on the eleventh hour on the eleventh day of the eleventh month, troops on both sides would cease fire, the Allies holding their positions while the German armies retired back to Germany. Nevertheless, fighting continued that morning in spite of the news, with the last Allied soldier reportedly killed being Canadian Private George Price, who was hit by a German sniper at 10.58 a.m. while the 3rd Canadian Division captured Mons.

Formally, a state of war existed beyond the armistice, until a series of treaties were concluded between 1919 and 1923 that finally brought hostilities to a close.

In the fifty-one months the war had been raging, the combined Allied (Entente) forces lost almost ten million military personnel and civilians killed and missing, with close to thirteen million more having been wounded. In contrast, the Axis (Central) powers had seen around eight million killed with a similar number injured.

On the home front, the news was greeted with rapturous enthusiasm. Local papers reported on the peel of village church bells, with crowds gathering in towns and cities to celebrate the news of the armistice. Thanksgiving services were well attended throughout the country, all sizes of Union and other flags appeared at numerous windows, and im-promptu patriotic choruses could be heard in town centres, outside fac-tories and wherever there was a gathering that included someone willing to burst into song. Even Second Lieutenant Adlam, a Victoria Cross winner from the 7th Bedfordshires, remarked how he was so caught up in the celebrations in Cambridge Market Square that he shimmied up the flagpole before realising how high he had climbed and freezing with fear. The crowd of revellers in Ampthill became so carried away that '*a brewery dray, making its way from Bedford Street, met with an enthusiastic reception from the soldiers, who started to tug at the barrels of beer*', forcing the drayman to beat a hasty retreat back to the brewery he had left moments earlier.[232]

By complete contrast, in the 5th Division billeting area, news arrived at 8 a.m. on 11 November that a ceasefire would come into effect three hours later. Runners were urgently despatched with orders to carry the tidings to each battalion with all speed, but the atmosphere was al-together more sober: '*There was hardly any cheering; indeed the news was received with apathy and perhaps a tinge of disappointment. … When compared with the hysterical excitement and joy which characterised the receipt of the news at home, the callous manner with which it was greeted by those closely concerned may appear strange. The lifting of the ever present cloud of death, which had been before them for four and a half years, was not at first apparent to the muddy, rain soaked, and exhausted troops.*'[233]

An unheard-of silence descended over the scarred battlefields running between the North Sea and Switzerland, unnerving many veterans who had become accustomed to the sporadic shelling and almost constant, distant sounds of gunfire.

**Occupation and demobilisation: 11 November 1918 to April 1919**
That afternoon the Bedfordshires collected their belongings and moved back through the forest into billets at Louvignies-Quesnoy, where they remained until a further move took them to Ramponeau, just outside Le Quesnoy. Training and sports were organised to keep the men occupied and the Third Army commander, Sir Julian Byng, sent the following

complimentary message to all ranks: *'Since 21st August you have won eighteen decisive battles, you have driven the enemy back over 60 miles of country, and you have captured 67,000 prisoners and 800 guns. That is your record, gained by ceaseless enterprise, your indomitable energy, and your loyal support to your leaders. … May your pride in your achievements be as great as mine is in the recollection of having commanded the Army in which you have served.'*

As if to dampen enthusiasm for the end of the war, at home that November, local and national newspapers were full of deaths caused by the new influenza epidemic. 'Spanish flu', as it was known, was nicknamed as such purely because neutral Spain was the first European country to record influenza deaths publicly as no media blackout existed there. However, the reality was that many other European countries were already suffering from the pandemic by then but were unable and unwilling to admit it in a time of war. The first wave had started to take its toll on the elderly and infirm in June 1918, but the more devastating second wave in the autumn affected predominantly younger people. In France it became clear that from August a new strain was wreaking havoc on the armies and civilian populations of both sides, exacerbated by closely grouped units of soldiers and the constant movement and resulting transmission of the virus across large distances. By the end of 1918, the virus had all but abated in Europe but was still being attributed to deaths as late as 1920. Estimates vary as keeping accurate records was almost impossible, but it is generally considered that between fifty and one hundred million people died, making it one of the largest natural disasters in history.

Back in France, inspections and preparations for a proposed move to Germany created a stir as the entire battalion smartened itself up in readiness, with Lieutenant Colonel Shearman rejoining from the Casualty Clearing Station on 19 November. A short move into billets in Le Quesnoy itself came on the 20th, where they would remain until mid-December, training, and being introduced to educational schemes as part of the demobilisation process. Plenty of recreation, sports and passes into town kept the men occupied outside of training regimes, and officer drafts joined to make their numbers up.

Over the coming weeks, news arrived that three of the battalion's Old Contemptibles had been awarded Distinguished Conduct Medals.

Acting RSM George Illot from Hertford had added the DCM to his Military Medal from Oppy Wood, the citation accompanying the award reading: *'For conspicuous gallantry and devotion to duty. After three unsuccessful attempts had been made to deliver a message during an action he went forward, through a heavy machine-gun barrage, collected the necessary information, and returned with it to battalion headquarters. Later, when part of the line was held up, by his example of courage and determination he succeeded in leading the attack forward.'*[234]

Corporal Jack Pennycook from Wootton Green was awarded his *'for conspicuous gallantry and devotion to duty during an enemy attack. He so distributed his platoon as to protect the left flank of his battalion, and successfully beat off three determined attacks on his position. By his fine leadership and cool courage under the hottest close-range fire he set a splendid example to his men.'* [235]

A further well-earned DCM was awarded to Acting Company Sergeant Major Joshua Trundley from Hampton Wick, his citation explaining how *'during operations he continually exposed himself under intense fire, dressing wounded and placing them under cover, at the same time carrying out his duties as Acting CSM with the greatest efficiency. Later, he assisted in reorganisation, and his fearless bearing materially assisted in keeping up the spirits of his men.'* [236]

Captain James Charles Abbott Birch rejoined from sick leave on the 21st, along with Second Lieutenant Keith William Pittman Harvey, who returned from the field ambulance. Seven more officers also arrived over the next week: Captain Howard Watson Wright, having previously served in the 1st, 5th, 6th and 8th Battalions of the regiment; Lieutenant Julian Kelk, formerly of the Royal Field Artillery and Bedfordshire Yeomanry; Lieutenant Archibald Young, after recovering from a wound sustained in the 2nd Bedfordshires and several subsequent operations; Lieutenant Robert Hall, after narrowly escaping death in February 1917 while in the 4th Bedfordshires, which was followed by a long illness attributed to his head wound; Lieutenant Mervyn Ernest Alexander Farr, from the Royal Field Artillery; Second Lieutenant John Critchley Taylor, from the 2nd Bedfordshires; and Second Lieutenant Ernest Charles Herberg, after recovering from his wound six months earlier.

HM the King passed through Le Quesnoy on 1 December, returning the following day from other engagements as he toured the area and visited his troops. A ceremonial parade saluted the King the next day, followed by the entire brigade being inspected by a royal party on 4 December, comprised of the King, the Prince of Wales and Prince Albert. The Bedfordshires and Norfolks lined the streets of Le Quesnoy near the Landrecies Gate and the Cheshires formed up in the town square, while the brigade were turned out again the following day to line the streets as the royal party drove through the town on the way to their next port of call.

Training, lectures and recreation resumed until orders arrived that would take the battalion 100km north-east to their new station in Belgium.

Under the terms of the armistice, the Second Army were transported into Germany to occupy the Cologne bridgehead, with the Fourth Army, including the 5th Division, moving into support on the line between Avesnes, Maubeuge, Charleroi and Brussels. As part of the relocation, the 5th Division were ordered to positions in the Gembloux area, 35km south-east of Brussels.

A series of route marches took the Bedfordshires to what would be their final destination of the war, with the inhabitants at every stop doing their best to make the troops welcome and as comfortable as possible. Overnight stops at Bellignies (3km north-west of Bavay), Neuf-Mesnil (west of Maubeuge) and Rousies led to them crossing into Belgium on the 16th and billeting in Croix-lez-Rouveroy for two nights before moving on once more. Resting in Haine-St-Pierre, south of La Louviere on the 18th, and 6km north-east at Manage the following night, another 12km march north-east in the northern European winter on 20 December ended with a welcome and inspirational sight.

Before sunrise on 18 December, some 400km to the north-west, a party of soldiers in dress uniform had assembled in the barracks at Kempston. After one final inspection of the group, the treasured colours of the 1st Bedfordshires had been brought, still encased, from their home of the last four years in the officers' mess. Once unfurled, they were ceremonially passed from the steps of the Keep to Second Lieutenants Archibald Sheldrake and Philip Odell, the colour-bearers, and paraded on the square behind the Keep. To the sound of the regimental march, 'La Mandolinata', the escort party presented arms before the parade marched past to salute the colours and send them on their way. Led by the band, the colour party marched to the railway station, where they boarded the 8.20 a.m. train and began their long journey to 'somewhere in France'.[237] Three of the battalion's Military Medallists completed the colour party, having arrived at Kempston on the 17th from France: CSM Harry Allison, MM; Sergeant Arthur Faulder, MM and Bar; and Sergeant Alfred Joseph Sale, MM.

After two days of travelling to meet the 1st Battalion, the colour party greeted the marching men as they reached their latest billets in Nivelles, less than 10km south of the famous Waterloo battlefield.

A 20km march along the Namur Road, passing the famous Waterloo battle site of Quatre Bras on the way, was rewarded with an overnight rest at Sombreffe on the 21st, before one last 8km march north-east that saw the battalion reach Gembloux. On arrival at the town limits, the colours were unfurled and, along with the band, led the Bedfordshires into the centre. Officers mounted their horses, gleaming bayonets were unsheathed and not a creased uniform was anywhere in sight as the entire brigade marched crisply past the saluting platform in the town centre, to the delight of the local inhabitants. With the pomp and ceremony completed, the men settled into their billets and were pleasantly surprised with how comfortable they were going to be over the winter.

The battalion was also unexpectedly reunited with another old friend, not seen for over four years. When Pâturages was recaptured in November 1918, the 63rd Divisional commander, General Nelson, happened to lodge in the house of a lady called Madame Chanoines. She told him of how she had kept something of value safe, as requested by a battle-worn British sergeant on 24 August 1914. When asked to explain further, she presented the 1st Bedfordshires' regimental drum, having hidden it in a hat box to keep it from sight of the constant stream of German soldiers who had billeted in her home throughout the occupation. Knowing that Major General Henry Jackson was commanding the 50th Division in the area and further knowing how he had served in the Bedfordshires during 1914, the story was relayed. General Jackson was so delighted that he rushed to the house and promised that a replica would be made and presented to her in gratitude, as it was the only battalion drum to have survived the retreat from Mons in 1914. Drummer Smith, the original owner of the drum, had survived and was reunited with it in time for a ceremonial parade a month later in Namur. Remarkably, this prized drum still takes pride of place in ceremonial parades today, holding the rear right flank position of the Escort to the Colours and being carried by the Mons Drummer of the 2nd Battalion, the Royal Anglian Regiment.

Over the next few days, divisional transport arrived in dribs and drabs, but most units had to wait until after Christmas Day for their dinners. The local roads were in such bad repair, having seen huge migrations of troops and civilians moving along them in recent weeks, that even the most experienced of transport officers were having a dreadful time making progress. After the festive break, training resumed and the 'Inter company association league football competition' started in earnest, while the first half of January saw leave to Brussels extended to all ranks.

Lieutenant George Colby Sharpin of Bedford, whose birthday was two days before the armistice and who had been with the battalion continuously since July 1916, was awarded the Military Cross in the New Year's honours list. He would be back in England in time for it to be presented to him by the King at Buckingham Palace on 31 May 1919.

Among those mentioned in despatches from the New Year was Second Lieutenant Howard George Baker, who had been with the battalion from 30 August 1917. Born on New Year's Day in 1890, Howard had been a commercial clerk from Stoke Newington before the war and initially enlisted into the ranks under the Derby Scheme of December 1915. He had served in several battalions of the regiment in France before being commissioned in July 1917. His actions throughout the final year of the war did not go unnoticed and Howard was discharged from the army in March 1919, fully fit despite the service he had been through.

While the 1st Bedfordshires remained in their winter station at Gembloux, several of their former comrades, some not seen for over four years, started returning home from captivity. Local newspapers were filled with stories of 'Hun brutality',[238] although others interviewed did not recall a single example of bad treatment from their captors.

Kempston's first prisoner to return home was Arthur Austin,[239] who was among those wounded and captured at La Bassée in October 1914. The Mons veteran *'received a warm welcome from friends and neighbours, and flags were flying from the windows of the houses'*. Among descriptions of life with no food or water, little shelter and being worked hard day after day, he relayed stories of how singing the national anthem enraged their guards to such an extent that they fired on them and bayoneted several of the prisoners, killing two and wounding four. Parcels were confiscated for the slightest offence and the only newspapers they saw were those they bribed their guards for, using soap sent from home to barter, as no soap had been seen in Germany for some time.

Frank Watson of Arlesey[240] had also been wounded and captured in September 1914 and returned home to share stories of being among *'that band of 500 British soldiers who were sent into the firing line in the Riga district, the Huns claiming that German prisoners were sent into the zone on the Western Front'*. None the worse for wear despite having suffered from frozen feet after his spell in the Russian front line, Frank had spent the rest of his war in the Berlin gas works.

When the local reporter turned up to interview another 1914 prisoner at his home in Baldock, Norman Howe[241] was *'sitting by the fireside, looking remarkably well considering the awful conditions under which he has lived for the last four years. He spoke of his sufferings without emotion, or, what is still more remarkable, without anger.'* Captured during the battalion's determined stand in the woods east of Ypres on 7 November 1914, the *'typical British Tommy and a man of whom we may well be proud'* told of their journey into captivity and how their trucks were decorated with a placard reading 'English Swine'. At each station, the civilians attacked the prisoners, forcing them into the back of the cattle trucks, but, being so crowded, someone always got hurt. Coal mines, farms and building work filled Norman's time in Germany, although his determination not to be treated unfairly led to a beating from the guard, who subsequently ended up in prison for brutality himself. Now a marked man, he was beaten, provoked and *'tied up, suspended from the ground, in the snow and cold, for two hours'*. Norman witnessed two prisoners with double pneumonia being forced into a cold bath in the snow, from which they died, in addition to an Irish Guardsman being unexpectedly shot and the guard being awarded the Iron Cross. Like so many of his peers, *'his experiences were related in a quiet, casual manner, without a trace of bitterness, but it was apparent that the memory of his taste of hell will never be forgotten'*.

Thursday 9 January 1919 became an important day for the former prisoners of war when 184 repatriated POWs were treated to a banquet at the Bedford Corn Exchange to celebrate their return home.[242] Initial plans only to include those within ten miles of Bedford were soon proven to be ambitious, as the old comrades from all over the county rallied around to enjoy being reunited with their chums once again. Hosted by the Bedfordshire Regiment's Prisoner of War Committee, which had been actively sending every ounce of help and support it could to those county men interred abroad for over four years, an array of local and regional dignitaries were present including the Lord Lieutenants of Bedfordshire and Huntingdonshire, and the Mayor of Bedford, in addition to senior regimental staff and officers from the regimental depot. Relatives and friends of the soldiers crowded into the few free spaces around the room and were joined by those who had 'adopted' the POWs and sent parcels to them regularly, while the 184 guests of honour thoroughly enjoyed a dazzling array of foods, drinks, cigars and treats. Speeches flowed, as did the wine, ale and port, followed by *'a splendid concert programme'*, with each of the men being presented with a pocket knife and case, both being inscribed with the date of the armistice.

With talk of local elections and arrangements for war memorials filling column inches in the county newspapers, the Bedfordshires in Belgium, like the rest of the army, started becoming restless. Concerned that the jobs at home were all being taken, and driven by the wish to return to family and civilian life, those not intending to make soldiering their chosen profession after the war were keen to return home. Although not the case in the Bedfordshires' area, increasing unhappiness with the sluggish rate of demobilisation boiled over into near riotous situations in various camps throughout France and Belgium. Distractions of every kind were built into their routines, with daily sporting events taking place every afternoon, weather permitting.

On 10 January group and individual photographs of the officers and NCOs were taken, although five days later, one of those in the group photos left the battalion on the grounds of ill health. Lieutenant Robert Hare was invalided home still suffering from the recurring problem of neurasthenia that had plagued him since 1917 – even though he had carried on performing his duties and tried to ignore the ailment – but in December he was retired because of it. He subsequently bought a business in Bedford, but six years later applied for employment at the War Office when the economy took a turn for the worst. In Robert's place in the battalion, Lieutenant John Kingdon rejoined from his posting to the Fifth Army School, although he would be released from service a fortnight later.

Another case of ongoing, untreated, neurasthenia came to a head on 13 January when Canadian-born Lieutenant William Hope, who had been in charge of the 5th Divisional railhead since before Christmas, was found to be AWOL [243] when his relieving officer arrived to take over duties. William had served as a Canadian mounted policeman for ten years before enlisting when war broke out and had seen combat in King Edward's Horse before being commissioned in 1917. Joining the 7th Bedfordshires in October 1917, he disappeared for eight days until found drunk, having *'got some bad news from home'*, after which he *'gave way to the alcohol'*. The medical officer's examination concluded he was *'suffering from delirium and tremors'*, his body showed the *'effects of over indulgence for a prolonged period'* and after a short time under medical observation, William was released to the battalion, only to be gassed eleven days later and returned to England. While in the 3rd Bedfordshires, William was kept on report, his *'continued zeal and self restraint'* being noted and influencing the board to treat him with leniency. The matter was closed and he arrived with the 1st Bedfordshires early in October 1918, two weeks later being subjected to the intense bombardment as the battalion assembled ready for their assault on 23 October. Although he survived unscathed and continued about his business, fellow officers later remarked that he was 'strange' afterwards, but did not dwell on it, having seen it so many times in their comrades before. After his absenteeism was reported in January, Lieutenant

Hope was found *'extremely drunk'* in a civilian's home in Gembloux and on 3 March was tried by courts martial for drunkenness, being unfit for duty, going AWOL for one week, and the matter of 9,950 Francs that was unaccounted for from the divisional railhead kitty. In spite of his fellow officers' evidence of the change to his character since October, he was found guilty of all charges and cashiered, but when the file was passed to the Judge Advocate General's desk in June, the matter was reopened. The Secretary of State personally quashed the findings that month, based on his *'medical problems and mental instability'* at the time of the offences and a letter was hurriedly sent to his home in Canada. Remarkably, William had already enlisted for service in the ranks in the north Russian campaign by the time the letter arrived.[244]

On 24 January their divisional commander visited and two days of rehearsal for an upcoming ceremony followed. On the 28th, a ceremonial parade took place in the Place St Aubyn, Namur, where the Bedfordshires and King's Own Scottish Borderers trooped their colours in commemoration of the two battalions being involved in the capture of the citadel way back in 1695. The IV Corps commander, Lieutenant General Harper, reviewed the parade, with the Bedfordshires' party comprised of Captain James Birch as the officer commanding the colour guard, Lieutenant Archibald Young acting as the lieutenant of the escort, Second Lieutenant Ernest Herberg being the second lieutenant for the colour and CSM Frank Mead being the NCO for the colour.

More photographs of the battalion and the colour guard were taken the next day and on 3 February trucks were arranged to take one hundred men to the Waterloo battlefield.

On 28 January, three days after his 20th birthday, Second Lieutenant Lawrence Cale was admitted to the local hospital with influenza and diarrhoea. Although remaining in Belgium, he was among the many thousands of soldiers taken ill with the latest strain sweeping Europe and spent much of his remaining service in and out of local hospitals, finally returning to England with the last divisional draft in April 1919 and transferring into the regiment's Territorial reserve of officers later that year.

The Lena Ashwell concert party performed in the Hotel De Ville on 9 February, and cross-country racing on 19 February saw the battalion win the competition and add another cup to their cabinet, with the individual winners each receiving a medal.

In response to the growing unrest among the Allied troops and following an intense period of several weeks of demobilisation drafts leaving for home, the process was practically completed by 22 February. Four days later, Lieutenant Leonard Hobson, one other officer and 143 men were transferred to the 11th Suffolks, who formed part of the Army of the Rhine, and at the end of March more of the battalion were moved to the Bedfordshire Brigade within the army of occupation. Lieutenant Colonel Shearman arrived at the 53rd Bedfordshires, with Captains George Betty, Wilfred Hobbs and Walter Campion, along with Second Lieutenants Frank Whateley-Knight and Robert Hall becoming part of the 52nd Bedfordshires. Acting Captain Arthur Fyson also joined them and was mentioned in despatches in July 1919.

Notices appeared in the *London Gazette* between February and July, listing more Military Medals issued to men from the 1st Bedfordshires, for gallantry during the final operations of the war. Four sergeants were honoured in the 11 February edition: Arthur Boston from Highams Park in London; [245] Alfred Coxall from East Ham, who had originally served in the battalion between November 1902 and November 1915, being recalled again under the new military service acts in the summer of 1917; [246] Frederick Faulder of Wantage, who had been with the regiment since 1901 and had landed in France in the first reinforcement draft on 30 August 1914; [247] and Alexander Lasenby, a resident of Kensal Green who had joined the battalion at the end of April 1915 and had been thrown straight into the brutal fighting for Hill 60. [248]

On 14 May, five more additions to the list of battalion honours were confirmed: Acting Lance Corporal Gilbert Robinson from Soham, who had been with the battalion since February 1911 and had been in the first wave to land in France in August 1914; [249] Acting Lance Corporal Thomas Shadbolt of Welwyn, who had survived on the front lines since the end of 1915; [250] John Bussingham of Oundle, who had enlisted in February 1915; [251] Derby Scheme enlister Henry O'Shea from Wealdstone, who had served in the Hertfordshires before joining the 1st Bedfordshires; [252] and John Fox from Redbourne, who had joined the regiment at the end of August 1914 and arrived with the 1st Battalion on the front in March 1915. John's Military Medal was won while recovering two wounded comrades from the open under fire, himself being injured in the process. After the war, he returned to his printing job, even acting as the local lollipop man after his retirement. [253]

The 17 June edition recorded five privates whose Military Medals had been confirmed: Richard Hoar from Hemel Hempstead, who had already won his first Military Medal at La Coulotte in April 1917, now adding a bar to the ribbon for his work as a stretcher-bearer;[254] Percy How, also a resident of Hemel Hempstead, who had answered his country's call to arms in September 1914, joining the 1st Bedfordshires on Hill 60 in April 1915;[255] Walter Hare of Hitchin, who had enlisted in January 1915 and initially served in the 2nd Bedfordshires from August of that year;[256] St Ives resident William Jakes, who had been on the Western Front since July 1915;[257] and Sidney Jasper of Fakenham, who had initially served in the 7th Bedfordshires from December 1914.[258]. The last two privates to be awarded with Military Medals were recorded in July 1919: James Clifton from Hemingford Grey, who had joined up just before the Derby Scheme in November 1915;[259] and pre-war reservist George Wilby from Irchester, whose foreign service had started in November 1914 when he had joined the 2nd Bedfordshires as a replacement for their heavy losses during the First Battle of Ypres.[260]

Even though the fighting had been over for many months, the effects of being under such extreme stress continued to show. In May 1919, Captain Walter Campion started displaying the signs of severe shell shock, delayed since being under the intense bombardment in October 1918 when he had won his Military Cross. Several medical boards differed in opinion, but Walter was pale, anaemic, constantly fatigued and experiencing vague pains all over his body. Suffering from insomnia, tension, trembling and with a poor appetite, he was observed as being subjected to unexpected jerking of his knees and other joints and was very jumpy at the most innocuous noises around him. He was returned to the UK in July, relinquished his commission on grounds of ill health that November, but lived until his 80th year, dying in 1968.

Among those being demobilised was the well-known Master Cook Bertie Washington, winner of the Distinguished Conduct Medal. He was released after twenty-one years of service in February 1919 but died in Wandsworth just six years later, aged only forty-five.

The first in a series of moves that would conclude in England began on 6 April, when the remaining officers and men moved to Gilly. While waiting for further orders, Captain William Searle left for the 52nd Bedfordshires on the Rhine on 9 April and two days later Second Lieutenant Ernest Howlett left for England. Second Lieutenants Lawrence Cale and Ernest Robinson joined the 5th Divisional Details Battalion, which formed what was left of the entire division.

Remarkably, Second Lieutenant David Lydle was still in post despite the length of his illness and the apparently negative opinions he had been exposed to from his superiors. His requests to resign had been in hand since mid-November 1918 yet he found himself in the final cadre of officers leaving for home shores in April. David's retirement was finally sanctioned in June, but two months later he had still not heard defini-tively, the tone of his letters to the War Office losing their politeness with every passing month. Remarking how it was a *'disgraceful way to be treated'* in his final communiqué with the War Office, Second Lieutenant Lydle's retirement was finalised in August and he returned to civilian life, still carrying three pieces of shrapnel in his chest from Trônes Wood three years earlier. [261]

The details marched to Hauteville station on the 17th, and were moved by train to Charleroi, then on to the Embarkation Camp in Antwerp by 7 a.m. on 18 April. Twelve days of waiting and amusing themselves in the camp and surrounding city followed, before the remaining Bedfordshires finally headed for England on 30 April 1919.

## The return of the Bedfords: 28 April to July 1919

The remnants of the battalion who had gone to France with the original British Expeditionary Force in 1914, bolstered by a selection of medal winners still actively serving, gathered at the Keep in Kempston and marched into Bedford on Monday 28 April 1919. The new regimental flag was unfurled and with the massed bands of the 1st and 2nd Battalions assembled to lead the parade, bayonets were fixed, ranks were dressed and Bandmasters Vince and Baxter set the procession on its way with a rousing delivery of 'La Mandolinata'. [262]

Around eighty soldiers formed the initial company, with fourteen of their old comrades bringing up the rear, but by the time the procession reached St Paul's Church in the centre of town, so many discharged soldiers had tagged on to the column that they far outnumbered those still in uniform. A local reporter [263] recorded how *'the delight of many of the old soldiers to "follow the band" once more was obvious, and one could not help ad-miring the way one ex-Bedford stumped along with his peg-leg. The first great cheer awaited the heroes as they emerged from the gates, to where Kempston had gathered in an enthusiastic crowd. Kiddies ran alongside waving miniature Union Jacks.'*

Local papers had announced the impending return of their senior county battalion as early as a fortnight before they physically arrived, so the procession was greeted by many thousands of well wishers who blocked every street and window along their course. Resembling an American ticker-tape parade, the entire route of march was a riot of colour and buntings, with the thronging crowd cheering continuously as they passed, then following on behind in their wake. The reporter, caught up in the celebrations, wrote how *'the original procession itself became only the centre of a great, moving mass of people'*. Crossing the bridge and proceeding into Midland Road, they passed the 5th Bedfordshires' 'Yellow Devils' flag, unfurled in their own salute to the senior battalion.

On reaching the High Street where the waiting crowd was the largest, the volume of cheering intensified to a deafening roar yet, miraculously, the mass of bodies parted to allow the soldiers through. The parade passed Shire Hall, before coming to a stop outside the Town Hall, where they were greeted by the Mayor and Corporation, Lord Ampthill, Major Bassett and many others. Entering St Paul's Church to the national anthem, the colour party took their post on the chancel steps and a mass of soldiers, ex-servicemen and well wishers quickly filled every available space, both seated and standing. The regimental chaplain, Reverend Landers, took the short service before the procession resumed its journey to the Corn Exchange. So many thousands had filled St Paul's Square that it took some time for the police to clear a path for the procession but, at length, the men formed up in a double line in front of the Corn Exchange, the King's and regimental colours unfurled for all to see in the bright sunshine.

Once settled, the Mayor gave a speech before the procession retired into the Corn Exchange for an official luncheon, the men being waited on by the *'Mothers of the regiment'*, formed by a willing group of army officers' mothers. The officers present were listed as Captain James Birch, Captain and Adjutant Alexander Riddell, Captain and Quartermaster John Hislop, Lieutenant George Sharpin, Lieutenant Claud Wilkins, Lieutenant John Taylor and Second Lieutenant Philip Odell.[264]

That evening, the party returned to the Corn Exchange for a banquet provided by the regiment's Comfort Fund Committee, of which Lady Ampthill was the president. An evening of feasting, drinking and several short speeches was rounded off by a concert, with each officer receiving a silver cigarette case and each of the men being presented with a knife.

Celebrations complete, the process of rebuilding the battalion for their peacetime role started once they re-formed at Colchester. Attractive terms and bounties were offered to those wishing to re-enlist, the resulting structure of the battalion being a healthy mix of veterans and new recruits.

## 1st Battalion, the Bedfordshire and Hertfordshire Regiment July 1919 onwards

In July the regiment was amalgamated with the Hertfordshire Regiment in recognition of the men of Hertfordshire's contribution to the Bedfordshire Regiment before and during the war. The resulting unit was renamed the Bedfordshire and Hertfordshire Regiment, which title would be used for the next thirty-nine years.

After an intense period of training, the 1st Battalion resumed its post in Ireland as part of the 5th Division in July 1920, where it was given the unenviable task of helping to police the increasingly unsettled countryside.

Joining the battalion in July was an old comrade, Captain Edward Small. Born in 1877, Edward had originally served in the ranks from August 1895 and had carried out duties in Gibraltar, Bermuda, South Africa, France and Flanders, and India and Burma. He had worked his way up through the ranks in a career that incorporated acting as a recruiting sergeant, colour sergeant and company sergeant major, before being commissioned in October 1914. Posts in the front as a combat leader and in the UK as a recruiting officer, as well as the adjutant of a garrison battalion, had seen him rise to the rank of captain by the end of the war. Captain Small's list of injuries and illnesses were as long as his postings and included a broken jaw from boxing, a dislocated knee cartilage, broken teeth sustained in combat, being badly gassed on Hill 60 in 1915 and a variety of ailments typical of the climates he had served in. Within months of arriving in Ireland, he was criticised for providing 'conflicting evidence' and showing 'indifference' while giving testimony at the inquest into the death of Michael Connolly, an Irishman who was shot and killed by the Black and Tans in September 1920.

Lieutenant Eric Chilver Wilson had enlisted into the ranks of the East Kents in September 1914 and was commissioned into the Bedfordshires a year later. Measles and an accidental gunshot wound in the foot while in No Man's Land in February 1917, as well as a stint in the Indian army in Afghanistan and on the North-West Frontier had meant Eric's war had certainly been busy. However, in 1920 he had returned to the British army and rejoined his old regiment in Ireland.

Returning from leading a raiding party on 4 March 1921, Lieutenant Wilson's convoy was ambushed by gunmen outside Carrick-on-Shannon. They came to a halt and jumped from the car to return fire when Private Greaves[265] heard his lieutenant call out, '*I am hit.*' Using his field dressing to stem the flow of blood, Private Greaves was also hurt, but the squad chased their attackers away before making their way back to Dublin. Lieutenant Wilson died from a gunshot wound to the head at the King George V Hospital in Dublin the next day, aged 25.

News also arrived that summer of the fate of Lieutenant Arthur Woodford, who had been injured at La Coulotte in April 1917. Service in the 2nd Bedfordshires followed his recovery, although he was wounded and taken prisoner in August 1918, serving the rest of his war out in Germany. After repatriation, Arthur had sailed to India with the 2nd Battalion and was in a car near Secunderabad at 2 a.m. on 29 June 1921 when it left the road and hit a tree. The driver and other passengers survived but Lieutenant Woodford's body took the full impact, killing him instantly.[266]

Lieutenant Woodford was not the only former 1st Battalion officer who died in India after the war. Lieutenant Philip Ralph Odell from Hertford had survived the last actions of the war, transferring into the 2nd Battalion in 1919 and sailing to India with them that October. On 29 April 1920 four officers, including Lieutenant Odell and two other former 1st Bedfordshires officers, Captain Mayne and Lieutenant Powell, went on a shooting trip with Sergeant Glenn and almost thirty locals. At 5 p.m. on 30 April, when the party had stopped around a small wood, a shot rang out into the still air. Lieutenant Odell's comrades rushed towards the sound, finding him lying on the floor having taken a bullet to the right arm, shattering the elbow and surrounding tissue in the process. When asked who had shot him, Lieutenant Odell replied *'I did; I am afraid it is all my fault.'* With no doctors in the party, Sergeant Glenn did what he could to dress the wound with makeshift bandages, the lieutenant being *'conscious and quite composed'* throughout. An improvised stretcher was made and he was carried for around 4½ hours back to the base camp in the hills. One of the group went on ahead, collected a car and met the stretcher party en route. Loading the wounded officer into the car, he was rushed to Wellington hospital but died on the way from blood loss, aged just 21.

The battalion's posting in Ireland came to a close and, returning with the 1st Battalion to Colchester on 4 February 1922, Captain Small had lunch with his friend William Nicholl on 28 April before they arranged to go into Brightlingsea for the afternoon. Dropping into the officers' quarters to retrieve his coat and a cheque, Captain Small was making his way back down the stairs when Mr Nicholl heard him stop and call up to his servant, Leonard Blow,[267] *'Blow, get my coat and one for Mr Nicholls.'* George Gear, a painter working in the building, was at the bottom of the staircase, watching Captain Small as he called up for his coat. Turning to continue his journey, he missed his footing completely and tumbled down the flight of stairs. Hearing the almighty crash his friend rushed to his aid, and Captain Small said, *'Nic, get me upstairs. I believe I am hurt'*, before passing out. The 45-year-old veteran of twenty-seven years' service in the regiment – with two South African war medals, three Great War medals, and an array of good conduct, wound and overseas stripes adorning his tunic – was rushed to hospital with a fractured skull. An operation at 7 p.m. failed to save the situation and Captain Small died at 8.40 p.m. as the result of his accidental fall down the stairs.

A posting in Aldershot followed in the autumn of 1923, which was the start of eighteen months of hard training under the watchful eye of many motivated and driven senior officers, some of whom would rise to great heights during the Second World War. The King reviewed the battalion and presented it with new colours on 11 June 1924, albeit in the gymnasium once heavy rain put paid to the plans to hold the ceremony outside.

November 1925 saw the battalion leave Aldershot for Malta, 636 men strong. A quiet, uneventful posting was broken only by the arrival of men of the 2nd Battalion on 14 April 1926, who were on the way back home after nineteen years of foreign service.

Shanghai in China beckoned in February 1927, forming part of the International Defence Force, tasked with protecting the port from the Nationalist threat presented by the Chinese civil war. By May 1928 the 1st Battalion had concentrated at Weihai, Shandong, before moving into northern China. Transported by sea to Chinwangtao (Qinhuangdao) and finally to Kuyeh by rail, they were assigned the role of protecting the mining facility there. By November the unrest has settled down and the battalion moved to Hong Kong.

On 25 March 1929 the battalion arrived at Mhow in central India, where they would remain for the next four years. A move in 1933 to Dehra Run, 230km north of Delhi, saw them become the British element of the Gurkha Brigade, and three years later a further move 50km north to Chakrata, India, found them manning a very basic hill station around 8,000 feet above sea level.

In 1938 the regiment celebrated its 250th anniversary and dozens of occasions were arranged both at home and abroad. In September the 1st Battalion were hurriedly transferred to Bombay amid rising tensions in Europe and embarked with two other battalions, bound for home soil. In the event, they were diverted and alighted instead at Haifa as the tensions in Europe were resolved. The following year a move to Cairo came in July, in response to the building threat of war, with another relocation, to Palestine, ordered in November.

The Second World War saw the 1st Battalion posted numerous times, including to Greece, Egypt, Syria, Tobruk, Bangalore and Burma. Serving in conventional units such as the 6th Division, as well as specialist units like the Long Range Penetration Group, or 'Wingate's Chindits', their war was certainly less static than the one their forebears fought over thirty years earlier.

In the period to 1950, the 1st Battalion continued their Grand Tour, serving in India, Chakrata, Libya and Greece before returning to England in February 1950. However, 1947 saw their sister battalion, the 2nd Bedfordshires and Hertfordshires, placed into 'suspended animation' and the following year it was amalgamated into the 1st Battalion, exactly ninety years after it had been raised.

In 1951 a draft was sent to Korea, although the battalion itself remained at Bury St Edmunds until posted to the Guards Brigade in Egypt in response to the Suez Crisis. They landed in Cyprus in November and waited for orders, finally moving to the Suez Canal in July 1952 to guard British military installations against the troubles caused by the country's transformation to a republic. The battalion were finally shipped home in December 1954, returning to Tidworth in Hampshire, and on 25 April 1955, their Honorary Colonel-in-Chief, the Queen Mother, presented them with new colours.

The year 1956 saw the battalion's first posting to Goslar in West Germany, to man the 'Iron Curtain' during what would be labelled the Cold War. However, the Defence White Paper of 1957 resulted in the reduction of the British army into a smaller force and on 1 June 1958, after 270 years of loyal service to the country, the 1st Battalion, Bedfordshire and Hertfordshire Regiment were merged with the 1st Battalion, Essex Regiment to form the 3rd East Anglian Regiment.

The Queen Mother remained the honorary Colonel-in-Chief of the new regiment and presented their new colours in 1959, before they moved to Malaya to serve in 28th Commonwealth Brigade in the operations against Communist guerrillas. Three years later the 3rd East Anglian Regiment was posted to Northern Ireland and on 1 September 1964 the three regiments forming the East Anglian Brigade were merged with the Royal Leicestershire Regiment into the first 'LARGE REGIMENT OF INFANTRY' unit in the British army. The 3rd East Anglian Regiment became the 3rd

Battalion (16th/44th Foot) of the Royal Anglian Regiment.

The date of 5 October 1992 saw the 3rd Battalion disbanded, its personnel being folded into the 1st Battalion ('the Vikings') and the 2nd Battalion ('the Poachers'). At the time of writing, D Company (Bedfordshire and Hertfordshire) of the 2nd Battalion are the direct ancestors of Douglas's Regiment of Foot, originally raised in 1688. Since the formation of the Royal Anglian Regiment, in addition to British and West German postings, it has served operationally in Aden, Cyprus, Malta, Northern Ireland, the Persian Gulf, Croatia, Bosnia, Sierra Leone, Iraq and Afghanistan. When exercises are added to the list of countries the regiment has been present in, there are not many parts of the globe unvisited.

# Chapter 12

# The End of an Era

*'They will hold the line.'*

And what of the men whose deeds, courage and steadfastness collectively maintained and enhanced the battalion's reputation throughout those intense years of war?

Of the tens of thousands who passed through the regiment between 1914 and 1919, the lives they went on to lead could easily be representative of any regiment who fought on the battlefields of Europe and elsewhere. Some became senior military figures, others held civil positions of standing, with most returning to everyday life, marrying, raising families and putting their experiences behind them as best they could.

Hundreds of those still serving in 1919 formed the cadre around which the post-war battalion was reformed and rebuilt. Those who thought they had 'done their bit' and wanted the end of army life returned home; even if they would go on to form the Home Guard two decades later in response to their country's new call to arms, in 1919 they were, at least, blissfully unaware of the future threat that would see them back in uniform.

Memorials sprang up at local and national level, providing a method of focus for those who had lost loved ones yet who had no final resting place to visit. Over and above the thousands of Imperial War Graves Commission (later the Commonwealth War Graves Commission) cemeteries and memorials to the missing, national monuments and those erected in towns or villages across the country, numerous personal methods of remembrance came to life.

Among the many examples of private memorialisation is that of

Second Lieutenant Frederick Lee Ray, who was killed in May 1918. He lies in the Tannay British cemetery at Thiennes and is remembered on the local Elstow Church memorial near Bedford. His father, also called Frederick Ray, was called on to use his transport expertise in the war effort, serving as an officer in the Bedfordshire Volunteer Corps and the Bedfordshire Motor Volunteer Corps. Unbeknown to him, he was gazetted as a temporary major on 17 May 1918, a day after the death of his son in France; the telegram sharing the bad news would have doubtless arrived the same day or a day later. Frederick senior ran a successful logistics company between the wars, being among those to embrace the Sentinel steam lorry at an early stage. His legacy was sufficient to establish the Frederick Ray Charity in memory of his son, which includes almshouses in Bedford, even naming the road on which they were sited as Ray's Close.

The post-war euphoria gave the returning veterans hope for a brighter future which, for a while at least, inspired many to embark on business ventures as they searched for the new life they had earned.

Ernest Charles Howlett was one such veteran who tried to make good in the 'land fit for heroes' that he returned to. Ernest had served in the army since enlisting aged 18, joining the 1st Bedfordshires as a private in November 1913. Landing in France in August 1914, Ernest served continually throughout the campaign on the Western Front until wounded in the left shoulder at Longueval in July 1916. Two months later he was back with his old pals and by the time he was granted leave to return home and marry in August 1917, had risen to the rank of sergeant. A commission into the Suffolks followed at the end of 1917 and, after months of service between the Suffolk and Norfolk regiments, Ernest rejoined his old comrades in the 1st Bedfordshires in July 1918. Surviving the last intense months of the war, Second Lieutenant Howlett retired from military service in April 1919, taking the opportunity to make a better future for his family by using the gratuity provided by the War Office. Unfortunately, by the end of the 1920s, Ernest, like many others in his position, was struggling with a wife and six children to support and no private income. In the lean post-war years, the army were unable to offer any gainful employment when he applied unless he repaid the gratuity provided, leaving him and many others like him in a no-win situation.

What would become labelled as the 'Roaring Twenties' came to a close in 1929 with the Wall Street Crash and ten subsequent years of global 'Great Depression' that ultimately contributed to the start of the Second World War.

The legacy left from the war continued to take its toll on the young men who had served through it, with many dying as a direct result of their service for years after the armistice was signed.

Lieutenant Charles James Hunter had joined the colours on 1 September 1914 and saw combat service in the ranks of the London Regiment and as an officer in the Bedfordshires. His second wound of the war came at Longueval in July 1916, after which Charles's war effort was restricted to administrative duties, courtesy of the loss of an eye and a series of illnesses. The second bout of 'Spanish flu' to ravage Europe in November 1918 hit Charles's system hard and he died on 4 November 1918, on the same day his former comrades were engaged in their final battle and just a week before the armistice was signed. He was 25 years old.[268]

Second Lieutenant Leonard Johnston Jones, who had been wounded on Hill 60 in May 1915, never regained fitness due to nerve, muscle and bone damage to his right arm. Staff posts and periods on half-pay while continuing with treatment had taken up the remainder of his war until a medical board in April 1919 declared him fit for active service once more. Leonard was posted to India with the 2nd Bedfordshires and Hertfordshires that September but within a few months it became clear that his injury was simply too restrictive for him to continue as a regular army officer. Returning to civilian life and taking a post as a stockbroker's assistant, Leonard fainted suddenly on 5 June 1921, his friend loading him into his motorcycle's sidecar and rushing him to Bedford hospital. Leonard died that evening, his death being attributed to syncope and heart failure. He was 25 years old.[269]

Also wounded and gassed at Longueval was Captain Frederick Vivian Parker, although he recovered from his injuries and delayed shell shock, joining the 2nd Bedfordshires early in 1918. The battalion conducted a series of remarkable fighting withdrawals during the German spring offensives two months after his arrival, during which Captain Parker was hurt and then captured. After receiving bad medical treatment while a prisoner, Frederick was repatriated with a long list of wounds and health issues that eventually took his life in January 1921, aged 29.[270]

Private Frederick Charles Cook from Stagsden had seen service in the 1st Bedfordshires from the end of 1916 and, other than being mildly gassed twice including at Achiet-le-Grand in August 1918, had survived the fighting. Being demobilised as medical category A1 in March 1919, Fred returned home to Civvy Street. However, pulmonary tuberculosis – which was attributed to having been aggravated by his war service –

overcame him late in 1920, eventually taking the 22-year-old's life on 5 July 1921.[271]

Over and above those whose lives were cut short long after the fighting had stopped, many continued into civilian life accompanied by well-documented psychological traumas, coping with varying degrees of success.

Second Lieutenant Stanley George Fisher, formerly a chartered accountant's clerk from St Albans had served in the ranks on the Western Front before being commissioned into the 1st Bedfordshires, joining them in September 1918. Although wounded in the thigh on 23 October 1918, Stanley had recovered and was medically categorised as A1 in November 1919. As was the case with many thousands of former servicemen in the years after the war had finished, it transpired that service in the war had *'aggravated his mental condition'*, which led to his wife having to move him into Camberwell House Hospital on 4 May 1921, suffering from *'delusional insanity and hallucinations'*. He was *'certified as unsound of mind'* and relinquished his commission on account of ill health two months later. Despite surviving the war, coming through the psychological trauma caused by his experiences and living through a second war, Stanley died on 17 January 1969, aged 74, from multiple injuries after a tree fell on to him.[272]

William Rankin had been among the Bedfordshire lads attracted to enlist in the Gordon Highlanders while they were billeted in the county during 1915. An officer's commission and subsequent service in the 7th and 1st Bedfordshires was cut short after being wounded during heavy shelling on the Somme in 1916. William had been thrown into the air by a close explosion and knocked unconscious. Concussion, hand and head tremors, stammering, insomnia, violent headaches and dreams, exaggerated reflexes and *'noises in his head'* plagued the 20-year-old until, remarkably, he was passed as fit for service again in 1917. His health deteriorated once more and by early 1919 William resigned his commission on account of ill health, although he still married his sweetheart a year later and lived well into his eighties, finally passing away in June 1980.[273]

Yet among the carnage, destruction and wrecked lives, others, against the apparent odds, survived the worst that warfare could throw at them.

Sergeant 8186 Frank Butler served in the regiment from 1905 until passing into the reserves in 1912. He was mobilised when war broke out and went to France with the 1st Bedfordshires in August 1914, winning the Military Medal on the Somme in 1916. Frank came through the war without a scratch, returning to life in Cambridge in January 1919.

Boxing Day baby Captain William Pottle had been *'born and raised in the regiment'*, his service in the ranks including campaigns in India in the 1890s and as a recruiting sergeant over and above his Great War service. After receiving a commission in the regular army in 1914, William had left the 1st Bedfordshires in 1915, joining the 1st Lancashire Fusiliers, of the '6 VCs before breakfast' fame from Gallipoli. He had gone over the top with them on 1 July 1916, being among 24 officers and 460 men of the battalion who became casualties that day. A year of home service had followed while he recovered, before rejoining 1st Bedfordshires again as they rested after their tour around Ypres in 1917, although he would see no more active service after spending months in hospitals in Italy, France and England. After a posting as adjutant at the Kempston barracks, his service was extended beyond his 45th birthday, courtesy of the 'high regard' he was held in by his peers. Posts in the defence force and in re-cruiting roles until 1928 took William to compulsory retirement age, and he remained in Bedford until his death from 'old age and heart failure' on April Fool's Day 1964, aged 87.[274]

John Stapleton from Sawtry had also been with the regiment since the 1890s and had been the battalion's acting RSM at one point, reverting to the role of RQMS, where he remained until discharged in June 1919. After twenty-four years of service, which embraced the entire period of the Great War, John came out with a single wound stripe in addition to an array of medals, including the Distinguished Conduct Medal.[275]

Lieutenant Colonel Percy Worrall added the CBE to his collection of medals which included the Distinguished Service Order, Military Cross, Queen's South African war medal with four clasps, a 1914 Star, Victory and British war medals. He went on to write *Smoke Tactics* in 1919 and served as the commanding officer of the King's Own Malta Regiment, retiring in 1936. Once the third war he would serve through flared up in 1939, he was sent to command the Alderney garrison in the Channel Islands until its evacuation in June 1940, and died in November 1950, aged 70.

Ernest Alfred Hague from Bedford had been an officer in the 8th Bed-fordshires initially, joining the 1st Battalion in August 1916. Weeks later he was on his way back to the UK after being wounded at Falfemont Farm, suffering from shrapnel wounds to the back, head and right arm, and deaf-ness to his right ear. Headaches, sleeplessness and stretched nerves would plague him for months and, although he returned to the 8th Battalion in February 1917, he was sent back for a medical report early in May, after exposure to another big battle with massed artillery had shredded his nerves further. Diagnosed as suffering from neurasthenia, Ernest was held back for administrative duties at No. 6 Camp in Calais as he recovered, joining the 7th Battalion early in 1918. While leading a patrol in May 1918, he was shot clean through the right bicep, which saw an end to his active service and he relinquished his commission on account of ill health caused by wounds in January 1919. Life settled down to relative normality, living on the Gold Coast, West Africa, for some years, marrying and starting a family in the 1920s. A twist of fate saw to it that Ernest was residing in Jersey when it was occupied by German forces in 1940 and he spent the first two years of his second world war on the island before being transported into captivity with his family in 1942. After repatriation in 1945, Ernest and his family settled on the Isle of Wight, where he passed away in January 1971, aged 75.

Lieutenant Colonel Charles Richard Jebb Griffith had led the 1st Bedfordshires on to the Western Front in 1914, having already spent many years in the 2nd Battalion and having come through the South African wars with a DSO. Service as the brigadier of the 108th Brigade in the Ulster Division until May 1918 followed, with a post in command of the Machine Gun Corps Training School rounding off his active service after the effects of wounds kept him from the front lines. His final posting on the Standing Committee of Enquiry into Prisoners of War came to a close in 1919, at which time he took retirement and returned to his family home on the Isle of Wight, dying there in August 1948, aged 80.

Others simply removed themselves from the hustle and bustle of society at the time, such as Lieutenant (temporary Captain) Arthur Topley, who served in the battalion during the Somme campaign of 1916 before going on to see Mesopotamia and Afghanistan through the eyes of an army officer. After the war he was demobilised and travelled to a cousin's farmstead in British Columbia, apparently not having found a profession that suited him. Eight years later Arthur was off on his travels once more, destination Hawaii. He lived on the isolated, tropical island for the remainder of his life, inadvertently raising considerable speculation and tales of his aristocratic background. With no visible form of income to his name and his extremely quiet, polite and typically reserved English gentleman's demeanour, his neighbours related stories of how he had suffered from being gassed and from the effects of shell shock during the war, the wounds leaving him a little 'barmy'. Local legend told of him being a 'remittance man', whose rich family had paid to keep away from home, the tales allegedly being confirmed by his unverified army rank of colonel,

in spite of having been a temporary captain. Arthur's eccentricities doubtless compounded the recurring tales, as he was never seen without his
heavy khaki woollen greatcoat, always carried a *'tan cloth bag, perhaps a
khaki fabric slung over his shoulder'*, and endlessly walked around the island,
although *'no-one really knew why he spent so much time just walking about'*.
Arthur *'lived alone in a room on the second floor of a boarding house'* and could
be seen sitting at his window every evening for hours on end, just looking
out over the sea. Naturally, young lads were tempted to tease him as he
certainly stood out, but their parents quickly put a stop to such behaviour, teaching their boys that *'war sometimes did strange things to people'*. The
generation of children from the 1950s called him 'Sir Arthur Topley' and
'The Duke' as, coupled with his very British accent, he was always incredibly kind and polite to them. He was described as *'an impressive looking
man, much like an English Lord … carried himself in such a manly but casual
manner that there was no question … that he was an aristocrat'*.

Decoration Day parades, which would later become Memorial Day
parades, also saw him appear in his somewhat shabby but impeccably
kept clothing as all local veterans were encouraged to participate; as the
parades were organised by rank and the locals were convinced he was a
colonel, Arthur would march at its head alongside an American army
colonel from the island, often to the minor annoyance of other former
servicemen. By 1960, Arthur's funds, whatever their source, had seemingly run out and he lived in Kimiville, a poor area of the island, still sporting much the same clothing he had worn for decades. The arrival of a
Tsunami in 1960 wiped the area from the map, killing 62-year-old Arthur
in the process. Despite his apparent condition by the end of his life, the
reserved, polite British 'colonel' certainly *'made a favourable impression on
those he came into contact with'*. [276]

Today, no survivors of the Bedfordshire Regiment remain, their deeds
and memories being confined to written memoirs and diaries, sound re-
cordings and the occasional filmed interview. Very few Bedfordshire and
Hertfordshire Regiment veterans are left, with the ranks of those men who
served in the Second World War and into the post-war era growing thin-
ner by the year.

Over half a century after the Bedfordshire and Hertfordshire Regiment passed into the historical annuls of the British army, it is perhaps
not entirely surprising that the Bedfordshire and Hertfordshire regimental association is winding down in August 2014 and the regimental
museum at Wardown Park in Luton is being scrutinised with a view to

reducing it in size. Although these are sad events in themselves, they also mark the 'passing of the baton' on to those who carry the regimental trad-itions into the future, namely the Royal Anglian Regiment.[277]

Concluding a story such as this is best left to a person who stood tall on the world stage at the time and shared in some of the events the 1st Bedford-shires lived through.

In 1928, Marshall Ferdinand Foch, formerly the Supreme Commander of the Allied armies in 1918, sent a message to the people of Bedford-shire; like most of Europe, they were finding it increasingly difficult mak-ing ends meet in post-war Britain.[278] In the message, he recalled several forms of contact he had with the regiment both on and off the battlefield, but one recollection typifies the spirit of the regiment.

At a time when the Germans were attacking the hinge between the French and British armies in force, with no reserves available to move into the threatened area, an urgent meeting was called with the colonel from the nearest unit who had any troops available to hold back the on-slaught. He was from a Bedfordshire battalion.

*In the presence of Marshall Haig, the Colonel of the regiment was asked if he could be sure that his men would hold the line until the critical moment had passed. His answer was:*

*'I am a Bedfordshire man; I know the men of the county, and I know that they will not betray the trust you have placed in them. I am going back to tell them what is expected of them, and though many of them have not been under fire before, I vouch for them.*

*They will hold the line.'*

*And they did, though the cost was a heavy one.*

# Notes from the Author

The approach, style and format of this volume has been consistent with the preceding volume (*1st Bedfordshires. Part One: Mons to the Somme*), hence the notes remain largely the same.

Compiling this story began with the source closest to the events, being the battalion, brigade and divisional war diaries. The resulting story was then developed using the sources listed below, including personal details from private letters, memoirs and diaries from those who were there.

Anyone who has researched a subject as complex as this will agree that the accuracy of sources cannot always be taken at face value. Laying out the parameters within which I have sought to verify facts is inappropriate here and would almost certainly result in a rather boring paragraph, so suffice to say that I have taken very little at face value, as even the 'official histories' are prone to errors with the benefit of that wonderful word – hindsight. When conflicts have occurred between facts, I have considered all angles and sought verification from other impartial sources that did not themselves draw on any of the conflicting ones. Quotations from those who were there are given as they appeared at the time, regardless of any inconsistencies with the facts available with hindsight; to my mind, they should have the privilege of recalling their memories as they choose and it is not for me to correct them.

Military Medals are a notorious subject for those researching when and how they were earned, even in which battalion the recipient won them. Those included in this volume are purely the ones I have been able to corroborate, but it is feasible that I have neglected to include some that belong in this story. Citations accompanying Military Medals were all destroyed so identifying the details surrounding their issue is often a difficult process. For example, of the 631 Military Medals I have identified as having been awarded to men in the Bedfordshire Regiment, I have been unable to find evidence to clarify in which battalion 22 of those from the period that this volume represents were won, let alone for which action they were issued.

There is a mixture of metric and imperial units of measurement throughout, depending on the source and context. For instance, a square on a 1:10,000-scale British trench map from the time is 1,000 yards, so any reference to a map is made in yards, as are any quotations from the time which use miles or yards. In contrast, distances between locations on the Western Front are given in kilometres and metres, as that is the measurement adopted locally.

Names of towns use the local, modern spelling, with alternative, anglicised spellings included in brackets. The notable exception to this is Ypres (Ieper), which is shown by the anglicised spelling to avoid confusion, as many official battles, memorials and other such titles are referred to using that spelling.

For those with a genealogical or personal interest to learn more, personally I am a huge advocate of physically standing on the sites where the events took place. Reading about them is one thing but standing on the very ground with the story in one hand and a map in the other while juggling a compass adds a dimension worth pursuing. Most of the aspects have not changed since our ancestors laid their eyes upon them, despite a century having passed. Many roads, woods and even buildings remain, so comparing features on a map from the war is often not as difficult as one may imagine. The difference, of course, is that we enjoy a landscape comprising green grass and farmers' fields instead of a vast swathe of grey-brown mud broken by shell holes and the litter of battle.

# Sources

The following sources have been incorporated while producing this story:

The 1st Battalion war diaries, held at the National Archives under reference WO 95/1570 and at the Bedfordshire and Luton Archives and Records Service (BLARS) under reference X550/2/5. Much cross-referencing was also undertaken from the National Archives WO 95 collection (predominantly in the range of WO 95/1510 to 1580), which includes diaries from other units within the 5th Division (including the 15th Brigade diary held under WO 95/1566 to 1569) as well as those from outside the division who were in the line next to the battalion during a given event.

The History Committee, the Royal Anglian Regiment (Bedfordshire and Hertfordshire): Lieutenant Colonel T.J. Barrow, DSO, Major V.A. French and J. Seabrook Esq. (1986), *The Story of the Bedfordshire and Hertfordshire Regiment (The 16th Regiment of Foot). Volume II. 1914 to 1958.*

Hussey and Inman, *The 5th Division in the Great War* (reprint of 1921 edition), Naval and Military Press.

The Bedfordshire and Luton Archives and Records Service (BLARS) houses various records and information on the regiment over and above their local and family history collections.

*The Wasp, the journal of the 16th Foot, the Bedfordshire and Hertfordshire Regiment,* Gale & Polden.

Service records held at the National Archives under WO 339 and WO 374 (officers), WO 363, WO 364 and WO 97 (other ranks, including pre-war discharges).

The Imperial War Museum archives hold several personal diaries and memoirs of men who served within the battalion and whose memories have been quoted within this story.

Trench maps are available from a variety of sources over and above those held within war diaries and independently at the National Archives. The Bedfordshire and Luton Archives and Records Service (BLARS), the Imperial War Museum, as well as commercial outlets such as the Naval and Military Press, all hold selections of maps, each collection seemingly having variances between them.

Newspapers from the time, held by local, regional and national libraries and archives: *Ampthill News; Bedfordshire Times and Independent; Biggleswade Chronicle; Herts Advertiser and St Albans Times; Hunts County News; Hunts Post; Illustrated London News; Kettering Leader; Leighton Buzzard Observer; Letchworth Citizen; London Gazette; Luton News and Bedfordshire Chronicle/Bedfordshire Advertiser; Royston Crow; St Neots Advertiser; St Neots and County Times; The Times.*

Appendix

# A Brief History of the Regiment: 1688 to 2013

The regiment that would become the 16th Regiment of Foot and later the Bedfordshire Regiment was initially raised during a period of turmoil in Europe. In the late seventeenth century, Europe was in the grip of religious, military and political upheaval, with several major powers vying for supremacy and the emerging American continent about to enter the world stage. Not four decades earlier the English Civil War had been fought, the Thirty Years War in Europe had finished, as had an eighty-year war between the Netherlands and Spain. The Ming Dynasty had come to an end in China, and war, famine and plague affected Europe and the New Worlds of the Americas, wiping out huge numbers of people. Only two decades earlier the bubonic plague swept London, killing an estimated 100,000 people, closely followed by the Great Fire of London one short year later.

Until the English Civil War, no standing army existed in England, with armies being mustered on an ad-hoc basis when needed. Parliament's 'New Model Army' was effectively the first permanent force but was disbanded when King Charles II reclaimed the throne. The year 1661 saw the first permanent Regiment of Foot raised by Royal Warrant, and several more followed in the next few years, which would form the foundation for the growth of the English and later the British army. In 1685 ten new Regiments of Foot were formed in England, and these would later become the 5th to 15th Foot inclusive.

Despite many achievements and much progress being made, including

Isaac *Newton's Mathematical Principles* being published, the 1680s saw numerous wars, sieges and plots to overthrow and assassinate various royalty and heads of state. By 1688 King Louis XIV of France had the Grand Alliance of England, Spain, Holland, Sweden, Savoy and the Holy Roman Empire arrayed against him and was at war with almost every European power.

During the autumn of 1688 and following his 'Declaration of Indulgence' towards Catholics and nonconformists, King James II was facing the threat of the Dutch William, Prince of Orange, who brought an army to England on the behest of seven English lords. In the last months of 1688 King James was in a precarious position and authorised the mustering of more regiments of pikemen and musketeers, which were later referred to as being the last of the 'senior' regiments. The first of these regiments was raised by the distinguished twenty-year veteran Scottish soldier Archibald 'Spot' Douglas and, although initially named after the colonels who commanded them, this regiment would in time become the 16th Regiment of Foot.

### Archibald Douglas's Regiment of Foot

A cadre of officers and professional soldiers who had served with Douglas in what would become the Royal Scots followed him and formed the nucleus of the new regiment on 9 October 1688. With the first men being enlisted from Uxbridge in Middlesex, they moved to Reading after five days of recruiting and completed the raising of Douglas's new regiment.

On 5 November 1688 the Prince of Orange landed in Torbay and the regiment was ordered to concentrate with the standing army at Southwark, where they remained as the political situation developed. The date of 11 December saw King James disband his army before fleeing to France ten days later, with William of Orange assuming the throne and reforming the army almost immediately.

Douglas's regiment were then quartered in Stony Stratford, Buckinghamshire, but their colonel remained loyal to the monarchy he had served for two decades and refused to take the 'Oath of Allegiance' to his new King. All bar five officers joined Douglas in his refusal, leaving the regiment temporarily in a state of flux.

### Robert Hodges' Regiment of Foot

Douglas's original second in command, Robert Hodges, assumed the colonelcy of the regiment on the last day of 1688. Being woefully short of officers, he turned to his former regiment, the Earl of Dumbarton's Foot (later known as the 1st Foot, or the Royal Scots). Dozens of officers and non-commissioned officers joined him and for many years they even retained the uniform of their old regiment.

Hodges' regiment were in action on the European continent from 1689 and would be engaged in European campaigns almost continuously until 1712.

Following initial training, Hodges' regiment sailed for Holland in 1689, and until 1695 were engaged in the War of the League of Augsburg against France. Credited with being the first of the new, permanent English regiments to fire a shot in anger in continental Europe, they were praised for their behaviour during the Battle of Walcourt in a despatch to King William IV, before moving to Bruges in October.

June 1690 saw them transfer to Brussels and they rejoined the main English army at South Brabant the following March. While engaged at the Battle of Steenkirk (Steenkerque) in 1692, Colonel Hodges was killed at the head of his regiment's advance by a cannon ball.

## James Stanley's Regiment of Foot

James Stanley, later the 10th Earl of Derby, purchased the colonelcy after Hodges' death and his regiment saw much action during the twelve years of his command. In July 1693 they were engaged at the Battle of Landen before being quartered at Dendermonde later that year. They rejoined the army in the field in May 1694 and returned to garrison Dendermonde after the year's campaigning came to a close. In 1695 they were involved in the siege and capture of Namur and rejoined the army at Brabant during 1696. The following year saw the Treaty of Ryswick bring hostilities to a close and the regiment came home to England, becoming a part of the Irish garrison in 1698.

The War of the Spanish Succession flared up in 1701 and would continue for eleven years. Also referred to as Marlborough's Wars, the regiment were among the English forces present throughout the entire conflict, embarking from Carrickfergus for Holland on 7 June 1701. The following year they moved to Rosendael (Rosendahl) and encamped at Cranenburg (Kranenburg) before a hectic campaigning season began. Stanley's regiment were engaged at the siege of Kayserswerth (Kaiserswerth) and afterwards marched to Nimeguen (Nijmegen). Several more sieges were conducted that year, at Venloo (Venlo), Ruremonde (Roermond) and Stevenswaert (Stevensweert). October saw their last action in a busy year when the regiment were involved in the capture of the citadel at Liege on 23 October. After wintering in Holland, April 1703 saw them move towards Maestricht (Maastricht) at the end of April and they were engaged at the siege and capture of Huy and Limburg before returning to Holland again for the winter.

A move into Germany in 1704 led to the regiment being present at the Battle of Schellenburg, during the Danube crossings, and the Battle of Blenheim, which would become synonymous with the regimental trad-itions in the centuries that followed. The survivors of the regiment re-turned to Holland after Blenheim and Stanley's military campaigning came to a close in 1705 in favour of service at the highest levels of the British monarchy.

### Francis Godfrey's Regiment of Foot

A nephew of the Duke of Marlborough, Godfrey took over the colonelcy in May 1705. Already an experienced soldier, he and his regiment were engaged during the assaults on Helixum and Neerhespen in Belgium. The year 1706 found the regiment heavily engaged at the Battle of Ramillies and during the surrender of the principal towns of Brabant, after which they were quartered at Ghent.

English and Scottish forces merged to form the modern British army as a result of the 'Acts of Union 1707', which also saw the creation of the 'Kingdom of Great Britain'. That year Godfrey's regiment were continu-ally in the field but their French opponents avoided any engagements.

On 21 March 1708 the regiment landed at Tynemouth to help repel the French invasion in support of 'The Pretender' but returned to Flanders soon after as the navy had already neutralised the threat. They were then engaged at the Battle of Oudenaarde and the siege and capture of Lille and its citadel on 9 December. On arrival at Lille, Sergeant Littler swam a defended moat armed with just a hatchet and released the drawbridge, thus allowing the army to move into the defences. For his gallantry he was granted the rare honour of being commissioned from the ranks into what would become the 3rd Foot (the Buffs).

In 1709 the regiment were engaged in the siege and capture of Tournay, and during the bloodiest confrontation of that century, the Battle of Malplaquet on 11 September. They later took part in the siege and sur-render of Mons, after which they were quartered at Ghent. The next year Godfrey's regiment found themselves forcing the French lines at Pont-à-Vendin, followed by several sieges – at Douay (Douai), Béthune,

Aire and Saint-Venant. They were quartered again at Ghent (Gent) that winter.

## Henry Durrell's Regiment of Foot
In February 1711 another Foot Guards' officer called Henry Durrell purchased the colonelcy and his regiment were committed to pressing the French lines at Arleux on 5 August, and at the siege of Bouchain, where they garrisoned for the winter. April 1712 saw them transferred to Tournay (Tournai) and encamped at Le Cateau-Cambrésis. In what would be the final summer of the war, the regiment were involved in the capture of Le Quesnoy in July and following the ceasefire were moved to defend Dunkirk.

## Hans Hamilton's Regiment of Foot
In 1714 the colonelcy passed to Hans Hamilton, who originally joined when the regiment were formed in October 1688. Hamilton's Foot were transported to Scotland in April, landing at Leith, and were stationed in and around Stirling from September.

## Richard Ingram's Regiment of Foot
In July 1715 the 5th Viscount Irvine assumed the colonelcy. His command saw the suppression of the Scottish rebellions in 1715 and 1716, although the regiment remained garrisoned at Fort William and did not take the field during the hostilities.

## John Cholmeley's Regiment of Foot
After a distinguished career in the regiment, John Cholmeley bought the colonelcy in December 1717 and led his regiment through a spell of home service in England, Scotland and Ireland.

## Henry Scott's Regiment of Foot
Cholmeley's death in April 1724 saw Lord Henry Scott, the 1st Earl of Deloraine, assume command as their period of home service continued undisturbed.

## Roger Handasyde's Regiment of Foot
In July 1730 Handasyde joined from the colonelcy of what would become the 22nd Foot, remaining the regiment's colonel until his death over three decades later. The regiment continued on home service until

mobilised in 1740 as part of the forces committed to the War of Jenkins' Ear against Spain. During 1740, some months were spent as marines with a detachment embarking for an expedition to the West Indies towards the end of the year. The regiment landed on Jamaica in January 1741 and a detachment were later involved in the unsuccessful expedition and Battle of Carthagena against the Spanish in modern-day Columbia, where almost the entire detachment were annihilated by disease.

Returning home to recover and rebuild their numbers, the regiment were held in England during the outbreak of the war of the Austrian succession in 1742 and remained on the English south coast in response to the threat of French invasion. In June they were sent to join the army in the field, being engaged in the minor action at Melle on 9 July 1745.

March 1746 saw the regiment shipped to Edinburgh following the Scottish victory at the Battle of Falkirk, although they remained off the coast while the Battle of Culloden was fought, moving to garrison posts at Elgin and Fort Augustus the following summer. By 1747 the regiment were ranked as the 16th Regiment of Foot during a reorganisation of British forces, although the title was not used officially for some years.

Two years later garrison duties in Ireland followed. The regiment were reduced to a peacetime contingent and remained in Ireland for the next eighteen years.

**The 16th Regiment of Foot**

On 1 July 1751 the regiment were officially named the '16th Regiment of Foot' and standardisation of 'Line Regiments' within the army, including the 16th Foot, took place. An order of precedence was established, with each regiment no longer bearing the name of its colonel, but carrying a numerical title according to seniority based on when it was originally raised. Their uniform became almost completely scarlet with yellow facings and trim, and two battle flags were issued and carried: the King's Colour (the Union flag, or Union Jack) and the Regimental Colour (a yellow flag with the Union flag in one corner and the golden Romanised numerals for the 16th Regiment in the middle). The regimental nickname 'The Old Sixteenth' also surfaced, reflecting the regiment's long service and position within the 'senior' regiments of the army.

Several expeditions were ordered during the Seven Years War and, although the men of the regiment were even embarked on to boats during one such series of orders, they were never committed and remained on duty in Ireland until moved to Florida in 1767. Here they enjoyed a relatively trouble-free period of service for nine years, with their headquarters based at Pensacola and detachments spread over the countryside.

In 1775 the (American) War of Independence broke out between the Kingdom of Great Britain and the Thirteen Colonies. The regiment were briefly rushed to New York but returned to Florida shortly after and resumed their garrison posting.

During hostilities with Spain in 1779 a detachment from the regiment were among those captured when the garrison at Baton Rouge was overrun. Other units of the regiment were engaged with French and American forces at Savannah, and drove back an attempt to seize Georgia in October. In 1781 the regiment were engaged in repulsing a Spanish attempt to take Pensacola.

### The 16th (the Buckinghamshire) Regiment of Foot

In March 1782, following their losses in the American actions, the regiment was returned to England to rebuild. On 31 August they were authorised to use the title 'The 16th (the Buckinghamshire) Regiment of Foot' to encourage enlistment from that region and create a county identity. It was around this time that the nickname 'The Old Bucks' surfaced, reflecting the regiment's long service.

Duties as a small, peacetime regiment in Ireland started in 1784, followed by a move to Nova Scotia six years later. In 1791 the regiment were moved to Jamaica in response to the unrest created by the French Revolution, where they would remain for five years. St Domingo joined the British Empire in 1793, with a detachment of the regiment garrisoning the island. The following year saw the garrison rejoin the main force in Jamaica, just one officer and one sergeant having survived rampant disease.

In 1795 the regiment were engaged in the Maroon wars and at the end of 1796 the seriously reduced regiment returned to England to rebuild once again. The years 1797 to 1799 were spent in Scotland and 1800 saw another spell in Ireland follow until the West Indies came round once again in 1804, as war with Napoleon's France flared up.

Other than the Battle of Surinam in 1806, the 16th Foot would waste away in the Fever Isles until 1811, losing 27 officers and over 500 men to disease, and hundreds more being invalided home with yellow fever.

### The 16th (the Bedfordshire) Regiment of Foot

In May 1809 the regiment exchanged county titles with 'The 14th (the

Bedfordshire) Regiment of Foot' and became known as 'The 16th (the Bedfordshire) Regiment of Foot'. This was on the request of the colonel of the 14th (Bedfordshire) Regiment – Colonel and Adjutant General Sir Harry Calvert – who owned large estates in Buckinghamshire.

Detachments started to return to England from Barbados and Surinam, departing from those areas in 1810 and 1811. In 1812, the last detachment left the West Indies, but their costly spell of duty there was not complete even as they approached the Irish coastline. The very last group were shipwrecked off the Irish coast with the loss of a few men, one wife and several children, along with all regimental documentation, equipment and property. After rebuilding with English and Irish volunteers they marched to quarters at Sunderland in July, moving to Perth in Scotland the following March and to Ireland in July 1813.

War with the United States flared up once more in 1814, the regiment embarking from Monkstown in Ireland in the spring for Canada as an advanced guard to the British army being sent there. Arriving in Quebec on 29 May before moving to Chambly, they relocated to Montreal and finally to Fort Wellington.

Urgent orders rushed the regiment home again in 1815, in response to Napoleon's revival. In the event, the boats were late and the regiment left Quebec in July, arriving at Portsmouth in August. They joined Wellington's army at Ostend and moved into the army of occupation in Paris before finally being sent back to England very late in December.

In 1816 the regiment returned to Ireland, landing at Monkstown on 3 February before being stationed at Fermoy, Limerick and Cashel in turn. The next year they moved to Kilkenny and relocated to Athlone in 1819.

Starting out on what would become a long period of colonial service around the British Empire, the regiment embarked from Cork on 25 August, bound for Ceylon. Having spent a month in Cape Town they finally landed at Columbo on 20 February 1820. In August 1821 they marched to Kandy, returning to Columbo in 1824. July 1826 then saw them leaving Columbo bound for Pont de Galle.

The regiment left Ceylon for Bengal in four detachments starting in November 1828, the final group landing at Calcutta by January 1829. In 1831 they were transported to Chinsura by steamboats and two years later marched to Ghazepore, although orders were altered en route and the regiment transferred instead to Cawnpore, arriving on 28 February 1834. The regiment were posted to Dinapore in January 1840 and moved to the Presidency in November.

After twenty-one years of foreign service the regiment returned to England in 1841 and were stationed at Dover. They were issued with the new-type 'Percussion' arms in August and sent to Winchester in December. They left Winchester in April 1842 for Gosport, then to Portsmouth in August. New colours were presented to the regiment on 22 September and the following July they were posted to Ireland.

The year 1846 saw the foreign service element of the regiment (six companies) move to Gibraltar in January, then on to Corfu in March 1847. They joined the remainder of the regiment on Guernsey in May 1848, returning to the West Indies two years later.

Garrison duties in Jamaica came round again and the regiment spent the next seven years there, missing the Crimean War and the Indian Mutinies as a result. In June 1857 the regiment returned to England and during a major reorganisation of the British army in 1858, the regiment raised a second battalion in Ireland. All line regiments up to the 25th Foot were expanded to include a 2nd Battalion following reforms to correct the glaring deficiencies shown up during the Crimean War and the Indian Mutinies.

The 2nd Battalion were initially stationed in Ireland, but in 1861 the 1st Battalion were sent to Montreal to defend the border with America against Fenian raiders. The 2nd Battalion joined their sister battalion, arriving in Halifax, Canada, on their first foreign service before moving to Nova Scotia. Both battalions remained in Canada in response to tensions between America and the British Empire, following the American Civil War.

During 1866, the 1st Battalion were involved in several small engagements along the borders around Niagara against the attempted invasion by American Fenians and in 1866 the 2nd Battalion moved to the West Indies. Three years later the 2nd Battalion returned home and moved to Curragh in Ireland, where the 1st Battalion joined them the following year.

In 1873 further military reforms divided the country into 'Brigade Districts', usually consisting of one or more county, with the 16th Foot being allocated the 33rd Brigade District, which included Bedfordshire. Each district had a permanent depot, with the barracks at Kempston being assigned as the Brigade District base. The depots became the base for 'paired' battalions, with one being held on home service while the other was assigned a post on 'foreign service'.

The Regimental Barracks and Depot were completed on the Kempston Road in 1876, about 1 mile west of Bedford town centre. The building cost around £50,000 at the time and stood on a 23-acre site, 13 of which were used for encampments, drill and recreation grounds. The main building was formed into three sides of a quadrangle, housing stores, powder magazines, officers' and men's quarters – including some married persons' quarters – canteens, mess halls and other such areas. The 1st Battalion remained stationed in Ireland while the 2nd Battalion were sent to Madras in India.

## The Bedfordshire Regiment

On 1 July 1881, the regiment was renamed 'The Bedfordshire Regiment' as a part of the Childers reforms, although the title the 16th Foot was still used for many years afterwards, even beyond the First World War. Bedford became the official centre for the regiment. The Bedfordshire Light Infantry Militia and Hertfordshire Militia formed the 3rd and 4th Battalions and the Rifle Volunteer Corps (RVC) units from both counties were also folded into the county regiment. As a result, the 1st and 2nd Battalions remained the regular units, the 3rd and 4th Battalions became the militia units, and the three RVC battalions formed the 1st and 2nd Hertfordshire Rifle Volunteer Corps and the 1st Bedfordshire Rifle Volunteer Corps. The regimental recruiting district was also expanded to incorporate Hertfordshire. In a strange twist, when Battle Honours were introduced to the new regimental flags that year, only the Bedfordshire Regiment had none of the recognised honours, despite having served through many wars and for over 200 years. A committee was hastily formed and several of their past battles were recognised, rectifying the embarrassing situation.

In 1881 the 2nd Battalion moved to Burma, relocating to Bellary, India, four years later and on to Secunderabad in 1889.

By 1887 the three Volunteer Rifle Corps units in the regiment had been renamed the 1st (Hertfordshire) Volunteer Battalion, the 2nd (Hertfordshire) Volunteer Battalion and the 3rd Volunteer Battalion.

The 1st Battalion started their 'Grand Tour', moving to Malta between February and December 1890, then on to India, reaching there on 20 December. Early the next year the 2nd Battalion returned to England, arriving at Devonport on the south-western coast.

On 3 April 1895, the 1st Battalion became engaged at Malakand Pass during the Chitral Expedition, naming the steep hill they took that day as Bedfordshire Hill, and the battalion's two senior officers were mentioned in despatches as a result.

In 1896 the 2nd Battalion moved to Litchfield, then on to Dublin two years later and the 1st Battalion relocated to Mooltan in 1899.

In response to the start of the South African wars (1899 to 1902), the 2nd Battalion landed in that country on 2 January, where they served in the classic infantry role as well as providing a mounted infantry unit throughout the campaigns. Elements from the 4th Militia Battalion arrived on 21 March as support, and many of the men from the 2nd Volunteer Battalion offered themselves for service, resulting in the formation of a foreign service company that served between 1900 and 1902. At home, a further Volunteer Battalion was raised, becoming the 4th (Huntingdonshire) Volunteer Battalion.

The 2nd Battalion returned to England in 1903 and started their own 'Grand Tour' with a posting to Gibraltar in 1907.

The 1st Battalion remained in India during the South African wars and moved to Jhansi in 1902, then on to Aden in 1907, before transportation home in 1908 and an eventual transfer to Ireland in 1913. Passing Gibraltar en route to England, they exchanged greetings with the 2nd Battalion and were stationed at Aldershot on their return.

Under the Territorial and Reserve Forces Act 1907 (a part of Haldene's reforms), the Territorial army was formed. The regiment's two militia units were renamed and reorganised into the 3rd (Reserve) and 4th (Special Reserve) Battalions; the 1st and 2nd Volunteer Battalions joined forces to become the Hertfordshire Battalion; and the 3rd and 4th Volunteer units merged into the 5th Battalion (TF). The Hertfordshire Battalion left the regiment in 1909, becoming the 1st Battalion, the Hertfordshire Regiment (TF).

The 2nd Battalion moved to Bermuda in 1910 and while they were preparing to leave there for Bloemfontein in South Africa on 16 January 1912, the German cruiser *Hansa* arrived and docked there for three weeks. Several parties were held and friendships formed between the Bedfordshire officers and German naval officers, who only two years later would be on opposing sides in a major conflict.

When the First World War broke out in August 1914, the regiment was expanded greatly as a consequence. Twenty-one battalions served at home and abroad, with around 60,000 men passing through the regiment during the four years of hostilities. More than one in ten of those men would lose their lives and tens of thousands more would be wounded, many carrying multiple-wound stripes on their uniforms.

In 1914 the 1st Battalion were in Ireland and the 2nd were stationed at

Pretoria, South Africa. Both were recalled immediately to fight in the war against Germany and her allies. The 1st Battalion landed in France with the first wave of the British Expeditionary Force and were heavily engaged at the Battles of Mons, Le Cateau, the retreat to Paris, the Marne, the Aisne, La Bassée and the First Battle of Ypres. The 2nd Battalion arrived in France early in October, within the 7th Division, who were to lose 90 per cent of their number before Christmas in stopping the Prussian Guard breaking through at the First Battle of Ypres. The 5th Battalion (TF) were in reserve in East Anglia and, although expecting to be deployed abroad, were held back until the following summer. The regiment's pre-war reservists were all committed before Christmas and replacements started to include men who, until August 1914, were civilians. Three 'service' battalions (the 6th, 7th and 8th) were raised within Lord Kitchener's New Armies, in addition to several supporting units. The 9th and 10th Service Battalions were formed to guard the British coast and provide replacements for the battalions abroad. A second-line Territorial battalion was also raised, being the 2nd/5th Battalion, to provide the 1st/5th with reinforcements and take over duties of providing home defence once the latter were mobilised and sent abroad.

In 1915 the 1st Battalion endured the atrocious fighting at Hill 60 in April and May, which saw Edward Warner win a posthumous Victoria Cross and the arrival of hundreds of replacement men who had enlisted from civilian life the previous autumn. The 2nd Battalion were heavily engaged at the Battle of Neuve Chapelle in March – during which Captain Foss won a Victoria Cross – in addition to the Second Action at Givenchy, the Battle of Festubert, and the Battle of Loos. In July the 6th and 7th Battalions arrived in France, followed by the 8th Battalion in August. Although the 6th and 7th spent their first eleven months away from any set-piece actions, the 8th found themselves thrown headlong into the Battle of Loos in September and in the week before Christmas were subjected to a ferocious barrage and raid, losing over 200 men in the process. The Territorial soldiers in the 1st/5th Battalion landed on the Gallipoli peninsular on 11 August and were heavily engaged in offensive actions north of Suvla Bay within days. They conducted a difficult bayonet charge against established Turkish positions, gained their objectives despite losing around 300 men, and were reduced to about 170 men by the time the British army withdrew in December. Two garrison battalions were raised and provided the garrisons in India and Burma until disbanded in 1919.

By 1916 all battalions on the Western Front were engaged in the Battle of the Somme, with the 7th being one of the few British battalions not only to make it into the German trenches, but also able to hold their gains despite the best efforts of the German defenders. The 4th (Special Reserve) Battalion were mobilised and sent to France in August and all six battalions on that front were employed in the ferocious battles of that year, losing many thousands of men between them. In September, Lieutenant Tom Adlam of the 7th Battalion won a Victoria Cross while leading his men during the capture of the 'impregnable' Thiepval village and the Schwaben redoubt. The 1st/5th Battalion were retired to Egypt and spent the first few months rebuilding their numbers around Cairo, before moving east and guarding the Suez Canal for the rest of 1916.

During 1917 many of the regiment's battalions in France were engaged in pursuing the German army back to the Hindenburg Line and stretcher-bearer Christopher Cox won the 7th Battalion's second Victoria Cross at Achiet-le-Grand in March. All six battalions on the Western Front were heavily committed to the Battle of Arras in April and May, with the 6th coming out of their final assault with just fifty-eight men. The Third Battle of Ypres and the Battle of Cambrai later that year saw all battalions in combat again, although two of them found themselves in attacks that were called off again and again, sparing them some of the carnage endured by other units. The 1st Battalion were rushed to northern Italy after the disastrous fighting there almost finished the Italian army. The 1st/5th Battalion advanced across the Sinai peninsular with the British and Commonwealth forces and were engaged in all three battles of Gaza. In July, they 'covered themselves in glory' during a raid against positions on Umbrella Hill opposite Gaza and were the northern flank of the entire assault against Gaza in November. They were also heavily occupied in defensive battles late in November as the Turkish army tried to force the weak section of the Allied lines while Jerusalem fell further south.

In February 1918 the 8th Battalion were disbanded as the British army reorganised, and March saw the German spring offensives fall on the southern end of the British lines on the Western Front. The 2nd, 4th and 7th Battalions were all greatly involved from the opening day of the battles, conducted often desperate fighting withdrawals over massive tracts of land, and found themselves a shadow of their former selves. Lieutenant Colonel Collings-Wells, in command of the 4th Battalion, won a posthumous Victoria Cross in the process. The 1st and 6th Battalions were among the units rushed into the area, but both arrived after the fighting had fizzled out or moved into other sectors. In May, the 6th and 7th were disbanded as the British army shrunk further, leaving just the 1st, 2nd and 4th on the Western Front. The 1st/5th were engaged in the March offensives in Palestine but, with many divisions being hastened to France after the German offensives began, operations in the Middle East paused despite the Turkish forces being close to defeat. A patrol almost ended in disaster in September but Samuel Needham saved the situation with his 'berserk fury' and won a Victoria Cross in the process. The battalion were engaged in the Battle of Megiddo and the armistice with Turkey was signed in October. On the Western Front, in August 1918 the Allies started their final '100 Days' offensives that would lead to the end of hostilities in Europe. All three battalions were embroiled in the ferocious fighting and by 11 November 1918 found themselves not far from where the Battles of Mons and Le Cateau were fought over four years earlier.

### The Bedfordshire and Hertfordshire Regiment

By the summer of 1919, all remaining battalions had been disbanded abroad and re-formed back in England, with 51st and 52nd (Graduated) and 53rd (Young Soldiers) Battalions being posted to the 'Army of the Rhine' (the British army of occupation in Germany), between them forming the 2nd Eastern Brigade. On 29 July the Bedfordshire regiment incorporated the title Hertfordshire into its name in recognition of the long-standing connection between the two counties. It became the Bedfordshire and Hertfordshire Regiment and was reorganised to its peacetime complement. The 1st and 2nd Battalions remained the regiment's regular, full-time units, with the 3rd and 4th being placed in suspended animation and never re-forming again in the real sense. The regiment's two transport workers' battalions were disbanded in August and September and its three garrison battalions were all brought home at the end of the year, finally being disbanded completely in January 1920. The 2nd Battalion moved to India in October, being based in Trimulgherry, Decan, until moved on to Secunderabad.

The 1st Battalion was posted back to Ireland from 5 July 1920 and spent the next eighteen months separated into detachments, policing a large area around Ulster. The Territorial army was reconstituted and the 5th Battalion reformed into a part-time, Territorial army unit once again.

On 11 November 1921, after a remarkable effort raising the funds to do so, the regimental memorial opposite the Keep at Kempston Barracks was unveiled.

The 1st Battalion left Ireland and returned to Colchester, arriving on 4 February 1922; they were moved to Aldershot in 1923. The 2nd Battalion in India were inspected by the Prince of Wales on 26 January and transferred to Kamptee shortly afterwards. At the annual camp in Cardington, the 5th Territorial Battalion were given a speech by the Chief of the Imperial General Staff, General the Earl of Cavan. In it he made the memorable remark: *'You men of Bedford, you began the war very little known. You ended the war the best known of the whole of the British line. No regiment has a finer record than you have.'* In April the regimental journal *The Wasp* made its first appearance.

King George V reviewed the 1st Battalion at Aldershot in 1924 and presented them with new colours, with no less than seventy battle honours being awarded to the regiment the following year.

The 1st Battalion left Aldershot in November, bound for Malta, and the 2nd Battalion withdrew from India and arrived at Baghdad, Iraq, on 13 January, to assist in training the local army to take over the policing of their country. The 5th Battalion (TF) represented the regiment in regular-army manoeuvres.

In March 1926 the 2nd Battalion left Baghdad for Karachi, moving back to England after a brief stop. On the way home, on 14 April, they met the 1st Battalion who were based at Malta, being a rare event in the regiment's history. On Sunday 20 June, while based at Dover, the 2nd Battalion held a commemoration service, having completed nineteen years of foreign service. On 16 November the 2nd Battalion were moved temporarily to Bedford for two ceremonies that saw them welcomed home to the town and, the following day, they were presented with new colours by the Prince of Wales at Luton.

In February 1927, the 1st Battalion left Malta for Shanghai, China, and formed part of the International Defence Force, who had the job of protecting the port from the Chinese Nationalist threat during the Chinese Civil War. By May 1928 they were concentrated at Weihai, Shandong, then moved into northern China. Transported by sea to Chinwangtao (Qinhuangdao) and finally to Kuyeh by rail, they were assigned the role of protecting the mining facility there. By November the unrest had settled down and the battalion were moved to Hong Kong.

The 1st Battalion arrived at Mhow in central India on 25 March 1929, where they would remain for the next four years. October saw the 2nd Battalion taking up residence at the Quebec Barracks, Borden Camp,

Aldershot.

In 1933, the 1st Battalion transferred to Dehra Run, 230km north of Delhi, becoming the British element of the Gurkha Brigade. Three years later they moved a further 50km north to Chakrata, India, which was a very basic hill station around 8,000 feet above sea level. In response to Italy's invasion of Abyssinia, British forces were reinforced in the Middle East. February 1936 saw the 2nd Battalion leave Colchester for Egypt and on 1 June they were sited in Palestine as tensions built between Arabs and Jews in the area, arriving at their camp just north of Jerusalem the same day. They took part in small-scale operations to quell revolts all over Palestine until leaving for England in late November. From 7 December until the outbreak of the Second World War, the battalion were based at Gravesend in Kent.

In 1938 the regiment celebrated its 250th anniversary and dozens of occasions were arranged both at home and abroad. In September the 1st Battalion were hurriedly moved to Bombay amid rising disquiet in Europe and were embarked with two other battalions, bound for that continent. In the event, they were diverted and alighted at Haifa instead as the conflict in Europe was eased, but the Arab–Jewish problems in Palestine were still very active.

On 3 September 1939, war with Germany was declared once again. The 1st Battalion, who had been posted to Cairo in Egypt that July, would serve the entire war in Eastern theatres and were moved to Palestine in November to prepare for the coming fighting. The 2nd Battalion were mobilised into the 10th Brigade, 4th Division, and transferred to Aldershot on 23 September, where the division concentrated. They were then sent to France, landing at Cherbourg on 1 October, then to Carvin on the French–Belgian border and 10km south-west of Lille. The battalion were posted to several positions along the Maginot Line during the phase referred to as the 'phoney war'. The 5th Battalion (TF) were mobilised on 25 August and C and D Companies from the Luton area were immediately separated to form the nucleus of a new battalion, called the 6th Battalion (TF). Both would be engaged in extensive guard duties in Bedfordshire and Hertfordshire and have little time for unit-level training over the next year.

By 1940 the 2nd Battalion were in Belgium, responding to the German invasion of Holland and Belgium and the beginning of the Battle of France. The battalion lined the canal bank around Escanaffles, 30km north-east of Lille, and made first contact with reconnaissance parties of the German army on 20 May. After two days of resisting German blitzkreig tactics, skirmishing and counter-attacking, the brigade flanks were overrun and they were ordered to provide the protective rearguard for the withdrawal late on 22 May. They moved due west until reaching positions north of Lille and held their lines between 23 and 26 May, clashing with the enemy as they patrolled the area. Orders to withdraw overnight on the 27th were issued and the battalion were heavily attacked that evening, pulling back through Ploegsteert to the Wijtschate region once darkness fell, places their fathers would have remembered from two decades earlier.

On the 28th they were engaged again and orders to retire north followed the next day, along with instructions to destroy all arms and ammunition as they did so. Moving through the growing chaos, they passed through Furnes and were once more employed in rearguard actions that day, south of Oust Dunkerque. On the 31st they were again in combat as the German army pressed forward, trying to capture the remaining Allied army being evacuated from the beaches around Dunkirk. At 2 a.m. on 1 June the battalion were ordered to evacuate through La Panne on the coast to the beaches, where they endured the attentions of the Luftwaffe who bombed and strafed the beach and all vessels evacuating troops across the English Channel.

At length, the battalion were re-formed at Yeovil in Somerset, having lost just 130 men despite being heavily engaged in several rearguard actions. By 1 July the elements of the 2nd Battalion who had made it back to England had been reinforced back up to strength and were in defensive positions around Bognor Regis, Sussex. In October they proceeded to Alresford in Hampshire, then on to Totton in November. In May the 5th Battalion were transferred to Norfolk in response to the invasion threat and were inspected by King George VI on 23 August.

In March 1941 the 1st Battalion were sent to Alexandria in Egypt, where they concentrated and moved on to Athens, Greece. Their isolated post was to be the island of Lemnos, where the 5th Battalion had spent time in 1915, but they were evacuated before it was possible for the advancing Germans to cut off their route back to Egypt completely. They were returned to Alexandria in April to provide anti-air defences and then located at a camp near the Suez Canal in May, where they became part of the 14th Brigade, 6th Division. A further move to Syria in June followed, to provide internal security as part of the army of occupation. In October the division became the 70th and transferred to Tobruk on the Libyan coast, where it fought during the defence of Tobruk. The 2nd Battalion returned to Alresford in February and took part in several big exercises over the summer. That October saw a further move to Barton Stacey in Hampshire and at the end of November they were posted to Fleet. The 5th Battalion spent between January and April in Galashiels, Scotland, before being sent to Uttoxeter, Staffordshire, for a few weeks in April and then on to Atherstone in Warwickshire. In September they relocated again to Litchfield, Staffordshire, before leaving home shores from Liverpool on 29 October. Although initially intended for the Middle East, Japan's entry into the war caused a fateful change of destination. Their meandering route took them via Nova Scotia, Trinidad, Cape Town and Bombay, before spending a week at Ahmednagar in India.

The 1st Battalion moved back to Egypt in February 1942, then left for Malaya on 1 March but were diverted to India as both Singapore and Rangoon had fallen by then. After a pause, they were sent inland to Ranchi, 200 miles west of Calcutta, and provided various security detachments. In February the 2nd Battalion progressed to Inveraray, Argyllshire, and spent almost a year in advanced training. The 5th Battalion left India on 19 January as the situation in the Far East deteriorated rapidly and landed at Singapore harbour on 29 January, only to be rushed east to Changi. Two days later the remnants of the Allied forces that had been fighting the Japanese were concentrated on Singapore Island, ready for a last stand. Within two weeks Singapore had fallen and the battalion spent the rest of the war in the notoriously brutal Japanese POW camps.

In August 1943 the 1st Battalion transferred to Bangalore, southern India, becoming part of the division's Long Range Penetration Group, also known as Brigadier Wingate's Chindit force, who were engaged in irregular Special Forces operations. The 2nd Battalion were moved to Carronbridge in Dumfriesshire in February and left for foreign service from Glasgow on 11 March. They landed at Algiers (El Jazair), Algeria, on 23 March as part of V Corps in the British First Army and were engaged in the Tunisian campaign from 7 April. Within a week huge gains were made but the battalion lost around 250 men, including their commanding officer. Between 6 and 13 May the battalion were also employed in Operation Vulcan and faced the elite Hermann Goring Parachute Division in the massive Battle of Tunis, intended to eliminate the Axis army in North Africa. By the end of operations, almost 240,000 Axis prisoners had been taken, with several thousand of them surrendering to the 2nd Battalion as they edged ever forward. Their division was left out of the initial Italian landings and spent until December resting and training in Algeria. In mid-December the battalion embarked from Algiers, arriving at Port Said, Egypt, on 22 December. They were sent to the Suez Canal, being based at Kubrit (Kubrr), a few kilometres north of Suez (As Suways).

In March 1944 the 1st Battalion left India for Burma, where they fought within the Chindits until August. They returned to Bangalore, India, in August and remained there until the end of the war. The 2nd Battalion's division were earmarked to assault Rhodes but the operation was cancelled and mid-February saw a move to Italy, landing at Naples (Napoli) on 21 February. They were engaged in the long, costly advance, including assaulting the infamous Monte Cassino in May. In December they went to Greece to help sweep Communist guerrillas from the island. The 1st Battalion was in India until August 1945, remaining in Dehra Dun until the end of hostilities. The 2nd Battalion spent the final period of the war in Greece and remained there afterwards while general stability resumed. The Japanese prisoners of war from the 5th Battalion returned home in several detachments late that year. Although exact numbers are unknown, around a third of those captured at Singapore died in captivity. The 6th, 9th, 70th and 71st battalions, who were all raised for the war and served exclusively in the UK, were all disbanded as the war closed.

On 14 February 1946 the regiment provided the Honour Guard for Princess Elizabeth's visit to Bedford. In April, the 1st Battalion moved back to Chakrata, the hill station at the base of the Himalayas where they had been posted before the war had started.

The Territorial army was re-formed at home on 1 January 1947 and after hostilities had ceased, the only battalions not disbanded were the 1st, 2nd and 5th (Territorial). However, the 2nd Battalion, who were in Egypt, were placed in 'suspended animation' from May, with the personnel being transferred to other units and the cadre returning to England in June.

The 1st Battalion, then the only regular contingent in the regiment, left Bombay for the last time in November 1947, following Indian independence, and were posted to Tripoli, Libya. In July 1948 they relocated to Greece and after ninety years of service, the 2nd Battalion were officially absorbed by the 1st at a ceremony in Salonika (Thessalonika), Greece, that October, being one of only a few occasions in their history that both battalions had met. This left just one regular and one

Territorial battalion in the regiment.

In January 1950 the 1st Battalion were the last British unit to leave Greece and they returned to Bury St Edmunds in mid-February. Blenheim Day in June saw them visit the depot at Kempston to mark their return home after twenty-five years of foreign service. On 11 November the regimental Second World War memorial at Kempston was unveiled in the presence of the Queen, the colonel of the regiment, and an assortment of other dignitaries. Soon after, the battalion moved to Warminster.

In 1951 a draft from the regiment was sent to the Korean War as replacements for British losses suffered during the Chinese offensives, but the 1st Battalion remained in England until posted to the Guards Brigade in Egypt in response to the Suez crisis. On 29 November they disembarked on Cyprus and waited for orders. The following July, the 1st Battalion arrived at El Balah (Ballah) in the Suez Canal zone, to guard British military installations amid the troubles while Egypt transformed into a republic.

On 25 October 1953 the Queen Mother (the regiment's honorary Colonel-in-Chief) presented the 5th Territorial Battalion with new colours.

In December 1954 the Guards Brigade in Egypt was broken up and the 1st Battalion were shipped home, arriving at Tidworth in Hampshire before Christmas. On 25 April 1955 the Queen Mother inspected the battalion and presented them with new colours at Tidworth.

The 1st Battalion was posted to a new location in 1956, being Goslar in West Germany, around 80km south-east of Hannover. Here, in a new type of war, they guarded the 'Iron Curtain' for the first time, in what would become known as the Cold War.

During what would be their last year before another major reorganisation to the British army, 1957 saw eighteen battle honours from the Second World War granted to the regiment.

## The 3rd East Anglian Regiment (16th/44th Foot)

After 270 years of continuous, loyal service to the country, on 1 June 1958 the 1st Battalion, Bedfordshire and Hertfordshire Regiment were merged with the 1st Battalion, the Essex Regiment to form the 3rd East Anglian Regiment, based in Dortmund, West Germany. The following year, the Queen Mother chose to remain the honorary Colonel-in-Chief of the new regiment and presented them with their new colours. Later that year they were moved to Malaya, serving in the 28 Commonwealth Brigade in the operations against Communist guerrillas.

In May 1961 the Territorial army was again reduced and the 5th Battalion joined forces with the 1st Battalion of the Hertfordshire Regiment, becoming the Bedfordshire and Hertfordshire Regiment (TA). Upon returning to home duties, the 3rd East Anglian Regiment was posted to help police the growing unrest in Northern Ireland in 1962 and just six years after their formation, another reorganisation loomed.

## The Royal Anglian Regiment

On 1 September 1964, the three regiments forming the East Anglian Brigade were merged with the Royal Leicestershire Regiment into the first 'Large Regiment of Infantry' unit in the British army, becoming the Royal Anglian Regiment. The 3rd East Anglian Regiment became the 3rd Battalion (16th/44th Foot) of the Royal Anglian Regiment. The Territorial battalions from all six counties within the regimental region were affiliated to the regiment.

Three years later the Bedfordshire and Hertfordshire Regiment (TA) were folded into the 5th (Volunteer) Battalion, the Royal Anglian Regiment and in 1970, the 4th Battalion were reduced to company strength. A year later the 6th and 7th Territorial Battalions of the Royal Anglian Regiment were formed and in 1975 the 4th Battalion were broken up completely.

The regimental structure remained stable until 1992, when the 3rd Battalion were disbanded on 5 October, its personnel being amalgamated into the 1st Battalion (the 'Vikings') and the 2nd Battalion (the 'Poachers').

By 1996 the Territorial battalions within the regiment had been reduced to just the 6th and 7th, and three years later the two remaining Territorial units of the regiment were merged and renamed the East of England Regiment. On 1 April 2006, the Territorial East of England Regiment were renamed as the 3rd Battalion (the 'Steelbacks') of the Royal Anglian Regiment.

As of 2013, D Company (Bedfordshire and Hertfordshire) of the 2nd Battalion (the 'Poachers') are the direct ancestors of Douglas's Regiment of Foot who were originally formed in 1688. Since the formation of the Royal Anglian Regiment, in addition to British and West German postings, they have served operationally in Aden, Cyprus, Malta, Northern Ireland, the Persian Gulf, Croatia, Bosnia, Sierra Leone, Iraq and Afghanistan. When exercises are added to the list of countries the regiment have been present in, there are not many parts of the globe they have not set foot on during the last decade. The documentary *Ross Kemp in Afghanistan* originally shown on television in 2007 featured the

1st Battalion in Afghanistan during their tour in 2006, and a well-reported 'friendly fire' incident in August 2007 killed three men of the 1st Battalion as well as injuring two others. On the lighter side, the band of the Royal Anglian Regiment played the 'Blackadder Goes Forth' theme for the comedy series. The 2nd Battalion still celebrate Blenheim Day on 13 August each year, having been the Bedfordshire Regiment's annual day.

# Acknowledgements

My personal thanks go to the following people who have shared information from their own fields of research or who have provided moral support in some way:

To my wife Liz, for her continued understanding, support and interest, and publisher Steve Darlow for his efforts in making this story known.

To the individuals who have helped with information, opinions and guidance from their own fields of interest: Nigel Lutt and his colleagues at BLARS, Kenneth Wood, Peter Epps, Lilias Odell, John Wainwright, Steve Beeby, Barry Elkin, Alec Foley (the Kilgallon collection), Sergeant Mike Bates (2 R. Anglian), Kate Wills, and any others I may have inadvertently left out.

To the relatives of those men who served in the battalion during the period this volume covers, and those with a personal interest that had led them to investigate specific individuals from the battalion: Julie Day (Sidney Wilson), David Downes (Thomas Haynes and Henry Downes), Paddy McHugh and John Law (Harold McHugh), Derek Lawman (Samuel Spicer), Roy Litchfield (for directing me to the Brightman brothers' story), Penny Maitland-Stuart (Hugh Courtenay), Karl Rachwal (John Fox), Chris Ray (Frederick Ray), David Sankey (Percival Hart), Claire Stockdale (Drummer H. Humphrey), Mark Turner (James Wright), Ron West (William Newbound).

The final acknowledgement must go to those men whose courage, fortitude, endurance and selfless actions provided the component parts of this story, as well as those whose contributions have not been identified or included. Even though a century has passed, you are all still remembered.

# Endnotes

1    The correct, localised spelling is Faffémont, although, like Trônes Wood and other places, it became anglicised to Falfemont over time.

2    The History Committee, the Royal Anglian Regiment (Bedfordshire and Hertfordshire); Lieutenant Colonel T.J. Barrow, DSO, Major V.A. French and J. Seabrook Esq. (1986), *The Story of the Bedfordshire and Hertfordshire Regiment (The 16th Regiment of Foot). Volume II 1914 to 1958*, page 142.

3    National Archives, reference WO 95/1570.

4    Lieutenant Robert Kenneth or Kays Wright.

5    Private 40020 Ernest Baalham.

6    Private 8414 Herbert Durant.

7    Private 19499 Frank Kefford.

8    Private 29355 Harold Oclee.

9    Private 25850 Herbert Francis Dicks; *Kettering Leader*, 5 October 1917.

10    Hussey, A.H. and Inman D.S. (reprint of 1921 edition), *The 5th Division in the Great War*, Naval and Military Press, page 139.

11    Private 18257 Herbert William Fish.

12    Corporal 13610 Harold McHugh.

13    Private 43031 Christopher Cross.

14    Corporal 18069 Frank Bradley.

15    Corporal 7175 Arthur Faulder.

16    Lance Corporal 3/7184 Frederick Payne.

17    *St Neots Advertiser*, 2 February 1917.

18    Private 33362 William Henry Bashford; references to Harry Bashford are taken from an interview held under IWM reference 9987, combined with his service record from the WO 363 series at the National Archives.

19    Sergeant 16454 Frederick Groom.

20    Private 13376 William Brown.

21    Private 33372 Arthur Thetford.

22    Corporal 18620 Fred Weston.

23    WO 339/38949.
24    Private 31815 Sidney Short.
25    Lance Corporal 7326 Frederick George Eames.
26    *Bedfordshire Times and Independent*, 4 May 1917.
27    Private 10352 Chris Runham; *Bedfordshire Times and Independent*, 4 May 1917.
28    National Archives, reference WO 339/44903.
29    Sergeant 20374, later Second Lieutenant Reginald Charles Humphries.
30    National Archives, reference WO 339/10166.
31    Private 20974 Edgar Gurney.
32    Corporal 43098 Frederick Ebenezer Hazelton.
33    *St Neots Advertiser*, 4 May 1917.
34    Lance Corporal 12039 James Daniel O'Brien.
35    *Letchworth Citizen*, 11 May 1917.
36    Lance Corporal 6535 Frederick William Rowley.
37    Corporal 32950 Herbert Ernest Ball.
38    *St Neots Advertiser*, 4 May 1917.
39    Sergeant 9885 Samuel Arthur Baxter.
40    Private 28207 James Sinclair.
41    Sergeant 7721 Walter Hilliard.
42    Private 3/7448 Robert William Brown.
43    *Letchworth Citizen*, 11 May 1917.
44    Service record under National Archives reference WO 339/52186.
45    Private 16957 Richard Ralph Hoar.
46    Private 14558 Frederick Sapsford.
47    Lance Sergeant 7373 Edward Flitton.
48    Company Sergeant Major 6521 Walter Freer.
49    Private 43473 Charles James Vowles.
50    Lance Corporal 19836 William Herbert Smith.
51    Lance Corporal 3/7450 George Henry Bland; *Bedfordshire Times and Independent*,
      11 May 1917.
52    Private 4/7118 Arthur Albert Izzard, also recorded as number 7718.
53    Lance Corporal 3/6712 Algernon Breed; *Bedfordshire Times and Independent*, 11 May 1917.
54    Corporals 22019 George Dilley and 33620 David Dilley.
55    Sergeant 19255, later Second Lieutenant George Howlett; National Archives,
      reference WO 374/35192.
56    Sergeant 8081 George Gazeley; *Bedfordshire Times and Independent*, 4 May 1917,
      reported this to be his fifth wound, although his service record only mentions four.
57    Private 13119 Arthur Jackson; *Bedfordshire Times and Independent*, 5 May 1917.
58    Gilbert, Martin, *First World War*, HarperCollins, London, (1995).
59    Blake, Robert (editor), *The Private Papers of Douglas Haig 1914–1918*, London (1952).
60    The actual figures are disputed as official French records are not available until 2017.
61    *Bedfordshire Times and Independent*, 11 May 1917.
62    'Trench strength' is the number of soldiers available to hold the front lines after
      headquarters, transport, and details are left behind.
63    CQMS 6756, later Second Lieutenant Frederick Halsey; National Archives,
      reference WO 339/122616.
64    Sergeant 10196 Herbert Hill; *Bedfordshire Times and Independent*, 15 March 1918.
65    Company Sergeant Major 9183 Walter James Summerfield, DCM.
66    Sergeant 8095 William Falla, DCM.

67 Private 31846 Herbert William Lovitt.

68 *St Neots Advertiser*, 19 July 1917.

69 Acting Colour Sergeant Major 8721 Reginald Thomas Lansbury.

70 Sergeant 10055 Reginald Henry Puddefoot.

71 Sergeant 28207 James Sinclair.

72 Sergeant 7175 Arthur Faulder.

73 Sergeant 10238 David Stone.

74 Acting Company Quartermaster Sergeant 8311 Harry Norman.

75 Corporal 8253 George Ilott.

76 Private 43038 Frederick Dighton.

77 Private 10667 James Houston.

78 Private 43460 Leonard King. The war diary mistakenly records his service number as 43023, which is the number of Ernest Gibbons.

79 Private 20337 William Clarke.

80 Sergeant 10052 George Edward Neale.

81 Lance Corporal 17425 Arthur Cox; *Bedfordshire Times and Independent*, 24 July 1917.

82 Lance Corporal 12365 James Charles Price.

83 Sergeant 20374, later Second Lieutenant Reginald Charles Humphries.

84 Hussey and Inman, *5th Division in the Great War*, page 168.

85 Corporal 3/6448 Sidney Charles Wilson, letter published in the *Royston Crow*, 13 July 1817.

86 Private 31007 John Catlyn.

87 Lance Corporal 10285 William Wrenn.

88 Private 37172 Charles Dukes, published in the *St Neots Advertiser*, 19 July 1917.

89 Lance Corporal 9390 Charles George Cross.

90 Quotations relating to Second Lieutenant Paul Christie are drawn from a privately produced booklet: *In Memoriam P.N.J.C.*, Riverside Press, Edinburgh (1917).

91 'We are the Bedford Boys' was a marching song certainly traceable back to the 1800s, and which appears to have been adapted to suit almost every regiment, the names of local streets being amended according to the regiment.

92 Private 32911 Albert Andrews.

93 *Letchworth Citizen*, 24 August 1917.

94 Private 22938 John Catlin.

95 Private 33595 John Thomas Bartlett, originally served as 2497 Bedfordshire Yeomanry.

96 Private 30167 William Charles Uffindell.

97 Corporal (Lance Sergeant) 7049 George Corbett.

98 Private 33755 William John Fairey.

99 RSM 7521 Cecil Ford Walker, DCM.

100 CSM 8306 Percy Folkard.

101 Sergeant 10190 Oswald Gentle; *Letchworth Citizen*, 19 October and 2 November 1917.

102 Lance Corporal 13904 George Pike, letter published in the *Letchworth Citizen*, 26 October 1917.

103 Private 203926 Frederick Dollimore.

104 Whether Harold Bashford was recalling the death of Second Lieutenant Reynolds or Fleming is unclear, although the latter appears the most likely.

105 Private 8325 Alfred Barker.

106 Sergeant 8186 James Bush.

107 Private 33605 Alfred Burridge.

108 Private 33616 Frederick Chessum.

**109**   Supplement to the *London Gazette*, 23 April 1918.

**110**   Private 29818 Walter Berry.

**111**   Private 15478 Thomas Neale; *Royston Crow*, 30 November 1917.

**112**   CSM 8341, later Second Lieutenant Henry Trasler, DCM.

**113**   Letter dated 20 October 1917 from Second Lieutenant John Dickinson to
          Second Lieutenant Christie's parents.

**114**   CSM 7623 Sidney Chamberlain; *Royston Crow*, 18 August 1916.

**115**   Private 29549 Samuel Thomas Spicer.

**116**   Private 9560 Albert Durham, MM.

**117**   *Luton News* and *Bedfordshire Advertiser*, 1 January 1920; Privates 3/6189 Alfred Brightman
          (killed 26 October 1914); 27656 Frank Brightman (killed 12 October 1916);
          23316 Herbert Brightman (killed 25 October 1917); 203259 Richard Brightman
          (wounded 30 October, dying 10 November 1917); 20451 Walter Brightman (survived);
          23647 George Horsler (killed 30 October 1917).

**118**   Sergeant 9502 Alfred Sale; *Bedfordshire Times and Independent*, 7 March 1919.

**119**   Sergeant 8186 James Bush.

**120**   Corporal 18844 Arthur Francis.

**121**   CQMS 8309 Howard Bourn (Bourne).

**122**   Private 4/7009 Leonard Arthur Ball.

**123**   Acting Regimental Sergeant Major 6863, later Second Lieutenant Edward Johnson.

**124**   Stewart Daniel Harrower, aka Stuart Dare Harrower, formerly CSM 8556.
          Service record held at the National Archives, reference WO 374/31517.

**125**   Service record of Basil Charles Williams, held at the National Archives,
          reference WO 339/35511.

**126**   Hussey and Inman, *5th Division in the Great War*, page 197.

**127**   Published in the *St Neots Advertiser*, 11 January 1918.

**128**   Published in the *St Neots Advertiser*, 18 January 1918.

**129**   Lance Sergeant 43122 Hugh Johnson.

**130**   Private 43012 Alfred Askew.

**131**   Private 32965 John William Boxall.

**132**   Private 14703 Joseph Harold Clark.

**133**   Private 15111 Ernest John Humbles.

**134**   Private 16957 Richard Ralph Hoar.

**135**   Private 43460 Leonard King.

**136**   Private 8036 James Sellers.

**137**   Published in the *St Neots Advertiser*, 8 February 1918.

**138**   Corporal 265418 George Harry Drury.

**139**   Possibly Private 20167 George Faraday.

**140**   Private 9091 James Bagnall.

**141**   Private 8128 George Hynard.

**142**   Private 8455 Arthur King.

**143**   Lieutenant Colonel John Stanhope Collings-Wells won the DSO and later
          a posthumous VC commanding the 4th Bedfordshires.

**144**   WO 374/31517.

**145**   Private 15568 Bertie Seymore Warwick.

**146**   Sergeant 9284 Richard Henry Wheeler, later served as 5944202 in the
          5th Bedfordshire and Hertfordshire Regiment.

**147**   Second Lieutenant William Francis George Perham.

**148**   Character assessment included in his 'Employment Sheet' within his service record, held at the National Archives, series WO 363.

**149**  Sergeant 4/7325 John Charles Cordell.

**150**  Corporal 18751 John Bass.

**151**  Corporal 3/6712 Algernon Breed.

**152**  Private 17479 Sydney Rawlings.

**153**  Private 10346 James William Smith.

**154**  Private 37574 George William Weston.

**155**  *Bedfordshire Times and Independent*, 5 July 1918.

**156**  Baker, Chris, *The Battle for Flanders. German Defeat on the Lys 1918*,
Pen & Sword (2011), page 95.

**157**  Private 15567 William Spicer.

**158**  Private 48023 Harry Lowe.

**159**  Private 27786 Harry Cotton.

**160**  Private 46990 William David Gray.

**161**  Corporal 2379, later 265418 George Harry Drury, DCM. The date his
DCM was won was recorded in the *Letchworth Citizen* on 30 August 1918.

**162**  Second Lieutenant Ambrose Ethelstone Peel;
*Bedfordshire Times and Independent*, 10 May 1918.

**163**  Private 8837 Henry Walter James Clarke.

**164**  Private 20539 Alfred Peacock; article published in the *Letchworth Citizen*, 19 July 1918.

**165**  Sergeant 43473 Charles James Vowles.

**166**  Private 268162 Harry Byatt, letter published in the *St Neots Advertiser*, 17 May 1918.

**167**  Privates 200925 Leonard Alwyne Gray and 10288 William Gray, published in the
*Biggleswade Chronicle*, 30 August 1918; also from Wood, Kenneth,
*Biggleswade and the Great War*, History Press (2009), pages 31, 103 and 124.

**168**  Master Cook 6187 Bertie Washington.

**169**  Corporal 18682 Henry Charles Boston.

**170**  Lance Corporal 15736 Edward Henry Rolph.

**171**  Corporal 9222, later Second Lieutenant Thomas Bradford Mills Connolly.

**172**  Sergeant 3/6527 Alfred Edward Page, published in the *Letchworth Citizen*, 28 June 1918.

**173**  Personal letter from Percy Worrall to Hugh Courtenay's widow, dated 28 August 1918.

**174**  Lance Corporal 32256 Fred Richards.

**175**  Sergeant 7944 William Felstead.

**176**  Hussey and Inman, *5th Division in the Great War*, page 227.

**177**  Lance Sergeant 43059 William Thomas Dighton.

**178**  Private 42069 George Sparrow.

**179**  National Archives, reference WO 339/62557.

**180**  Second Lieutenant Ernest Charles Howlett, formerly Private 10341.

**181**  National Archives, reference WO 95/1569.

**182**  National Archives, reference WO 95/1569.

**183**  Private 8974 Herbert William Creighton.

**184**  Sergeant 13610 Harold Albert McHugh, MM; extract from a personal memoir,
courtesy of John Law.

**185**  Extracts from personal letters held by Lieutenant Colonel Courtenay's family.

**186**  National Archives, reference WO 374/2280.

**187**  *St Neots Advertiser*, 27 September and 11 October 1918.

**188**  Corporal 3/6712 Algernon Breed; *Bedfordshire Times and Independent*,
6 and 20 September 1918.

**189**  CSM 7459 Harry Allison; *Bedfordshire Times and Independent*, 20 September 1918.

190  Private 7170 Edward Davis.

191  Corporal 7099 Charles Meakins.

192  Lance Sergeant 18751 John Bass; *St Neots Advertiser*, 7 February 1919.

193  National Archives, reference WO 374/32078.

194  Private 8259 Edward Jarvis.

195  National Archives, reference WO 339/119689.

196  National Archives, reference WO 339/103186.

197  Private 15753 Charles Frederick Kidby.

198  Private 4968, later 266610 Frank Burch.

199  Sergeant 43407 William Papworth, formerly 844 Huntingdonshire Cyclists Battalion.

200  National Archives, reference WO 374/73372.

201  National Archives, reference WO 374/73372.

202  Company Quartermaster Sergeant 9209 William Austin.

203  Hart, Peter, *1918 a Very British Victory*, Phoenix (2009), page 464.

204  Private 12975 Edward Strudwick.

205  Private 23417 Frederick Breed; *Bedfordshire Times and Independent*, 18 October 1918.

206  Corporal 20952 Percy Appleby, MM.

207  National Archives, reference WO 339/95628; no further details are recorded.

208  National Archives, reference WO 339/62557.

209  National Archives, reference WO 95/1569.

210  Company Sergeant Major 10339 Frank Mead, DCM.

211  Citation published in the *London Gazette* supplement, December 1918.

212  National Archives, reference WO 95/1569.

213  Medical reports from National Archives, reference WO 339/120900.

214  Medical reports from National Archives, reference WO 374/47028.

215  Sergeant 8338 Reuben Jeffries (Jefferies).

216  Private 32116 Herbert John Dean, formerly 3362, 5th Battalion; *Bedfordshire Times and Independent*, 8 November 1918.

217  Lance Sergeant 16631 George Bellamy; *St Neots Advertiser*, 15 November 1918.

218  Corporal 17425 Arthur Cox, whose photograph was carried in the *Bedfordshire Times and Independent*, 27 December 1918.

219  Private 43876 William Price.

220  Private 271017 George Thatcher.

221  Lance Corporal 16750 Owen Albert Brown; *Letchworth Citizen*, 29 November 1918.

222  Private 10241, later 5942334 Thomas Haynes.

223  Private 47366 William Walter Jones.

224  Private 51158 Sidney Fred Bryant.

225  Sergeant 10052 George Edward Neale.

226  Private 29026 Arthur Newton.

227  Private 271125 Edward Lawson.

228  CSM 200970 John James Ryan.

229  Corporal 19554 James Tuckey.

230  Private 43242 Alfred E. McDougall.

231  Private 10346 James William Smith.

232  *Bedfordshire Times and Independent*, 15 November 1918.

233  Hussey and Inman, *5th Division in the Great War*, page 163.

234  Acting RSM 8253 George Illot.

235  Corporal 3/7352 William John 'Jack' Pennycook (not Pennycock).

236  Acting CSM 6897 Joshua Trundley.

237   *Bedfordshire Times and Independent*, 20 December 1918.

238   *Letchworth Citizen*, 22 November 1918, among others.

239   Lance Corporal 9985 Arthur Austin; *Bedfordshire Times and Independent*, 29 November 1918.

240   Private 8994 Frank Watson; *Bedfordshire Times and Independent*, 20 December 1918.

241   Private 10170 Norman Howe; *Letchworth Citizen*, 29 November 1918.

242   *Bedfordshire Times and Independent*, 10 January 1919.

243   Absent With Out Leave.

244   National Archives, WO 339/98853.

245   Sergeant 12538 Arthur John Boston.

246   Sergeant 45845 Alfred Coxall, initially numbered 7317.

247   Sergeant (later CSM) 7003 Frederick Faulder.

248   Sergeant 15124 Alexander Richard Lasenby.

249   Acting Lance Corporal 9725 Gilbert Robinson.

250   Acting Lance Corporal 18623 Thomas Shadbolt.

251   Private 19738 John William Bussingham.

252   Private 7955, later 268054 Henry William O'Shea.

253   Private 13256 John William Fox; information supplied by John's descendants.

254   Private 16957 Richard Ralph Hoar.

255   Private 16936 Percy How.

256   Private 18716 Walter Hare.

257   Private 18461 William Jakes.

258   Private 12793 Sidney Jasper.

259   Private 22922 James Clifton.

260   Private 3/7133 George Wilby.

261   National Archives, reference WO 339/62557.

262   'La Mandolinata' was the regimental march, originally taken from an Italian opera.

263   *Bedfordshire Times and Independent*, 2 May 1919.

264   Elements of this march can be seen in a film held by the East Anglian Film Archive, reference 216864. Visit www.eafa.org.uk to view or learn more.

265   Private 5943725 C. Greaves; account held at National Archives, reference WO 339/72726.

266   National Archives, reference WO 339/46403.

267   Private 5944327 Leonard Blow; account held at National Archives, reference WO 339/13456.

268   National Archives, reference WO 339/32962.

269   National Archives, reference WO 339/15567.

270   National Archives, reference WO 339/22355.

271   National Archives service record, held within the WO 363 section.

272   National Archives, reference WO 374/24448.

273   National Archives, reference WO 339/43731.

274   National Archives, reference WO 374/54828.

275   RQMS 5362 John Stapleton.

276   Mike Weight and an article by Roy Kodani in the *Hawaii Herald*, 3 October 2008.

277   Colonel (retired) Tony Winton, OBE, DL.

278   *Bedfordshire Standard*, 21 December 1928.

# Index of Personnel